MW00445211

Making It *Easy* for Patients to Say "Yes"

A Complete Guide to Case Acceptance

Making It *Easy* for Patients to Say "Yes"

A Complete Guide to Case Acceptance

Dr. Paul Homoly, CSP

First printing 2005
Revised 2017
ISBN 0-9776289-4-9

Cover and text design by Breiding Marketing, LLC

Dedication

This book is dedicated to my family: my mom, Wanda, whose spunk ignites any room she's in; my older brothers, Clarke and Guy, who have been my heroes ever since I can remember; my sister, Bonnie, who's shown more courage than most; my son and daughter, Adam and Kristen, of whom I am so proud; and Joseph Paul, my first grandson. If he inherits only half of the "oomph" of his immediate ancestors, he is in for quite a life.

Contents

Acknowledgment

Do you remember the story of the little blue train engine that could? She (yes, the engine was a "she") had a full load of freight and chugged her way up to the top of the mountain all the while puffing, *"I think I can, I think I can, I think I can..."*

This book has been a trip up the mountain for me and I've had a lot of help pulling the load—my team in Lansing, Michigan, Nanette Morel and Sue Corden, who ran my business and kept things on track; and my team in Charlotte, North Carolina, Sharon Hutchison, Janet Plantier and Julie Potter, who now keep fires stoked.

I want to thank the many dentists and team members who've attended my workshops and whose interest and suggestions have propelled this work. Drs. Phil Potter and John Gordon, along with Barb Herzog, have served as faculty members at many of my workshops and have been reliable sources of innovation and good cheer. A big thank you to them.

And for the nuts-and-bolts work that makes every author look good, a hearty thanks to my design team, Tim Breiding (Breiding Marketing) and Nikki Harrison; and my editor and source of mental health, Juliette Kurtz.

Prologue
Dr. Romeo and Dr. Juliet

Once upon a time there were two dentists, Dr. Romeo and Dr. Juliet. They both were "bread-and-butter" general dentists and practiced together for many years. They had similar clinical skills and experience, plenty of happy general care patients, and successful practices.

Although they were pleased with their general practices, they both wanted to provide more complex care dentistry. However, Drs. Romeo and Juliet were discouraged because, in spite of all they did to boost their clinical skills, they still did only very few complex-care cases.

One day Dr. Romeo said to Dr. Juliet, "*We need to do something to get more new patients who need complex care.*"

"*Absolutely,*" replied Dr. Juliet.

So Dr. Romeo and Dr. Juliet went off to see the famous Wizard of Marketing.

"*There's no doubt that I can help you two,*" grunted the Wizard after listening to their requests for more complex care patients.

"*In fact, I can absolutely guarantee you I can attract many new complex-care patients to your practice. But I'll do it only on one condition,*" said the Wizard, raising an eyebrow.

"*What's that?*" both dentists asked.

With a wry smile the Wizard said, "*The condition is this: one of you will* treat only those complex care patients who are ready to accept your entire treatment plan the first time it's offered. The other one will treat no patients who are ready the first time it's offered; however, those patients will remain in your practice and when they become ready, they'll ask you to do their complete care. Choose now and choose wisely."

Dr. Romeo was quick to speak, "I'm glad to take all the patients who're ready. That's an easy choice–get 'em when they're hot!"

"I guess that means I get ones who aren't ready," said Dr. Juliet, not too sure of what she had just gotten herself into.

And so Dr. Romeo focused on making patients ready. He bought all the latest high-tech equipment, took sales courses, and learned how to "close" the sale. He took patient education to new heights, making sure every new patient had a thorough examination and an in-depth consultation. He told every patient every little thing that was wrong with their teeth and how he'd fix it. "The more educated they are, the more ready they become," he thought.

Dr. Juliet didn't worry about making patients ready; after all, if they were ready she didn't get to treat them. Instead, she focused on building good relationships with them and did what she could for them, so when they did become ready for complete care, the treatment process was easy with minimal stress.

A few years later, the Wizard appeared in their office. "How's it going?" he asked, in a way that suggested he already knew the answer.

"I've done some very nice cases," said Dr. Romeo. The biggest frustration, though, is that most people don't get it. I tell and show them what they need, but most patients still prefer to spend their money on other things rather than to take care of their teeth. And if the insurance doesn't pay for their dentistry, a lot of patients just walk out the door. It's very frustrating at times."

"And how about you?" the Wizard asked Dr. Juliet.

"*It was rough in the beginning when all my new patients weren't ready,*" said Dr. Juliet. "*But life changes—weddings, new jobs, divorces—have a way of making people ready. It would sometimes be years after I first offered complete care that they came back, waving my treatment plan, saying, "I'm ready!" During that time they had gotten their lives in order so that finances, family, and work issues weren't too much of an obstacle. Over time I was doing complete care cases every day on patients I had first examined a few years earlier. It really seems to be working out.*"

Who Are You?

None of us have met the Wizard, yet many of us act like we have, in that we've made some strong choices on how we offer compete care dentistry. Are you more like Dr. Romeo, or Dr. Juliet? There are many dentists who focus on technology and tasks, are quick to give advice, and are looking to "close" the sale. However, there also are a growing number of dentists who focus on relationships, are quick to listen, and who look to understand "readiness" and wait for the right time for the patient to undergo treatment.

This book is about offering complete care dentistry, a topic that is rich in diverse opinions and processes. It is not about one "best way," but rather, the many ways in which patients can enter complete care. You have the freedom to make a choice to be like Dr. Romeo or Dr. Juliet. My advice is to choose the best of both. By showing you how to be a leader, and how to practice like one, this book will make it easier for your patients to say "Yes."

Chapter One
Leadership: The "Friendly Spirit" of Case Acceptance:
The Role of Leadership in Case Acceptance

There used to be times when I'd swear that my dental practice was haunted. Odd things would happen and nobody could explain why: patient records would vanish, then reappear months later; team members would fight like demons one day and hug each other the next; one day we'd make lots of money, the next day we'd be giving it back. The biggest mystery, though, was the patients. Some were angels, others were "phantoms of the operatory"—especially during case presentation. Some would hear my treatment recommendations, smile, and say "Yes." Others would sit there listening to me and as I'd get more into the technical aspects, they'd enter into an altered state as if they were hallucinating.

There was no doubt about it—my office was haunted. I had poltergeists—mischievous spirits that would make things happen for which there was no explanation. How about you? Do you have things going on in your office for which there is no explanation, especially concerning case acceptance? I'll bet you do. This chapter will help you solve some of the "mystery" in your office by introducing a way to get rid of your hidden demons: *leadership*. Leadership is the friendly spirit that makes case acceptance—and everything else that's good—happen in your practice. Leadership makes it easy for patients to say "Yes."

What is Leadership?

In *Principle-Centered Leadership*, author Steven Covey states that "leadership is the organization of people while management is the organization of things (i.e., systems)." The profit center in dental practices revolves around the dentists doing dentistry, not managing systems. Thus a dentist's ability to organize people to manage the systems in the practice is fundamental to his or her profitability. Let's further define *leadership in dentistry* as the ability to organize people to create a blend of clinical, organizational, and relationship/communication expertise. So the greater the complexity of care you offer, the more necessary it is for you to do this. The fundamental truth about advanced restorative dentistry is this: the greater the complexity of care you offer, the greater the demand for leadership skills.

Excellence Versus Leadership

Throughout this book I will make several distinctions. The first one is *excellence* versus *leadership*. Excellence is not a substitute for leadership. Most advanced continuing education (CE) courses do a great job of teaching clinical excellence. However, there are many aspects of excellence that patients don't perceive, such as perfect margins, tensionless flap approximations, tertiary anatomy, to name a few. In many ways, excellence is a personal experience enjoyed by you and your team. Often we alone know how good our restorations are. The impact of leadership, on the other hand, is immediately apparent to patients—great teamwork, supportive/nurturing relationship skills, on-time appointments, etc. Leadership must be the constant companion of excellence because it signals the presence of excellence, which may otherwise be imperceptible to the patient.

> **Leadership must be the constant companion of excellence because it signals the presence of excellence, which may otherwise be imperceptible to the patient.**

The Leadership Curve™

The Leadership Curve is a unique way of looking at leadership in dentistry. It illustrates how leadership requirements advance dramatically as the clinical complexity of care increases. It demonstrates how leadership is a prerequisite to practicing profitable, low-stress, advanced clinical care.

Figure 1-1 shows clinical skills, organizational skills , and relationship/communication skills. The vertical axis of the Leadership Curve represents the level of leadership. The horizontal aspect represents clinical range—the level of care you wish to provide.

FIGURE 1-1

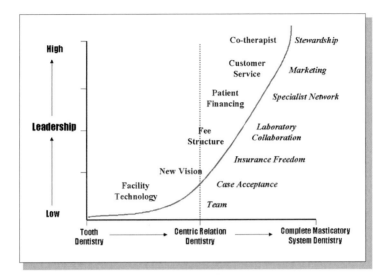

The Leadership Curve begins at *tooth dentistry*. Tooth dentistry means simple operative and general dental procedures, treating one tooth at a time. The level of leadership required for tooth dentistry is relatively low compared to that for complex care. Many dentists who are early in their career, exclusively doing tooth dentistry, are associates or are in residencies where they have little or no leadership responsibility. A good facility, reasonable overhead control, and staff that can manage the processes of delivering simple dentistry can get the job done.

As we move from left to right on the complexity of clinical care axis, tooth dentistry evolves into *quadrant dentistry*, where more than one tooth at a time is restored. Typically, quadrant dentistry involves two or three teeth. Fees for quadrant care are higher, laboratory relationships are more critical, and appointment control gets more complicated. Overall, the leadership requirement for quadrant care is greater than that for tooth dentistry.

Notice how the Leadership Curve turns sharply upward as the clinical complexity of care increases past the vertical line labeled "Centric Relation Dentistry" in **Figure 1-1**. It's at this point that the complexities of the conditions in the patient's mouth require the dentist to alter one or more of four critical clinical variables: anterior guidance, plane of occlusion, vertical dimension, and condylar position. Typically these alterations are necessary when more than four teeth per quadrant are restored. When one or more of these variables are changed, the complexity of care dramatically increases, as does the demand for better leadership (organizational and relationship) skills. Notice the labeled aspects of organizational and relationship skills along the ascending Leadership Curve. Don't assume, however, that this implies a rigid implementation sequence of these skills. Rather, this sequence is marked in a way that makes sense for most dentists.

Left-Side Versus Right-Side Patients

Throughout the remainder of this book I will make a distinction between procedures and patients relative to the centric relation line on the Leadership Curve—left-side and right-side (Figure 1-2).

FIGURE 1-2

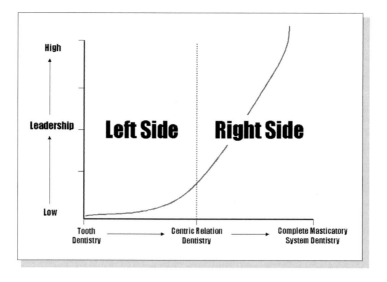

Left-side patients are those with minimal conditions who do not require changes in their anterior guidance, plane of occlusion, vertical dimension, and condylar position. Operative dentistry, single crowns, and quadrant dentistry are examples of left-side procedures and occur to the left of the centric relation line. Other left-side procedures include simple periodontics, endodontics, and tooth whitening.

Right-side patients are those whose clinical conditions require changes in anterior guidance, plane of occlusion, vertical dimension, and condylar position. Typically these procedures include cosmetic rehabilitations, partial and full reconstructions, and implant dentistry.

The descriptors *right-side* and *left-side* are used to make an important distinction between patients. These descriptors are not intended to suggest that right-side patients are better, smarter, more worthy of high-quality dentistry, or more deserving of your respect. Right-side and left-side simply are easy-to-remember labels for distinctions among patients. By making this distinction we can create the best possible experience for both right-side and left-side patients.

The "Making It Easy" Process

Most dentists do well with case acceptance for left-side patients; it's the right-side patient for whom we need a solution. This book shows you how to make it easy for right-side patients to accept treatment. You'll be able to apply the lessons learned here to left-side patients as well, making the entire case acceptance process a better experience for you and your team... and making it much easier for patients to say "Yes."

Different Strokes for Different Folks

Your experience of practicing dentistry is significantly different on the left and the right side of the line (**Figure 1-3**).

FIGURE 1-3

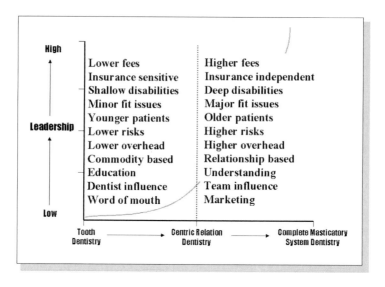

The differences between left-side and right-side dentistry are significant both from the perspective of the technical requirements of care and the organizational and relationship aspects. Right-side dentistry has much higher fees attached to it. Consequently, the impact of insurance is minimized; how the dentistry (fees, schedule, hassle factors) fits into the patient's life is pivotal; the level of customer service must be higher; there is a much greater need for relationship skills; and the influence of the team is critical. Because right-side dentistry is associated with more complex dental conditions, the technical and medical/legal risks are greater, the disability of the patient (how the disease affects his or her life) is deeper, and the overhead for producing the care is higher. Right-side care usually involves older patients, many with compromised medical issues. Older patients also require a special set of relationship skills, less emphasis on patient education, and a greater emphasis on empathy and understanding the issues of aging. Because this is a unique target market, marketing for right-side patients requires a very different message than that for left side patients.

The "Wall"

Many dentists expect that clinical training alone is enough to make rehabilitative care a big part of their practice and they therefore don't pursue leadership training. This belief is misguided, however, as the issues on the right-side require much greater leadership skills than those on the left. Inevitably, these dentists, avidly pursuing clinical education, slam head-first into the "wall" separating left- and right-side dentistry (**Figure 1-4**).

FIGURE 1-4

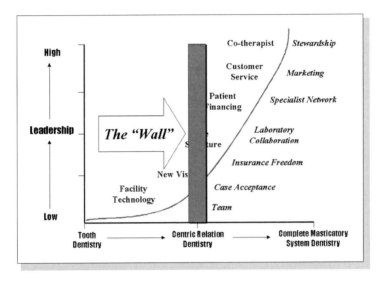

These dentists find that their typical accepted treatment plans top off with two to three units of crown and bridge, accompanied by some operative and hygienist-delivered periodontal care (in 2005 dollars, approximately $3,500–$5,000). This level of care is just short of centric relation dentistry. As a result, many patients with more complex needs and higher treatment fees go home to "think about it" and never return, leaving the dentist in his office to sulk. Some dentists blame the patient, others blame their team, and some blame themselves. Trying to grow a right-side practice without awareness of leadership skills is like fighting a ghost—you'll strike out at what you think is the problem, only to hit at thin air.

Leadership is the only way through the wall! Your ability to lead your practice affects the dentistry you do, the patients you treat, the team surrounding you, the prosperity you experience, and the legacy you leave.

> *Your ability to lead your practice affects the dentistry you do,
> the patients you treat, the team surrounding you,
> the prosperity you experience, and the legacy you leave.*

Unfortunately, there is minimal emphasis on leadership training in dentistry. You might accumulate hundreds of CE hours learning the technical side of dentistry, hoping that clinical savvy is your ticket to success. Sadly, if you're like most dentists, you discover that your success is stalled. You're not stalled by the clinical issues you've been so well-trained to deal with; rather, it's the issues of leadership—motivating team members and patients, managing entrepreneurial issues, communicating with impact, implementing the right vision—that hold you back. Like one unforeseen pothole after another, Leadership problems, if patched with trial-and-error solutions, keep your road to success a rough one. Sound familiar? You're not alone. Consider a new path and invest in your personal leadership skills. The real path to complete care is along the Leadership Curve, and clinical training is only one road on that journey. This book will help to give you the necessary tools to ascend the Leadership Curve.

Stress Distances People

Stress reduction is essential when creating quality relationships with patients. To paraphrase John Gray, Ph.D., author of *Men Are From Mars, Women Are From Venus,* "The greatest distance between people is stress."

Stress makes us our least authentic and likable selves. Again according to Gray, stress tends to make men contract (talk less and disconnect) and women expand (talk more and disconnect). When stressed, our truer nature is camouflaged by the stress-induced behavior; hence, patients never get to experience our true selves. Can patients sense when we're stressed? Of course, and their intuition leads them to draw conclusions about us and our team, such as, *"They're too busy here"* or *"Something's wrong."*

When we're not stressed, we become more authentic. Patients sense authenticity and love it. Authenticity is a form of disclosure. It gives patients a glimpse of our real selves and it's the sharing of our real selves that encourages them to share *themselves*. It's through this mutual sharing that relationships are formed and trust is earned. When trust is present you experience the best dentistry has to offer—great relationships with patients and team members and the satisfaction of doing the dentistry you love to do.

When you're doing the dentistry you love and have great relationships with the people around you, you'll experience greater fulfillment and peace. The sense of fulfillment and peace is contagious—it spreads to those around you and within your influence. People close to you, especially patients and team members, intuitively know your state of mind. When you're feeling satisfied with yourself, they want to be around you because they can start feeling the same way and feeling better about *themselves*.

Brian DesRoches, MBA, Ph.D., a psychologist and human systems consultant, talks about how leadership is a process where you help create positive self-experiences for your followers, motivating them to want to follow. Case acceptance is a form of leadership—patients need to have positive self-experiences when they're with you. When patients accept care, it boosts your confidence and adds to your inventory of wisdom in dealing with people (emotional intelligence). More confidence and greater wisdom leads to additional case acceptance.

The idea that case acceptance is a form of leadership—*helping people feel better about themselves in your presence*—is a key concept in this book. With traditional forms of case acceptance in which the emphasis is on describing disease and treatment processes, raising the patients' dental IQ, selling techniques, and visual aids, the intention of helping patients feel better about themselves can be missed. Often the reverse is true—patients feel *worse* about themselves after their diseases and troubles are laid at their feet...with a hefty price tag attached. We think we're doing the right thing by educating and explaining things, thinking we're motivating patients to receive care. Maybe not.

You've heard it a million times: *"Patients don't care how much you know, until they know how much you care."* Based on this maxim, we put considerable effort into impressing patients with our thoroughness: complex examinations and lengthy case presentations, and customer service: flowers, spa amenities, attempting to impress them with what we do and who we are. I'm all for thoroughness and customer service, but I wonder: Do our efforts to impress patients sabotage the richer experience of helping patients feel better about who they are? It's the *good* dental team that helps patients feel good about the team; it's the *great* dental team that helps patients feel good about themselves.

I believe this principle of leadership operates in all areas of life—what works in the dental office works in other aspects of life as well. Helping people feel better about themselves is a life skill and the dental office is a great place to learn it. Learn it at work and you'll be able to use it no matter what you do or where you go.

In a Nutshell
Chapter One—The Role of Leadership in Case Acceptance

- There is an important distinction between excellence and leadership. Excellence is not a substitute for leadership.

- Leadership in dentistry is the ability to organize people to create a blend of clinical, organizational, and relationship/communication expertise. The greater the complexity of care you offer, the greater the demand for leadership skills.

- There are many aspects of excellence in dentistry that patients don't perceive. The impact of leadership, however, is immediately apparent to patients—great teamwork, supportive/nurturing relationship skills, on-time appointments, etc.

- Left-side patients are those with minimal conditions who do not require changes in their anterior guidance, plane of occlusion, vertical dimension, and condylar position. Right-side patients are those whose clinical conditions require changes in anterior guidance, plane of occlusion, vertical dimension, and condylar position.

- The differences between left-side and right-side dentistry are significant. Because right-side dentistry has much higher fees, the impact of insurance is minimized and how the dentistry fits into the patient's life is pivotal. Therefore, the level of customer service must be higher and there is a much greater need for relationship skills.

- It's the lack of leadership, rather than the lack of clinical skills, that keeps many dentists from reaching the success they desire.

Chapter Two
Dollars (and Sense):
The Risks of Complex Dentistry

O f course right-side dentistry has rewards, but it also has risks. It's exciting to see beautiful photographs of right-side cases in lecture halls, and thoughts of big fees rolling in may be intoxicating, but I guarantee you that right-side dentistry is not all roses. There's plenty of hard work, stress, and risks. If you want to do more right-side dentistry you have to be willing to do the work and pay the price.

If you want to do more right-side dentistry you have to be
willing to do the work and pay the price.

This chapter offers simple ways to determine the percentage of right-side dentistry you currently perform. It also addresses the economic risks of evolving your practice from tooth care to complete rehabilitative care. Knowing what your financial risks are and how to manage them can be the difference between your experience of right-side dentistry being heaven or hell.

The 70/30 Mix
During seminars and workshops, I poll participants and my experience is that most dentists have practices that are left-side dominant. Many dentists tell me that 90 to 95 percent of their patients are left-side patients.

I believe what makes sense for most general dentists is to have a practice that is approximately 70 percent left-side patients and 30 percent right-side patients (**Figure 2-1**). Here's why.

FIGURE 2-1

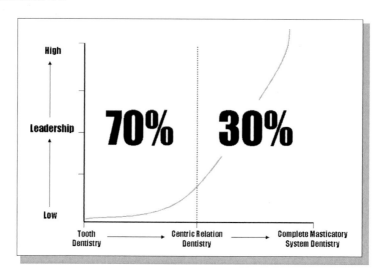

Having 70 percent of your practice on the left side protects you from downturns in the economy. Diversifying your technical mix provides some safety and stabilizes cash flow in tough times. Left-side patients, over time and with worsening conditions, may become right-side patients. Additionally, associate dentists can be fully engaged with the left-side patients. You can delegate hygiene examinations and simpler treatment plans to them, freeing you to focus more on right-side patients. Having 30 percent of your practice on the right side provides the professional stretch and the sense of accomplishment many of us seek. Although a 70/30 mix may not seem too sexy compared to celebrity right-side practices, a 70/30 mix means that one-third of your patents have four or more units of restorative dentistry. Most general practitioners I know would be very happy with this.

A good way to conceptualize the 70/30 goal is to think of it as two practices. The 70 percent left-side portion is steady and predictable—the cash flow side of your practice. It pays your bills, funds your retirement, and helps a lot of patients.

The 30 percent right-side portion is the "juice" side of your practice. It provides the excitement and energy for growth. On the right side we stretch our professional skills and experience significant rewards, both financial and spiritual, that help make dentistry fun and purposeful again.

The Making It Easy process is about building the 30 percent right-side practice and/or refining an existing right-side practice.

I'm cautious about recommending that dentists pursue a predominantly right-side practice. I believe it's far more practical for most general dentists to have a diversified technical mix. It's more achievable and less stressful. And when the time comes, diversified practices are easier to sell.

Determining Your Practice Mix

Determine what percentage of your practice is right side by totaling the collections from patients who are in active complex treatment where changes in anterior guidance, vertical dimension, plane of occlusion, and condylar position are required. Compare this number to the total fees collected (dentist only) over a specified interval, two or three months. Another way to estimate right-side percentage is to total the number of patients in active treatment whose accepted treatment plans exceed four or more restorative units (more than $5,000) and compare them to the total of patients with accepted treatment plans of fewer than four units (less than $5,000). After doing this computation, most dentists say that their percentage of right-side cases is much lower than they expected it to be (typically, most of the general dentists I've had do this computation discover that they have 2 percent to 10 percent right-side practices).

I'm well aware of practices that are far more than 30 percent on the right side—cosmetic, implant, TMJ specialty-like practices. My recommendation is that if you want a predominantly right-side practice, build it within a large left-side practice—a "practice within a practice." Bring in another dentist or dentists to sustain and grow the left side, while you focus your attention, energy, and time on the right side. For the last 18 years, I have focused exclusively on right-side patients while my associates developed the left side. Many general practitioners have done this successfully.

Progressing from Left Side to Right Side

Let's take a look at the typical progression from tooth dentistry to rehabilitative dentistry that a dentist goes through when building a right-side practice (**Figure 2-2**).

FIGURE 2-2

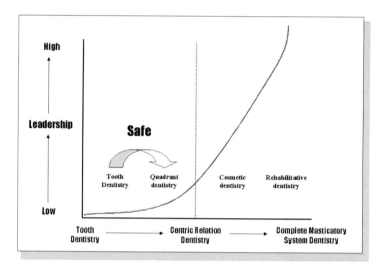

The first step is to evolve from tooth dentistry to quadrant dentistry. This is a very safe move from the point of view of profitability and patient care. You have all the elements in your office to do this—no new technology or materials are required. For most general dentists the jump from tooth care to quadrant care yields a huge jump in profitability and patient satisfaction. In fact, the most profitable process for most general dentists is to do three crowns in the same quadrant at the same time—only one quadrant to anesthetize, one impression, one opposing model, one bite registration, one laboratory, and one straightforward insertion appointment ten days later. Life is good!

However, to evolve from quadrant care (left side), to centric relation dentistry (right side), where you are altering anterior guidance, vertical dimension, plane of occlusion, or condylar position, is risky (**Figure 2-3**).

FIGURE 2-3

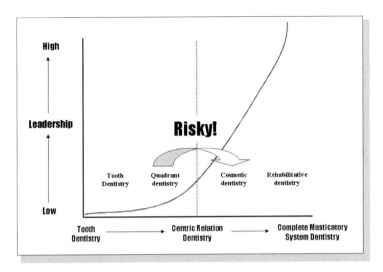

The risks reside in the loss of profitability. Right-side dentistry requires more time (patient chair time and planning time) laboratory fees, clinical risks, and remakes that our fees may not take into account. When the fees for right side dentistry do not account for the additional costs, time and risks, the profitability for right-side dentistry can be less than that for left-side dentistry.

When you practice right-side dentistry with insufficient leadership skills you take a big risk. The leadership deficits most responsible for these negative side effects of right-side dentistry are related to team issues, case acceptance/patient relationships, fee model, third-party payers, and laboratory relationships. Let's look at a fee model that helps take some of the risk out of right-side dentistry.

The Right Fee Solution™

The Right Fee Solution, which I developed with Ken Mathys, CPA, and Dental Practice Advisors LLC (Green Bay, WI), is a fee model for complex (quadrant, cosmetic, implant, and reconstructive) dentistry. It's designed to help you determine the right fee in the real world of advanced dentistry where outcomes aren't certain, treatment plans are complex (and may change mid-treatment), laboratory fees are variable, the probability for partial and total remakes is high, and fee models based on local comparisons and insurance limitations don't apply. (To learn more about how the Right Fee Solution can be customized for your practice, visit my web site at www.paulhomoly.com).

The Right Fee Solution is based on the premise that the greater the complexity of care you provide, the greater your profit per hour deserves to be (**Figure 2-4**).

FIGURE 2-4

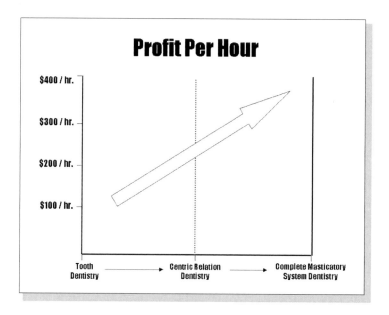

For example, let's say for the quadrant care case (three crowns) discussed earlier, you charge $800 a unit for ceramo-metal crowns. Your laboratory charges are $600 ($200/unit), and it takes you one-and-a-half hours to prepare and make temporaries and one hour to cement the crowns. Assuming a 56 percent overhead (not including lab expenses), your profit yield is $314/hr. This is an excellent profit yield, with minimal risk or potential for remake.

Quadrant Dentistry—Three crowns
>   Patient fee: $2,400
>   Lab fee: $600
>   Total time: 2.5 hours
>   Total profit: $314/hr.

> *The big mistake most dentists make is taking their fee for*
> *doing a single unit and simply multiplying it by the number*
> *of units to calculate the total fee for a right-side case.*

Now, let's do some right-side dentistry: 16 veneers under the same overhead and fee model. The big mistake most dentists make is taking their fee for doing a single unit and simply multiplying it by the number of units to calculate the total fee for a right-side case. For example, your unit fee for a veneer is $900. The lab fee is $300 per unit. Your total time to complete this case, including patient consultations, diagnostic wax-ups, treatment planning, lab consultations, imaging, photos, trial equilibrations, tooth preparations, insertion appointment, adjustments, etc. is 21 hours. (If this seems high to you, put some effort into tracking your time—you may be unpleasantly surprised.) Here's how the 16-veneer case looks:

Sixteen Veneers
>   Patient fee: $15,200 (unit fees plus diagnostic fees)
>   Lab fee: $5,200 (unit fees plus diagnostic lab fees)
>   Total time: 21 hours
>   Total profit: $208 / hr.

The 16-veneer case under these patient fee, lab fee, time, and practice overhead conditions yields a profit of $208/hr. (roughly two-thirds the profit yield for the quadrant case previously discussed. Now what if you had to remake part of this veneer case? Let's say you remade 10 percent of it, using 10 percent more lab fees, overhead, and time. Your profit yield now sinks to $143/hr., which is only a little more than if you were doing a $150 composite. Compounding all of this is that in order to do this 16-veneer case, you increased your overall overhead by attending continuing education classes, purchasing equipment, and training your team. After you've spent significant sums on all the necessary apparatus (digital cameras, diagnostic equipment, articulators, etc.), your overhead probably is higher now than when you started!

In order to get back to the profit-per-hour level of quadrant care ($314/hour) you need to raise your fee for this 16-veneer case to $20,300. To cover your costs in the event of a 10 percent remake, your fee needs to be $24,800, which works out to a unit fee of $1,550 per unit. As painful as that sounds, however, it's still not enough. Why? Because the skill needed and risks of the 16-unit veneer case are much greater than those for the quadrant-care case and you should be yielding higher profit/hr., even with remakes. How much more? Most dentists say at least 15 percent more, which now brings the fee to $28,520, or $1,782 per unit–almost twice your original unit fee of $900. (Note: Do not increase your unit fee in insurance claims or in patient communications. Add the additional fees necessary for appropriate profit in other categories such as occulsal analysis, equilibration, consultation, diagnostic provisionals, photography, etc.)

Figure 2-5 represent the profit yield of a 16-veneer case compared to left-side operative dentistry and quadrant dentistry.

FIGURE 2-5

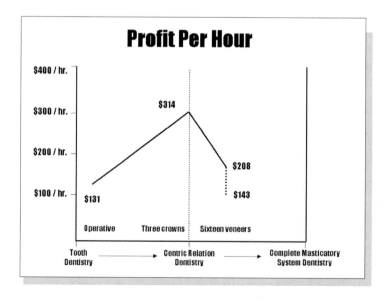

Operative dentistry in this example yields $131/hr., quadrant care (three crowns) yields $314/hr., 16 veneers yield $208/hr. and $143/hr. with remaking 10 percent of the case. What isn't shown in this Figure are the increases in overhead and stress. Right-side dentistry, because it harbors more risks and requires far more skill, needs to yield much greater profit than left-side care. A right-side practice with proper leadership and fee models should show profit yields on the right side consistently greater than those on the left side. In many practices, however, the profit from left-side dentistry subsidizes the lack of profit from right-side dentistry.

FIGURE 2-6

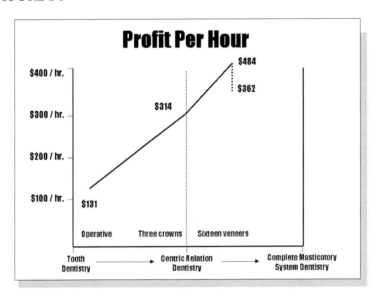

Figure 2-6 represents the 16-veneer case done with a fee model that provides increased profit as the complexity of care increases. The profit yield is $484/hr. and $362/hr. with a 10 percent remake of the case.

The original fee of this case using a unit fee approach was $15,220. The Right Fee Solution using a profit per hour approach is $28,520. Most dentists, when they see this jump in fee, think, "*I have enough problems selling a case for $15,000, let alone for $28,000*" and get depressed. Think about the fee demands of right-side dentistry as the first domino to fall in a line of other demands of the right side. Because you need to charge premium fees, it underscores the absolute requirement of building your relationship skills with patients and team members. In other words, the premium fees that right-side dentistry demands require premium case acceptance skills and all the other leadership skills on the Leadership Curve.

> *The premium fees that right-side dentistry demands*
> *require premium case acceptance skills and all the other*
> *leadership skills on the Leadership Curve.*

Finally, **Figure 2-7** shows the profit yield plotted along side of the Leadership Curve. Notice how the two curves escalate as the complexity of care increases. The greater the complexity of care, the greater the profit yield deserves to be.

FIGURE 2-7

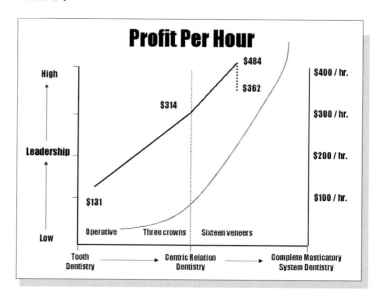

Here's the point. "Wannabe" rehabilitative dentists practicing with left-side fee models and undeveloped leadership skills end up with some very pretty photos of cosmetic cases but suffer intellectually, emotionally, and financially. Without leadership and appropriate fee models, right-side dentistry is no picnic.

Leadership is the Answer

If you're searching for the answer to the question, *"How do I get to the next level?"* I'll bet you're taking lots of courses, mostly clinical continuing education. If you spent half the time and money on advancing your leadership skills as you do advancing your clinical skills you'd be happier, more profitable, and do more right-side dentistry. Remember, the greater the complexity of care you offer, the greater the demand for leadership skills.

In a Nutshell
Chapter Two—The Risks of Complex Care

- What makes sense for most general dentists is having a practice where approximately 70 percent of your practice is left-side patients and 30 percent is right-side patients. The 70 percent left-side portion is the cash flow side of your practice. The 30 percent right-side portion is the "juice" side of your practice.

- For most general dentists, the jump from tooth care to quadrant care yields a huge jump in profitability and patient satisfaction.

- To evolve from quadrant care (left side) to centric relation dentistry (right side) is risky. The risks reside in the loss of profitability. When the fees for right-side dentistry do not take account of the additional costs, time, and risks, our profitability for right-side dentistry can be less than that for left-side dentistry.

- The Right Fee Solution is based on the premise that the greater the complexity of care you provide, the greater your profit per hour deserves to be.

- If you spent half the time and money on advancing your leadership skills as you do advancing your clinical skills you'd be happier, more profitable, and do more right-side dentistry.

Chapter Three
The "Jigsaw Puzzle" of Right-Side Case Acceptance:
Fitting the Pieces Together

I remember getting jigsaw puzzles as gifts when I was young. My older sister, Bonnie, and I would stand at the kitchen table and dump all the pieces out, then we'd prop the cover of the box up so we could see the big picture of how the puzzle was supposed to look when we were done. I liked the puzzles of tall pirate ships being tossed about in the high seas with their cannons blazing; Bonnie liked puzzles of horses.

Case acceptance for complete dentistry is like a puzzle—there are lots of little, but important, pieces. This chapter is the "big picture" on the cover of the puzzle box. It's important to understand the big picture, otherwise it's too easy to get lost in all the little pieces.

The Traditional Approach
Case acceptance for right-side dentistry traditionally has been taught using a linear process as depicted in **Figure 3-1**.

FIGURE 3-1

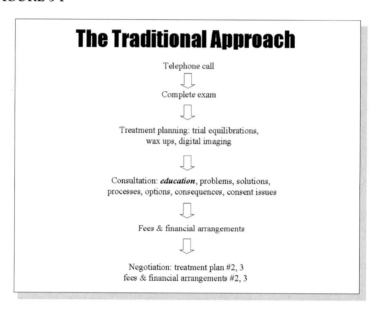

The traditional approach focuses on patient education. We educate patients with the intention of raising their dental IQ so they can understand and appreciate the processes (crowns, bridges, implants, etc.) they need. Chances are good that if you've taken advanced CE courses in occlusion, cosmetic dentistry, or implant dentistry you've been exposed to this traditional process and might be using something like it in your practice.

The traditional process begins with the telephone call. New adult patients are scheduled for a complete examination; this is based on the belief that all complete care must start with a thorough examination.

The new patient typically is seen by a team member who'll review medical history, get an idea of what the patient is interested in, and take full-mouth radiographs. Following this, the dentist will do a complete examination, study models, facebow record, etc. The patient is then dismissed and rescheduled a week later for a consultation appointment.

In the interim, the case is diagnosed and treatment planned by using insights gained through trial equilibrations, diagnostic wax ups, digital imaging, CT scans, etc. Based on the treatment plan, a fee is established.

A week later the patient returns for the treatment presentation. The focus of this consultation appointment is patient education, based on the premise that raising the patient's dental IQ increases the likelihood of case acceptance. The dentist or treatment coordinator starts the consultation with a complete description of all the existing pathology and other conditions that are outside of normal and healthy limits, usually accompanied by a show-and-tell using the patient's radiographs and study models. After describing what's wrong with the patient's mouth, the solutions (crowns, implants, etc.) are discussed along with the processes for their completion (tooth preparation, surgeries, etc.). Once the solutions and processes are described, alternative treatments are discussed, along with *their* processes. Finally, informed consent is established by discussing the benefits, risks, and consequences of all the potential treatment plans.

After the patient has heard treatment recommendations, financial disclosures are made—time in treatment, fees, insurance, and financial arrangements. Based on the patient's financial health and multiple other factors, a treatment plan and its fee are negotiated.

What Really Happens
The traditional process looks good on paper, and under ideal conditions is a predictable way of processing new adult right-side patients. All too often, however, conditions are not ideal and the textbook approach to case acceptance is not successful or realistic. Here are a few ways in which the traditional process can stall.

All too often, however, conditions are not ideal and the textbook approach to case acceptance is not successful or realistic.

The initial appointment for right-side patients in the traditional approach is a complete examination. The problem here is that often the new right-side patient believes she is best served, not by a complete examination, but rather by relief of a condition causing her a problem—a dark tooth, a loose partial denture—or she simply may want her teeth cleaned.

Forcing patients to adhere to an office policy that every new patient must go through a complete examination before any dental work is performed will on many occasions cause a contest of will between the patient and the dentist/team.

The consultation appointment is another area of the traditional approach that invites disaster. The root of the problem is in the assumption that the patient is ready for and wants complete care. Compounding this is the mistaken belief that our role as dentists is to "save" people from their dental disease and that motivating and educating them is for their own good. The truth is most patients aren't ready for right-side care, not because they have low dental IQs, but because the costs and time factors simply don't fit into their lives at that point. When their life issues are not taken into consideration and hefty fees are quoted for procedures they aren't ready for, it's no surprise that many patients leave the practice frustrated and angry. And when they do decide to get their teeth fixed, they go elsewhere.

The truth is most patients aren't ready for right-side care, not because they have low dental IQs, but because the costs and time factors simply don't fit into their lives at that point.

Patient education is a major theme throughout the traditional new patent experience, theoretically preparing patients to make informed choices about their healthcare. Typically no efforts are made to understand patients' lifestyle requirements and limitations—budgets, work schedules, family issues. The single greatest issue that impacts patients' decisions to accept complete care is how it fits into their lifestyle, but we spend our time educating them on how the dentistry will fit into their mouths. Often treatment plans are accepted based on lifestyle and financial circumstances, not what is the superior clinical solution.

A big part of the stress for the dentist and team is dealing with the financial issues. Because financial issues are usually the last thing to be discussed at the consultation appointment, stress escalates as we approach the financial discussion (**Figure 3-2**). This stress robs us of our authenticity just when we need it most. Financial discussions are important and if the dentist and/or team member is handicapped by their stress, patients sense it, consciously or unconsciously, and are negatively influenced by it.

FIGURE 3-2

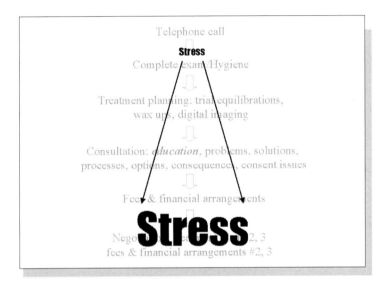

A huge problem with the traditional approach is that fees and affordability issues usually don't surface until after the dentist, team, and patient have invested hours in the processes of examination and consultation. Let's look at the time involved in the traditional case acceptance process **(Figure 3-3)**.

FIGURE 3-3

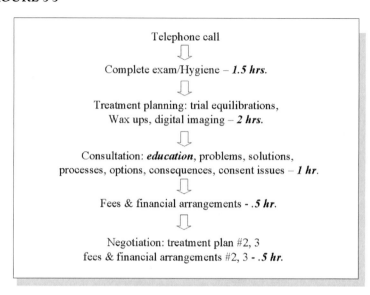

For a complex case, it's not unusual to spend up to five hours in the entire process. If the patient says "yes," then the five hours have been well spent. If the patients says "no" and does not go through treatment in the future, then the five hours have been lost, along with a big helping of your profitability. How many times have you spent several hours working up a case only to have the patient go home to "think about it"... and never return? Too many, I'll bet. How much could you have collected if you were doing left-side dentistry for five hours instead of the right-side examinations and planning? Try not to think about it.

Results of the Traditional Approach

The traditional approach can be an excellent one under the ideal circumstances (the patient is ready, willing, and able to accept care). Unfortunately these are rare circumstances in most bread-and-butter general practices. Here are some typical responses to the traditional approach when presenting complex right-side care (the first is a good response, the rest aren't!):

- *"Yes—when can we start?"*
- *"Yes, but I need to go home and think about it."*
- *"I don't know, I'll have to think about it. I'll call you back."*

- *"Wow, I had no idea it would cost this much."*
- *"Do I really need this much work?"*
- *"No, all I really wanted was to get my front tooth fixed."*
- *"Hell, no!"* (and calls three days later and asks for his records)
- *"Yes, when can we start?"* (but fails to keep the first appointment)

Do any of those negative responses seem too familiar? If they are, it might be time for you to think about presenting right-side care from a different point of view. In the traditional approach to case acceptance, we educate patients with the intention of raising their dental IQ so they can understand and appreciate the processes (crowns, bridges, implants, etc.) they need. The traditional approach focuses on educating the patient and tooth-fixing processes. This book focuses on understanding patients and their lifestyle issues.

The "Making It Easy" Approach

The focus of the Making It Easy approach is on understanding, not educating, patients and realizing that their lifestyle issues must be taken into account when presenting high-fee procedures. This approach is designed to avoid the potential contests of will, surprises, embarrassment, and stress of the traditional approach. (I referred to it as the "No Contest" case presentation technique in my first book, *Dentists: An Endangered Species*, and continued to develop the theme in my second book, *Isn't It Wonderful When Patients Say "Yes."* Since then I've coached hundreds of dentists and team members and have had the pleasure of working with truly talented practitioners who have helped me continue to evolve the concepts of case acceptance that you're about to read about.)

The Five Critical Dialogues

At the heart of the process are five Critical Dialogues (CD-1 through CD-5): Identity, Choice, Advocacy, Warm-up, and Financial Options. (Don't confuse references to CD-1, CD-2 etc. throughout this book with compact discs; they are simply referring to the sequence of the Critical Dialogues–CDs.) Each dialogue is designed to advance right-side patients to their next step toward complete care.

The five critical dialogues are woven throughout the experience of case acceptance for the right-side patient. Some right-side patients might need only two appointments—examination and consultation—to accept care. More commonly, however, the right-side patient may take months to years to become ready to accept complete dentistry. Either way, the critical dialogues guide the dental team in building the relationships with right-side patients, however long it takes to complete their care. (The dialogues are also useful for left-side patients, and I will point out their appropriateness throughout this book.)

The five dialogues are not rigid sales scripts; scripted responses to patients' questions and comments sound like selling and rob you of your authenticity. The critical dialogues are driven by their intentions and once you embrace the intention of the dialogue, the words you use become your own.

FIGURE 3-4

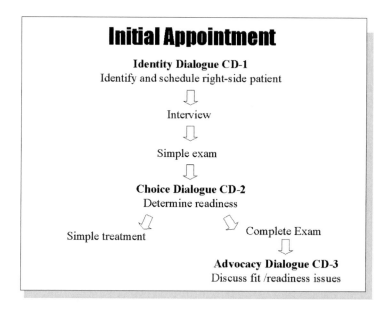

The Identity Dialogue, CD-1

Figure 3-4 illustrates the structure of the new patient initial appointment. The right-side process starts with the new-patient telephone call (Identity Dialogue, CD-1). The Identity Dialogue occurs during the patient's initial telephone call to your office. Its intention is to identify whether the caller is a left- or right-side patient and to schedule the caller appropriately.

Determining the left- or right-side status is critical because it governs how this patient is processed at the initial visit. Right-side patients are scheduled at the first appointment in the morning or afternoon, with nothing else on the dentist's schedule. This allows the clinical team a wide variety of options on how to best serve the patient, ensures the new patient is seen on time, minimizes stress, and helps create the best opportunity to make an outstanding first impression on the patient.

The new patient interview. The new right-side patient's initial appointment starts with the new patient interview with the dentist. The goals of the interview are to review medical and dental history; clarify the patient's expectations for the initial appointment; and to begin to discover the patient's attitudes toward, past experiences with, and goals for dentistry. The conversation is not focused on the dentist, treatment recommendations, or practice-centered activities (i.e., reciting mission statements or patient education). Resist making treatment recommendations during the new patient conversation. Its focus should be on listening to the patient's story and learning how we can best make this new patient happy with her first experience with us. It can be useful to have a team member present to document the critical aspects of the conversation, such as significant current events, dental history issues, goals for dental health, and financial concerns.

Limited initial examination. When the new patient interview is complete, the new right-side patient is put in an operatory for a limited initial examination. Typically as part of this limited examination (CDT-5 D0140) a panoral radiograph is taken, plus an oral cancer examination, a periodontal screening, and general charting of the dentition is completed. The goal of the limited examination is to gain an overall understanding of the patient's dental health, identify any clinical conditions currently bothering the patient (chief complaints), meet the standard of care, move through the clinical aspects of the new patient experience, and return to the communication/relationship aspect.

Choice Dialogue, CD-2

Post-examination discussion. Immediately following the limited examination is the post-examination discussion, the objective of which is to discover the right-side patient's level of readiness for accepting complete care. For example, new right-side patient Tom is concerned about a dark front tooth. His daughter is getting married in three weeks and he wants to look good for the wedding. During the simple examination you notice his discolored front tooth, along with many other conditions that he is either unaware of or not concerned about. You know from the interview that he is most interested in doing something about his front tooth, but you're concerned about the rest of this mouth. Many complete-care dentists face this problem: Should they do what will make the patient happy in the short run (fix the front tooth), or recommend complete care and risk offering the patient too much dentistry he might not be ready for?

The Choice Dialogue, CD-2, solves this problem of determining patient readiness. The Choice Dialogue is a question you ask during the post-examination discussion that reveals patient readiness for complete care. It sounds like this:

"Tom, today you have a choice. We can make your front tooth look great
for your daughter's wedding or, in addition to that, would today be a
good time for me to look at all the conditions in your mouth and begin to
develop a plan for a lifetime of dental health? What's best for you today?"

The assumption is, of course, that the new patient's chief concern is met within the standard of care, both your personal standard and the medical/legal standard.

The Choice Dialogue gives the patient a choice between addressing his chief concern (dark front tooth) or, in addition to that, starting the process for comprehensive care (a complete examination).

Notice the phrase in the choice dialogue, *"...in addition to...;"* this makes the choice an inclusive one. It's not an either/or choice. The patient hears that his main concern is being addressed and has the choice of also beginning a comprehensive process. The choice the patient makes reveals his level of readiness for complete care. Patients who are not ready will choose only to fix their chief concern. Patients who are more ready typically elect to address their chief concern and also start the process for comprehensive planning.

Under the traditional circumstances, this flexibility of structure at the new patient's initial visit is hard to manage. However, because we identified this patient as a right-side patient during the telephone call (Identity Dialogue) we are able to easily accommodate the patient's choice because we have plenty of time and no other patients waiting for us.

If Tom elects to fix only his front tooth at this time, we do it cheerfully (at this appointment or additional appointments) and when he is satisfied, we re-offer comprehensive care:

> *"Tom, now that we have your front tooth looking good, go and enjoy your daughter's wedding. My recommendation is that after the wedding you return here and have us do a complete examination for you. You have conditions in your mouth that, if left untreated, can give you problems in the future. Let's talk to Ginger at the front desk and get you that examination appointment."*

The Choice Dialogue guides us to the care that the patient is ready for. It also demonstrates our willingness to provide great service and reduces our frustration and wasted time by eliminating the long complete examination and consultation appointments for patients who aren't interested or ready. The toughest part about the Choice Dialogue is accepting their choice. Our role in the Making It Easy process is not to make patients ready for complete care, but to recognize those who are, and for those who aren't, maintain an excellent relationship so when they do become ready, they will choose us.

The complete examination. If our new right-side patient chooses to pursue complete care, then we begin our complete examination. If you combine the complete examination with treating a chief concern, you might not have time to finish your examination. If so, reschedule the patient.

One of the big differences between the traditional approach and the Making It Easy approach is that we are diagnosing readiness for complete care *before* we diagnose the mouth for compete care. When patients aren't ready for care, and they're forced to go through a complete examination and consultation, you'll hear objections (*"Why do I need so many x-rays?" "How much is all this going to cost?"* etc.), and you and your new patient will be disappointed with the outcome. When patients are ready for a comprehensive approach, the complete examination and consultation appointments flow more easily.

The Advocacy Dialogue

The Advocacy Dialogue, CD-3, immediately follows the complete examination. This dialogue begins to explore how comprehensive care fits into the current aspects of the patient's life—budget, work schedule, vacations, family events, stressors, etc. As every complete-care dentists learns, often treatment plans are accepted based on lifestyle and financial circumstances, not on what is the superior clinical solution. Consequently, it's smart to know what's going on in your patient's life before you recommend complex, time-consuming, and expensive dentistry.

To deliver the Advocacy Dialogue as it's intended, it's important to learn what significant life issues/events exist for the patient. We learn about the patient's life by being interested and curious about it and learn to listen for those things that compete with and/or are obstacles to complete care.

> *We learn about the patient's life by being interested and curious about it and learn to listen for those things that compete with and/or are obstacles to complete care.*

The Advocacy Dialogue links what's going on in patients' lives with what's going on in their mouths. For example, we learn from telephone conversations, the interview, and chitchat during the examination process that Donna's two sons are starting college this fall, and she travels extensively because of her job. We also know from her examination that she's aggravated by her mandibular partial denture, especially during business meals. The Advocacy Dialogue links her life with her dental needs and encourages a conversation about how dentistry fits into her life now.

> *"Donna, I understand that you've got a lot on your plate right now with your two boys starting college this fall and your heavy travel schedule. I also know that you're frustrated with your lower partial and it's embarrassing during business meals. Next time [consultation appointment] we'll sit down and talk about your choices and let's find the best way to fit fixing your teeth into what's going on in our life. Can you help me understand that better?"*

The last sentence, *"Can you help me understand that better?"* is designed to encourage a response from the patient that opens a conversation about how much treatment costs, how much time it takes, how much insurance pays, etc. For right-side dentistry we want to give the patient a ballpark estimate of costs, time, and other fit issues before we spend a lot of time (ours and the patient's) in treatment planning and consultation. We want patients to have an idea of how complete care will or will not fit into their lives. If it fits, then we can have confidence proceeding with our treatment planning and consultation appointment. If it doesn't fit, or if only part of it does, then we adjust our treatment recommendations. The dentistry that doesn't get done now is completed when it fits.

The Advocacy Dialogue reassures the patient that her life circumstances are respected; it alerts the dentist and team to the realities of the patient's life as they impact treatment planning; it results in the patient having a ballpark estimate of costs, time, and financial arrangement and insurance issues; and it avoids the embarrassment and anger that can result from offering complete care to patients whose life circumstances make it impossible for them to say "Yes."

Treatment planning. The case acceptance process continues in the patient's absence, with treatment planning. From the Advocacy Dialogue we have a sense of how our recommendations fit into the patient's life. At this point we don't know exactly how the patient will proceed, but we certainly have more insight into the patient's fit issues than with the traditional approach. During the treatment planning process, it's very useful to survey your team to be sure all known fit and readiness issues are documented. These issues are critical to the consultation appointment, which is ideally scheduled within a week following the examination.

The Consultation Appointment

The consultation appointment has three parts—the Warm-up Dialogue, CD-4; the Financial Options Dialogue, CD-5; and the technical case presentation (Figure 3-5).

FIGURE 3-5

Consultation Appointment

Warm-up Dialogue CD-4:
offers hope and opens fit/readiness conversation

Financial Options Dialogue CD-5:
total fee, total time, affordable options,
negotiation

Technical Case Presentation:
informed consent

The Warm-up Dialogue

The Warm-up Dialogue, CD-4, begins the consultation appointment and is a short discussion that gives the patient:

- our acknowledgment of why she is unhappy about her teeth
  (*"Michelle, I understand why you're not confident in the appearance of your front teeth..."*)
- our understanding of the patient's readiness/timing issues (*"Michelle, I also know that you're anxious to get your teeth looking great before the big business event you're hosting in three months."*)
- a clear statement of the chief benefit the patient is seeking (*"After reviewing your photos and models I am certain that I can restore your confidence in the appearance of your teeth."*)
- a brief description of the technical process in laymen's language
  (*"We'll remove the dark fillings and chipped enamel and replace it with a new enamel-like material. This is pretty easy for you and it takes about*

two appointments.")
- a reminder that the patient's care will be done with her lifestyle in mind ("*Of course, Michelle, before we start any of this, let's make sure this fits into what's going on for you at work and at home.*")
- an offer to address her questions about fees, insurance, scheduling, etc. ("*Michelle, what questions or comments about your care do you have for me?*").

The Warm-up Dialogue is not intended as a substitute for the ethical and medical legal requirements of informed consent. Rather, it's a simple way of discussing treatment recommendations and exploring how the recommendations fit into the patient's life at that point. The Warm-up Dialogue intentionally avoids going into any technical detail; we want the patient's response to be related to cost and time issues, rather than questions about confusing technical processes she doesn't understand. The objectives of the Warm-up Dialogue are two-fold: to give the patient hope that she will be happy with her result and to reopen the discussion about cost and time issues.

The Financial Options Dialogue

Most patients, after hearing the Warm-up Dialogue and the offer to answer any questions or comments ("*Michelle, what questions or comments about your care do you have for me?*"), will ask about the fees and administrative issues of care: time, insurance, number of appointments, etc. The Financial Options Dialogue, CD-5, answers these questions.

A written financial options form supports the Financial Options Dialogue. It's completed during the treatment planning phase, presented during the Financial Options Dialogue, and given to the patient to take home. The Financial Options Dialogue is the negotiation aspect of the consultation appointment. It's similar to the negotiation within the traditional approach except for one major difference. Within the Making It Easy approach, patients have a good idea of what the fee for care is from their previous appointment (The Advocacy Dialogue), and are rarely upset or embarrassed about the fees and financial arrangements when they hear them a second time. They might not be ready for complete care, but they won't be angered or embarrassed and leave your practice.

When the patient asks about fees, the Financial Options Dialogue provides information about:
- the total fee (including specialists fees)
- the total time in treatment
- the financial arrangement options.

"Michelle, your total treatment fee is $10,000 and it will take about three months to complete your care. Most patients prefer to begin their care with no initial payment and then make monthly payments. We can do that for you, and I estimate your payments to be $315 a month. Another option for you would be to pay one-third of your fee when we begin your care, one-third in the middle, and the final third when we're finished. If you prefer to pay in advance, we offer a 5 percent professional courtesy. Which option is best for you?"

Note that in this dialogue I'm offering an installment payment plan through a dental-financing service provider. Patient financing is critical for right-side care. Without it, a significant number of patients will not be able to fit complete care into their lives.

After the Financial Options Dialogue the patient, dentist, and financial coordinator come to an agreement on how to proceed with care. The financial coordinator can do most of the Financial Options Dialogue. Once the details of the financial arrangements have been completed and the next appointments have been set, the patient is ready for the technical aspects of case presentation.

The Technical Case Presentation

The technical case presentation is designed to meet the medical/legal standard of informed consent, telling the patient the benefits, risks, alternatives, and potential consequences of not being treated. It can be supported with visual aids, photographs, multimedia, and clinical diagnostic records and radiographs. The technical case presentation in the right-side process differs from the case presentation in the traditional model in that it occurs *after* the patient has accepted the financial and time commitments to care. Consequently it's a lot shorter and the patient is a better listener because any nagging fears about affordability have already been addressed. The stress normally associated with case presentation using the traditional model is completely absent. There are very few surprises and upsets. When the right-side process is done well, the technical case presentation can be an effortless conversation with the patient. Once the patient has acknowledged her understanding of the informed consent process (verbally or in writing), she is ready to begin complete care.

Overview

Figure 3-6 and **Figure 3-7** present an overview of the initial appointment and the consultation appointment with a new right-side patient. Listed are the processes, dialogues, and tools. It will help you to refer to these two charts as you progress through this book.

FIGURE 3-6

Process	Dialogue	Tools
Telephone Initial telephone contact *Identify right- vs. left-side patients* *Schedule for impact*	Identity Dialogue CD-1	Telephone call slip Discovery Guide side one
Initial appointment New patient interview *Disability, fit, and readiness issues* ↓		Discovery Guide side one & two
Limited examination *Condition(s) responsible for disability* ↓		Discovery Guide side one & two
Post limited examination discussion *Discovery Guide sequence 4,3,2,1* *Discover readiness* ↙ ↘	Choice Dialogue CD-2	Discovery Guide side one & two
Simple treatment Complete examination ↓		Discovery Guide side one & two
Post complete examination discussion *Reassure patient – link fit* *to disability issues*	Advocacy Dialogue CD-3	Discovery Guide side one & two
Treatment Planning		Discovery Guide side one & two Clinical treatment plan

FIGURE 3-7

Process	Dialogue	Tools
Consultation appointment		
Warm-up Dialogue *Give patient hope and reopen discussion about fit issues* ↓	Warm-up Dialogue CD-4	Discovery Guide side two
Financial arrangements *Total fee, duration of treatment, payment options* ↓	Financial Options Dialogue CD-5	Financial options form
		Clinical treatment plan
Technical case presentation *Informed consent issues*		Consent forms
Review of findings letter *Treatment recommendations*	Warm-up Dialogue in written form	Warm-up Dialogue letter
Patient Recall System		
Huddle work *Identify right-side patients Determine next step Agree how to manage*	Hygiene Choice Dialogue Hygiene Hand-off	Discovery Guide side one & two Clinical treatment plan

In a Nutshell
Chapter Three—Fitting the Pieces Together

- The traditional approach to case acceptance and the "Making It Easy" approach differ in significant ways. The greatest difference is that the emphasis of the traditional approach is making patients ready for complete care through educational processes. The Making It Easy approach recognizes that most right-side patients aren't ready for complete care because of their life circumstances. The Making It Easy approach emphasizes maintaining a good relationship with the patient who isn't yet ready.

- Another problem practitioners face with the traditional case acceptance process is that it is too rigid, requiring all new patients to undergo a complete examination at the initial appointment. Forcing patients to go through a complete examination before any dental work is performed will on many occasions cause contests of will between the patient and the dentist/team.

- Most patients aren't ready for right-side care, not because they have low dental IQs but because the costs and time factors simply don't fit into their lives at that point. When issues of their life are not taken into consideration and hefty fees are quoted for procedures they aren't ready for, it's no surprise that many patients leave the practice frustrated and angry. And when they do decide to get their teeth fixed, they go else where.

- Typically, no efforts are made to understand patients' lifestyle requirements and limitations. The single greatest issue that impacts patients' decisions to accept complete care is how it fits into their lifestyle, but we spend our time educating them on how the dentistry will fit into their mouths.

- A huge problem with the traditional approach is that fees and affordability issues usually don't surface until after the dentist, team, and patient have invested hours in the process of examination and consultation.

- At the heart of the "Making It Easy" case acceptance process are five Critical Dialogues (CD-1 through CD-5): Identity, Choice, Advocacy, Warm-up, and Financial Options. Each dialogue is designed to advance right-side patients to their next step toward complete care.

Chapter Four
Some Dentists Are More Influential Than Others:
How to Speak Like a Leader

Y ou're at a party and this guy starts telling a joke. He says, *"Two guys walk into a bar and... no, wait, it was three guys and one guy says... I think it was a guy...or was it a girl? Anyway, he says... no, wait, it wasn't a guy, it was the bartender. So he says to this horse... that's right, I remember it now! It was a horse at a bar and the bartender says, 'Why the long nose?' No, that's not right... he said, 'Why the long face?' I think that's what he said."*

Ever notice how some people can tell a joke and some can't? Taking it a step further, ever notice how some people can light up a room when they speak, while others dim it? Being able to speak in a compelling, appealing fashion is key when it comes to influencing and leading right-side patients and leading a right-side practice. A big part of great leadership is your ability to speak like a leader. My experience is that when dentists speak like leaders, they reach the hearts and minds of their patients, team members, and the profession. How about you—do you speak like a leader? If you'd like to become a more interesting, persuasive, and memorable communicator and be more leader-like in your speaking style, you've made a good decision. This chapter is about helping you to speak like a leader using a communication tool called the Spectrum of Appeal.™

In my previous book, *Isn't It Wonderful When Patients Say "Yes,"* I received incredibly positive feedback on the chapter on the Spectrum of Appeal. This is a revision of that chapter, including new material. You'll notice, too, that the concepts of this chapter will be sprinkled throughout this book, using the Spectrum of Appeal to illustrate various points.

The Spectrum of Appeal

If you study the art of influence you'll discover that there is consistent agreement among experts that influence is a combination of logical and emotional appeal. Much has been written on how the brain assimilates information and sorts and responds to logical and emotional stimulation. To be influential, many authors say, means weaving logical and emotional appeal into your communication style. Well, that's easy to say, but tough to do. It's like when you go to your physician and she says, *"In order for you to lose twenty-five pounds you need to optimize your diet and make your daily caloric intake 50 percent carbohydrates, 25 percent fats, and 25 percent protein."* Sounds great... now how do you do it? Several years ago I developed a tool to help blend logical and emotional appeal when speaking and writing. It's called the Spectrum of Appeal and I've used it with consistent success coaching dentists, attorneys, CEOs, marketing and salespeople, members of the clergy, financial planners, and entrepreneurs.

To understand the Spectrum of Appeal, imagine that language is like a beam of light. When a beam of light strikes a prism, it diffracts into its primary colors. The beam of language, when it strikes a prism—in the case of this metaphor, the prism is the listener's mind—also diffracts and separates language into its primary colors. The primary colors of the beam of language are blue and red (blue represents logical appeal; and red, emotional appeal (**Figure 4-1**).

FIGURE 4-1

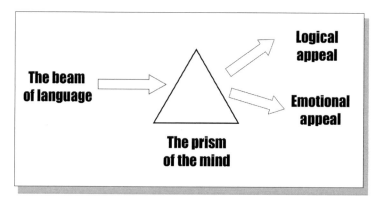

To expand on this metaphor, if language is like light then it can be analyzed by spectroscopy. **Figure 4-2** is a simple graph illustrating the blue and red spectrum. Since influence is a combination of logical and emotional appeal, this depiction is called the Spectrum of Appeal.

FIGURE 4-2

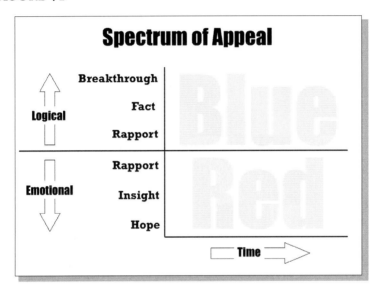

The vertical axis in **Figure 4-2** represents appeal: logical appeal above the middle horizontal line, emotional is below. As you move up the logic line, the intensity of the logical appeal increases. As you move down the emotional line, the intensity of the emotional appeal increases. This graph notes different levels of logical and emotional intensity. The horizontal line through the midpoint of the illustration separating logical and emotional appeal represents neutral appeal. The horizontal axis at the bottom of the illustration represents sequential time, the time between the beginning and end of your communication. Let's look at the various levels of logical and emotional appeal.

Establishing Rapport

The first order of logical appeal is rapport (when you establish similarity, agreement, and harmony). Establish rapport in the logical spectrum by introducing rational statements about yourself: name, location, history, occupation, role, age, and so forth. These statements establish common bonds with your listener, thus creating a similarity and affinity between the two of you. You may be similar to your patient in education, occupation, and where you live. If you were to build rapport with a patient in the logical spectrum it might sound like this: *"Hello, I'm Dr. Dennis Leonard. I've practiced dentistry for twenty years here in Charlotte. My wife, Stacy, and I have three kids: Shaun, Adam, and Kristen."*

You don't build rapport by talking about your mission statement or state-of-the-art dental remedies, or by sticking patients in front of a video monitor and having them watch a video on periodontal disease.

Getting the Facts

The next higher level of logical appeal includes facts: ideas, data, and information. Facts are the most common level of the logical spectrum. It's at this level that patient education, consent, home care instructions, explanations of procedures, and so forth, take place.

Making the Breakthrough

The highest order of logical appeal is *breakthrough*. A breakthrough is an "ah-ha!" experience, which occurs when the listener understands and sees new relationships among the facts, figures, ideas, and other data. Breakthroughs take us beyond the facts. Breakthroughs are the biggest truths, realized when we see ideas strung together like pearls on a necklace. We no longer see the individual pearls, we see their combined beauty. Einstein's famous formula $E=MC^2$ is a breakthrough. For dentists, mastering occlusion, esthetics, and biomechanics are examples of breakthroughs that string many facts together.

I experienced a breakthrough twenty years ago when I was attending the Pankey Institute. It was 6:30 in the evening, and I was struggling with an equilibration exercise on a plastic mannequin. Dr. John Anderson strolled up and leaned over to watch me work. *"Do you mind if I show you a few things?"* he asked. What happened in the next thirty minutes was the purest, clearest teaching I ever experienced. That day I achieved a breakthrough in my understanding of occlusion and equilibration.

Building Emotional Rapport

The emotional spectrum also has levels of intensity. The first level of emotional appeal is *rapport*, and just like logical appeal, rapport in the emotional spectrum fosters familiarity, similarity, and affinity. For example, I build rapport in the emotional spectrum with many patients by telling them a little about my own dental history:

"Betsy, I understand very well your discouragement with your teeth.
When I was in my twenties I had a severe misalignment of the teeth and
jaws. In many ways I was a dental cripple: I had trouble eating,
speaking, and I was embarrassed every day about my appearance."

Notice the differences in building rapport in the logical and emotional spectrum. Logical rapport addresses the issues of how, what, when, and how many. Emotional rapport focuses on reasons and is more visual in its language than logical rapport. Emotional rapport includes expected, familiar, and comfortable emotions.

Gaining Insight

The next level of emotional appeal is insight, which is an understanding or perception of things. Insights reflect how we feel about the facts, and may include unexpected, unfamiliar, and uncomfortable emotions or realizations. Typical examples of emotions at this level are surprise, humor, sorrow, conflict, fear, frustration, passion, depression, love, hate, excitement, boredom, greed, generosity, envy, and respect. Emotions that are opposites, like happiness and sorrow, are found together in this spectrum. This level does not qualify emotions as desirable or undesirable, but organizes them based on their effect on us.

Creating Optimism: Hope in Action

The deepest level of emotional appeal is hope. Hope is and always has been the most fundamental motivating emotion. The optimistic—hope-filled—person thrives emotionally. Without hope, there is no life. You have a wonderful opportunity to bring hope to your patients. Hope is the ultimate benefit of dental healthcare. Right-side patients need to experience hope as soon as possible in their new patient experience with you. You'll see how the Making It Easy approach incorporates hope in various ways, including the Choice Dialogue, positive framing, and the Warm-up Dialogue.

You have a wonderful opportunity to bring hope to your patients.

Defining *Blue* Versus *Red*

What blue spectrum tools do we use in the dental office? What has logical appeal? How about study models, radiographs, photographs, periodontal charting, patient education, diagnosis, treatment plans, insurance forms, technical explanations, brochures, records, oral hygiene instruction, medical history, and on and on. In fact, just about everything we touch and see in the dental office, along with most of our conversations, are based in logical appeal. We use an abundant number of blue spectrum tools. Most of our dental school and continuing education is blue spectrum, so it's easy to see why dentists and staff use blue spectrum tools almost exclusively and are the most comfortable with them.

If a major part of appeal is emotional, what red spectrum tools do we use with the same ease and consistency as our blue spectrum tools? Make a list of all the red spectrum tools you use. The list isn't as long nor does it come to mind as readily, does it? What this tells us is that if we want to optimize our appeal, then we need to recognize, develop, and use more red spectrum tools; these include humor, storytelling, colorful comparison, metaphors, attitude, visual language, and tone of voice. Remember, persuasion, leadership, sales, motivation, and any change in behavior or growth result from a combination of logical and emotional appeal.

You've heard it many times: people buy on emotion and justify with logic. What the Spectrum of Appeal creates is a visual representation of blending logical and emotional appeal. The broadest appeal combines both logic and emotion.

Charting the Language Path

Imagine that the Spectrum of Appeal graph is like an electrocardiogram on a long strip that turns on a barrel with an ink pointer positioned with its tip on the center neutral line. Now imagine that we connect this "electrocardiograph" to a speaker, and as he speaks the ink pointer oscillates between the blue and red spectrum, drawing a solid line indicating when he says something logical (facts, figures, data, information) and when he says something emotional (stories, humor, metaphors).

In **Figure 4-3**, notice the solid vertical line crisscrossing the center horizontal line. This is the language path of leader-like speaking that begins in the blue spectrum at the level of rapport and oscillates between blue and red, each time increasing the intensity of the appeal, ending with a call to action, indicated by the starburst "Yes"—indicating the listener is influenced to take action.

FIGURE 4-3

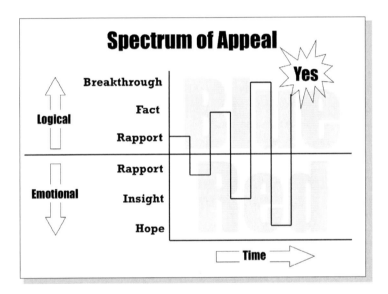

Creating the Spectrum

The intention of the Spectrum of Appeal is to graphically illustrate how the best leaders speak. I developed this tool because I was looking for a process to teach speakers how to be more influential and leader-like. As a member of the National Speakers Association and National Storytellers Association, I've listened to hundreds of speakers and have stacks of audio CDs of the best speakers. As I listened to the best speakers, I'd look for the foundational underpinning of what made them influential, but due to the wide variety of speaking styles and content differences it was tough to put my finger on any one thing. Then one day I was listening to a CD of a B.B. King concert. As you know, good blues has a certain attitude and influence to it. As I listened to B.B. King, I thought, how could a speaker hold the attention and influence his listeners as well as a musician does? What if I looked at communication and writing a speech like a musician looks at music and writing a song? That thought led me to consider other metaphors for speaking and eventually led me to the metaphor of the spectrum of light and its individual colors. Ultimately, combining the spectrum of light with the oscillatory rhythms and structure of music led me to the Spectrum of Appeal. I then went back to my stack of audio CDs of the greatest speakers, and analyzed their work using the Spectrum of Appeal. I immediately discovered the common denominators of the structural underpinnings and patterns of what makes speakers sound like leaders.

Understanding How it Works

Using the Spectrum of Appeal, let's examine and analyze the common denominators of what makes for leader-like speaking.

First, notice the block arrows (**Figure 4-4**). They indicate the logical and emotional content of the communication. They occur in an alternating order: blue, then red, then blue, etc.

FIGURE 4-4

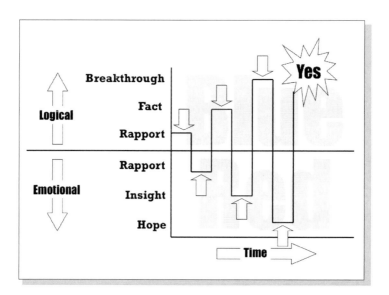

This alternating sequence of logical and emotional appeal creates contrast in the beam of language, creating interest and holding listeners' attention. In fact, the greater the contrast, the greater the interest. When dissimilar elements are put side by side, it creates interest and holds attention. We see this occurring all around us (e.g., seasonal differences, life cycles, architecture, art, literature, music). To speak like a leader you must learn to alternate your content from logical to emotional appeal. For example, state a principle (logic), then tell a story that illustrates the principle (emotion), then use statistics to support the principle (logic), then use a creative and humorous video to show the principle in action (emotion), etc.

Escalating Appeal

When leaders speak, the intensity of the appeal escalates as their communication continues: The logical appeal gets stronger and the emotional appeal gets more compelling. The two arrows in **Figure 4-5** illustrate this divergence.

FIGURE 4-5

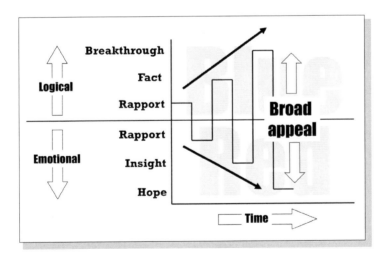

The greater this divergence, the broader the total appeal. Broad appeal creates a wide band of influence on its listeners. A key point to understanding broad appeal is this: in the presence of broad appeal, asking the listener for action sounds and feels like you're offering great advice. In the absence of broad appeal, asking for action sounds like you've got something to sell. This principle of speaking like a leader means that you must know what your strongest logical and emotional appeals to your listeners are. Once you know this, discuss them immediately before your call to action; this will result in the broadest appeal at the most critical time in your talk—just before you ask your listener to do/believe something.

In the presence of broad appeal, asking the listener for action sounds and feels like you're offering great advice. In the absence of broad appeal, asking for action sounds like you've got something to sell.

The principle of offering the broadest appeal immediately prior to asking for action is critical to case acceptance. In the chapter on the Warm-up Dialogue, I'll show the Spectrum of Appeal that offers a patient broad appeal immediately before I quote the fee, which is, in essence, asking for action. I can't overstate the importance of building appeal before asking for action.

Noting Spectrum Patterns

When mapping out the Spectrum of Appeal, patterns emerge. For example, **Figure 4-6** is a typical pattern most dentists create during case presentation (I call this a "flat-liner," after the EEG brain pattern that accompanies death).

FIGURE 4-6

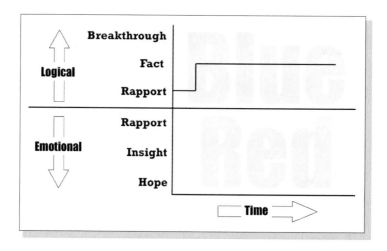

In this case, it's the "death" of persuasion, interest, and memorability. The "flat-liner" describes 95 percent of continuing education lectures. When a speaker "flat-lines" an audience, the listeners escape the dreariness by falling asleep. Have you ever been "flat-lined" at an association meeting or while in dental school? Join the club. Too many dentists don't alternate their appeal. The spectral patterns of their traditional case presentations are flat and predominantly blue, resulting in a narcotic effect on the listener—zzzzzzzzzzzz.

As audience members in dental continuing education, we've all experienced great intellectuals who are rotten speakers. Their logic is so compelling, however, that we forgive the death-like delivery, chalk it up to eccentricity, and are happy to escape with a few "pearls." Patients are not as forgiving. If you have great intellect, are in private practice, and have a death-like delivery, you'll have hungry kids. Logic alone does not inspire people to act. If that were the case, no one would smoke or eat red meat, and we'd all have fully-funded pension plans.

Logic alone does not inspire people to act. If that were the case, no one would smoke or eat red meat, and we'd all have fully-funded pension plans.

I work with highly educated professionals and CEOs in other industries such as engineering, financial services, and sales. These individuals share the fear that emotional appeal may compete with their credibility, perhaps diluting the impact of their message. However, the appropriate amount of time spent in the emotional spectrum enhances credibility and strengthens the message because it makes the logic more digestible, interesting, and vivid. The more vivid your language, the more memorable it is. Remember, no one ever lost credibility by being interesting.

Keep in mind that the "flat-line" red spectrum is as bad as the "flat-line" blue spectrum. The pattern in **Figure 4-7** is typical of people-pleasers who so much want to be liked that they can't bring themselves to get to the point. In fact, they have no point.

FIGURE 4-7

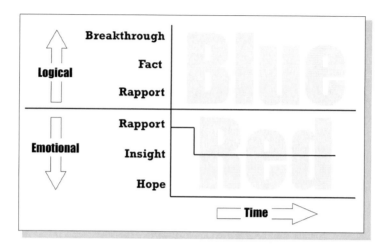

Too much emphasis in the emotional spectrum is called "baloney." Too much "baloney" sends a mixed message: *I like my dentist to have a sense of humor, but I don't want Jerry Seinfeld rebuilding my mouth.*

Diagnosing Spectral Patterns

Like ECG and EEG patterns that show what's going on inside the heart and brain respectively, spectral patterns demonstrate what's going on inside the heart and mind of the listener. You can use these patterns to diagnose the style and impact of the speaker. When discussing these patterns, I'll use blue for logic and red for emotion.

The spectral pattern in **Figure 4-8** shows a blue and red ratio of about 80/20 (80 percent blue, 20 percent red). When giving spectral ratio, I'll always state the blue spectrum first.

FIGURE 4-8

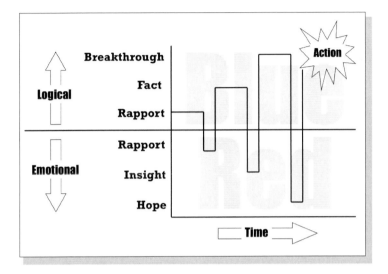

This pattern belongs to one of the leading speakers in dentistry, Dr. Carl Misch, founder and director of the Misch Implant Institute. Notice that the distribution of this speaker's logic is compelling and he backs up his ideas and conclusions with considerable research and experience. This appeals to audiences of dentists, who feed on new information. Notice, too, that from time to time Dr. Misch will drop into the red spectrum. Usually this takes the form of an amusing story illustrating his points. He provides just enough red appeal to keep our attention and break up the abundance of blue appeal. He's a pleasure to listen to and is very inspiring.

The pattern shown in **Figure 4-9** is that of Dr. James Pride, founder of the Pride Institute. Dr. Pride passed away in August of 2004 and was a dear friend and a gift to dentistry. He was one of the first people I showed the Spectrum of Appeal to and it was his enthusiasm that encouraged me to develop it further.

FIGURE 4-9

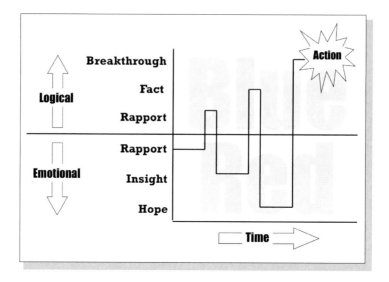

Notice his distribution of blue and red appeal was about 20/80, the opposite of Dr. Misch's pattern. Dr. Pride presented a concept, then beautifully and effortlessly illustrated his logic with wonderful stories. His stories were true accounts of dentists who have followed or not followed the concepts he was discussing. Dr. Pride would go into the blue spectrum to make his point, and then justify and illustrate it in the red spectrum. Dr. Pride enjoyed worldwide recognition for many decades using this speaking style.

Mapping the Language of Leadership and Management

Let's use the Spectrum of Appeal to map the patterns of management and leadership. Dr. Misch's pattern is a management pattern. This pattern shows an instructing, mentoring language, with the most emphasis on the blue spectrum: facts, how to, when, where, how many, and so forth. The blue/red ratio is about 80/20 (**Figure 4-10**).

FIGURE 4-10

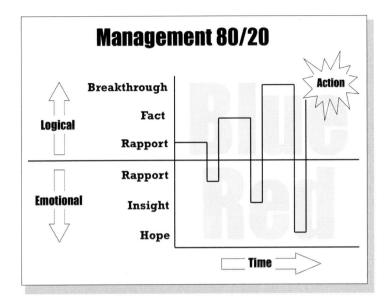

This 80/20 pattern is also the pattern of traditional sales techniques. Many of the techniques of sales—prospecting, getting the appointment, presenting benefits and features, overcoming objections, closing—are blue spectrum. Spectra of management, traditional sales, and the traditional case acceptance processes are quite similar.

Dr. Pride's pattern was a leadership pattern. This pattern shows a coaching, illustrative, intuitive pattern with most of the emphasis on the red spectrum—reasons, encouragement, character, vision **(Figure 4-11)**.

FIGURE 4-11

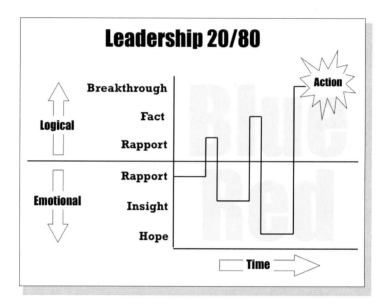

The blue-red ratio is about 20/80. Think back to the person who made the biggest difference in your life. Chances are excellent that he or she had a leadership pattern. When you stimulate the appropriate emotion, when you show someone the possibility for hope, growth occurs. That's what happened to you.

Academic and Emotional Intelligence

In a book I highly recommend, *Working with Emotional Intelligence*, Daniel Goleman, Ph.D., offers a compelling discussion on the difference between academic and emotional intelligence. Figure 4-12 shows how academic and emotional intelligence look on the Spectrum of Appeal.

FIGURE 4-12

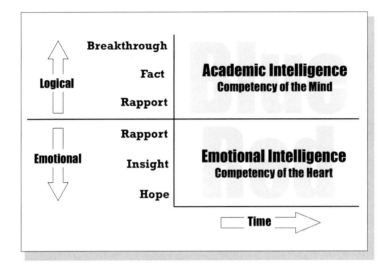

Academic intelligence, which includes our IQ, training, and expertise, is blue spectrum. Academic intelligence is what qualified us to get into dental school. Academic intelligence drives our intellectual ability, cognitive skills, technical know-how, and clinical treatment decisions. Academic intelligence is the competency of the mind.

Emotional intelligence is red spectrum. It includes self-awareness, motivation, self-regulation, empathy, and social skills. Emotional intelligence allows us to build relationships with others, understand ourselves, have a drive to succeed, persuade others, and effectively use intuition. Emotional intelligence is the competency of the heart.

To succeed in dentistry, you need both academic and emotional intelligence. However, as Dr. Goleman notes in *Working with Emotional Intelligence*, the irony is that academic intelligence is a less accurate predictor of success than is emotional intelligence among people in the most cognitively demanding fields.

To dentists and staff, the greatest leverage and opportunity we have to build our careers involve learning to think, communicate, and act in the red spectrum. Dental school focuses on academic intelligence. Because we are rewarded and advanced in school based on academic intelligence, our emotional intelligence can atrophy in the process. But remember the adage, "use it or lose it." It applies to emotional intelligence, too.

Dr. Goleman explains that emotional intelligence does not mean just being nice to people. Emotional intelligence is the way to leverage our knowledge and skills; it's another way of being smart. Lack of emotional intelligence makes smart people look stupid.

Lack of emotional intelligence makes smart people look stupid.

Academic and Emotional Memory

Has this ever happened to you? You're driving down the street, turn on the radio, and hear an old song you used to listen to years ago when you were in loooooove. From deep inside, emotion and fond memories pour out like a river. Did you have to struggle to recall those memories or did they just leap out on their own? What you experienced was emotional memory.

FIGURE 4-13

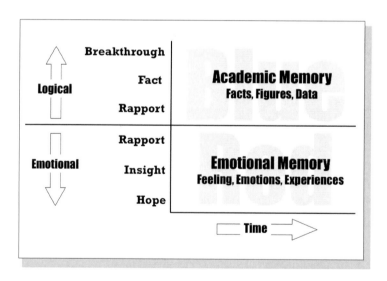

Figure 4-13 illustrates the differences between emotional and academic memory. Emotional memory contrasts with academic memory, which involves recalling facts, figures, and data. This is the memory we use to get through school and jump through the hoops related to licensure and certifications. Academic memory is what we are rewarded for in the social, political, and academic structure of dentistry.

Have you ever forgotten someone's name, your ATM code, or the combination to your health club locker? Of course you have—memory lapses of this type are so common we think of them as routine. But have you ever forgotten how you feel about any person, place, or thing? It requires no effort to access emotional memory and it endures for a lifetime. When emotion is attached to an experience, it anchors the memory.

What do you want patients to remember about you? Most of my dentist clients spend their time and effort with patients reciting treatment recommendations, information, and patient education. Of course we'd like patients to remember our treatment recommendations and information, but what they actually remember is whether they liked you and your staff and how they feel about the process. Patients will forget what you said to them, but they'll remember whether they liked you or not.

> *Patients will forget what you said to them,*
> *but they'll remember whether they liked you or not.*

Academic and Emotional Speed

Academic speed is blue spectrum; emotional speed is red spectrum (**Figure 4-14**). Our capacity to cognitively process information—academic speed—is fast.

FIGURE 4-14

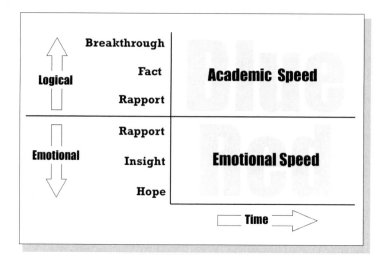

According to estimates, we can think at a rate of several hundred words per minute. Prove this to yourself. Visualize (a cognitive process) the following items as fast as you can read them: hill, house, barn, dog, cat, snake, cloud, raisin, and mother. No problem. Now try to experience the following emotions: hate, love, fear, confidence, loneliness, and bravery (the feelings I'm talking about here are the ones that require complex thought processes). You notice it takes much longer to identify your feelings.

Complete care patients may not fully understand how they feel about you until well after they hear your treatment recommendations. Give them time; don't push for treatment acceptance decisions too fast. Most people need time to process the information and impressions. I am against "going for the close." Slick closes that offer a list of alternative choices push people into decisions they may not be ready to make. A quick decision may be fine for left-side dentistry; but before I start a major rehabilitation, I want my patients to feel good about their choices, and those choices take time. In the dental office, dentists and staff think, act, and speak at academic speed. But complete care patients operate at emotional speed. Respect their speed.

Experts and Novices

When an expert is trying to influence another expert, the language pattern is 80/20. This is the management/sales pattern. If I'm a dental equipment dealer (an expert) and am trying to sell you (also an expert) a digital x-ray unit, I will try to influence you using what is most familiar to you, the blue spectrum. You and I speak the same language: logic. Although great salespeople can leverage their logical appeal with emotional appeal, the bulk of the dialogue in this situation falls into the blue spectrum: benefits, features, costs, delivery, maintenance, warranties. Another word for blue spectrum dialogue is jargon. Experts and managers speak jargon to each other because they understand its meaning. If I were making a case presentation to a dentist, I would speak in the blue spectrum using a management pattern and communicate well.

When an expert is trying to influence a novice, the expert must speak the same language as the novice. The spectral pattern here is 20/80, the leadership pattern. For example, if you're a real-estate salesperson and you're dealing with first-time buyers, you'll do well if you focus your language on topics most familiar to your buyers: neighborhood, schools, shopping. The smart real-estate salesperson doesn't use words like easements, footings, deeds of trust, or eminent domain. Jargon doesn't work on novices. Words like *centric relation*, *equilibration*, etc., don't work on patients. With the novice, the expert minimizes blue spectrum language because it has little meaning, hence, little appeal. Case acceptance is an expert-to-novice dialogue. Structurally, case acceptance for complete dentistry is the leadership pattern.

Do sales and leadership have different meanings to you? Look at **Figure 4-15**.

FIGURE 4-15

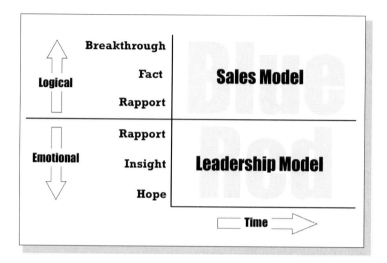

Traditional selling is a blue spectrum skill. Traditional sales skills include asking questions to evaluate the prospect's needs, uncovering buyer motivators and "hot buttons," presenting features and benefits, overcoming objections, asking for the order, asking for referrals.

Leadership is a red spectrum skill. Leaders show confidence and self-control, are motivational, are aware of others' feelings, and are adept at influencing others. Case acceptance is a blend of selling and leadership, with greater emphasis on leadership.

Are you more comfortable selling something, or leading someone? Most dentists are far more comfortable leading than they are selling, but structurally the two skills are similar. The difference is in the attitude of the expert. If you feel better when leading as opposed to selling, then lead your patients into case acceptance; don't attempt to sell them into it. When your intention is that of a leader, the fear of sounding like a salesperson disappears.

Questions and Objections

Let's put typical blue spectrum questions and objections on the Spectrum of Appeal, shown in **Figure 4-16**.

FIGURE 4-16

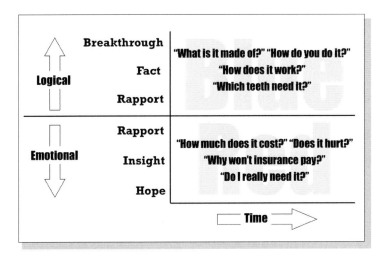

"What is the cap made of?" "How do you do it?" "How will you fix my tooth?" "What makes my tooth hurt?" These are common blue spectrum questions or comments. They seek information.

Let's put typical red spectrum questions/comments on the Spectrum of Appeal. "Why is it so expensive?" "I'm afraid it will hurt." "I'm disappointed my insurance won't pay." "Do I really need this much dentistry?" "How much longer will it take?"

Compare the blue and red spectrum questions/comments. Which spectrum represents the questions/comments that make or break case acceptance? Red, of course. But where do we spend most of our time explaining things and where are we the most comfortable? Blue, of course.

In terms of case acceptance for complete dentistry, we spend most of our time and energy in the areas that matter least. Be aware that some questions may sound like blue spectrum information-seeking questions, but may be red spectrum questions based on emotions, such as fear or loss of control. For example, "How much does it cost?" sounds like a request for facts, in this case the cost of the dentistry itself, or on the surface, blue spectrum information. But for most patients the red spectrum question

"Can I afford it?" lurks in the background. The concept of affordability, literally, the ability to buy, relates to safety, which is a red spectrum issue for most people.

Stay in the Patient's Spectrum

The key to answering questions and comments using the Spectrum of Appeal is to give your answer in the same spectrum as the question. If you hear a blue spectrum question, "When is my appointment?" reply in the blue spectrum: "Your appointment is tomorrow." If you hear a red spectrum question or remark, "I'm afraid it will hurt," reply in the red spectrum: "It's normal to feel afraid, and many of my patients are afraid. We make sure everyone is comfortable and safe in our office. We'll do the same for you." Answer questions and objections in the spectrum in which they originated. Don't make the patient come to you; you go to the patient. If your answer doesn't work, change the spectrum.

If your answer doesn't work, change the spectrum.

For example, your patient asks, *"How long will my care take?"* You interpret this as a blue spectrum question and respond in the blue spectrum, *"Your care will take one year to complete."* He rejects your answer and tells you that his job won't allow him to take the time. Instead of staying in the blue spectrum and proceeding to recite reasons and facts why quality care takes time, change your spectrum to red: *"Adam, I've treated many business-men like you and I'm great about respecting your work schedule and commitments. I recently finished a CEO just like you, and he missed very little work. I will do the same for you."*

Most dentists have a "default spectrum," one that they're most comfortable with. Usually it's blue. When confronted with objections, questions, or stress, dentists usually slip into the default blue spectrum because it's easy.

Think about all the objections you've heard. In which spectrum do most fall? Red. Most objections that are case acceptance-busters are in the red spectrum. To enjoy case acceptance of complete dentistry, a dentist and staff must learn red spectrum skills.

Overcoming Objections

The phrase **overcoming objections** comes to us from the world of sales. The inference we can draw is that I, as the salesperson, will use my logic and wit to change your mind about your resistance to purchase what I'm selling. For example, if my buyer has issues related to costs, I'll give him facts, data, and proof that the purchase is worth it, is a good investment, and so forth. I may use emotion and push a few hot buttons or remind the buyer of his motivators.

In dentistry, I challenge the concept of overcoming objections; specifically, the word *overcoming*. To overcome something connotes a contest of wills or breaking a barrier, in this case, a contest between the dentist and patient. It's almost as if patients are wrong in stating their objections, and it's our job as dentists to correct them. Considering that most objections are red spectrum, that is, emotional objections, we breed animosity if we tell our patients that how they feel is wrong.

The fastest way to make others mad is to tell them they're wrong about how they feel. Instead of "overcoming" the objection, acknowledge it. Don't make patients wrong because they are afraid, or believe the care is too expensive, or are disappointed by the lack of insurance coverage. Acknowledge their emotions and give them the space to be right. Your job as the professional is to move to their emotional place and then offer an insight that may help them see another way of looking at the situation.

Answering Questions and Acknowledging Objections

No rigid pattern for answering patient questions and concerns exists, so do not spend time looking for one right answer. The secret to creating the most appeal is to recognize where the patient is and comfortably move between spectrums. **Figure 4-17** provides a helpful template that illustrates three basic ways to respond: direct, defer, or illustrate.

FIGURE 4-17

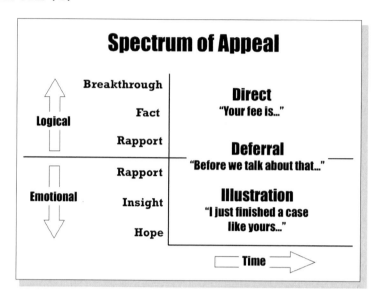

Direct response. The direct answer occupies the blue spectrum. It is the best response to a direct question. For example, you're asked, *"How much will my insurance pay?"* A direct answer would be: *"Your insurance limitation is $1,200 per year. In your case, insurance will pay 50 percent of the total fee for this crown."* Blue spectrum question, direct blue spectrum response.

Deferral. There are times, however, when a direct answer will take your dialogue down a path you don't want to travel. Deferring the answer might be a better strategy. For example, you're asked, *"How much will my insurance pay?"* A deferral sounds like this: *"I'll know better how much your insurance will pay after I've planned your care."* Deferring this question will give you more opportunity to build rapport with this patient, so when you do answer this question directly, there's a greater chance the patient will take your advice over the insurance company's. A deferral occupies a neutral spectrum, with no commitment to blue or red.

Answering a question with a question is a form of deferral. For example, you're asked about insurance. A deferral in the form of a question may sound like: *"Is insurance coverage an important concern for you?"* Your answer to your patient's question now guides you to your best response, either a direct answer or an illustration.

Illustration. The third way to answer a question is to use an illustration—a story, metaphor, simile, humor, comparison, or testimony. The illustration answer is a red spectrum response. I recommend using an illustration whenever it's clear that you have a red spectrum question. For example, your patient says: *"I am so disappointed that my insurance isn't going to pay for my dentistry. I've worked all these years paying for it and you'd think it would be worth something."*

You must realize that there is no graceful and effective way to answer this objection directly or with a deferral, and the situation would likely become worse. Instead, use an illustration:

"Joe, many patients are disappointed in dental insurance, too. It's a problem. I have a patient who was just as disappointed in his insurance and he put off his dentistry. Then a cap on his front tooth came off. We fixed it for him and insurance helped some and he used our patient financing service to pay for the rest. We can do the same for you."

The illustration does not provide a lot of blue spectrum information. Rather, it shows how another patient was frustrated but overcame the frustration and now is happy with the result.

Effectively use the three ways to answer a question by being aware of where the patient is and where you are in the Spectrum of Appeal. And if your answer doesn't work, change spectrums. Let's say you have a new patient and from what your staff tells you, she is a right-side patient. You've done an initial examination and she has advanced dental disease in all areas of her mouth. You'd like the opportunity to study her case and create a treatment plan for her. However, patients sometimes act in normal yet unacceptable ways (from your viewpoint), and this patient asks point-blank how much you will charge to fix her teeth. Here's a sample dialogue using all three ways of answering the same question: *"How much will it cost to fix my teeth?"*

Using deferral, I answer: *"I'll know better after I study your case,*   Mrs. *Mehran. I suggest I study your case when you're not here, and when you return, I'll know your case by heart."* *"Yeah, I know,"* she says, *"but you've done cases like mine before; give me a ballpark estimate."* She's pushing for an answer.

Using a direct answer, I say: *"A case like yours will cost $12,000 and will take about a year to complete. We have some flexible financial arrangements and payments would be about $xxx dollars a month. Does that fit within your budget?"* "I had no idea dentistry could cost that much. What makes it so expensive?" she asks.

Using illustration, I say: *"Many patients tell me the same thing. You remind me of Sally. We finished her case three years ago. She suffered with bad teeth all her life. It was after she saw what wearing dentures did to her husband that she started her care with us. Yes, it's expensive, but Sally considered losing her teeth worse. We stayed within Sally's budget and we'll do the same for you."*

When deferring an answer, be prepared for an objection to the deferral. If you hear one, give a direct answer or an illustration.

Don't be like a deer caught in the headlights with your default blue spectrum direct responses. These often work to make patients appear wrong and, therefore, a contest of wills starts. I'm not saying that blue spectrum responses are wrong. But as I've said before, they're incomplete with respect to using the entire range of the Spectrum of Appeal™

Case Presentation Patterns

A typical traditional case presentation spectral pattern is shown in **Figure 4-18**.

FIGURE 4-18

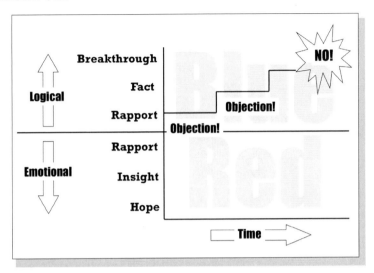

This is a dominant blue spectrum presentation. The dentist begins the presentation in the blue spectrum by reciting the findings and diagnosis. Sometime soon the patient asks a question, makes a comment, or raises an objection. Most of the time these questions/comments/objections fall in the red spectrum. Most dentists I work with will respond to red spectrum issues in the blue spectrum and give more facts and proof, escalating the logic. The presentation continues until the next questions/comments/objections, at which point the dentist escalates the logic again, providing even stronger evidence that supports treatment recommendations. Patients get the facts, but they don't experience emotional appeal. Why should it surprise us that patients say "No?"

When you're presenting recommendations for care, minimize blue spectrum language because it has little meaning (hence, little appeal).

Michael Sunich, Ed.D., a psychologist practicing in Charlotte, North Carolina, proposes the illustration shown in **Figure 4-19**. It shows the spectral pattern of the dentist (blue) while also showing the emotional response (red) of the patient during a traditional blue spectrum case presentation.

FIGURE 4-19

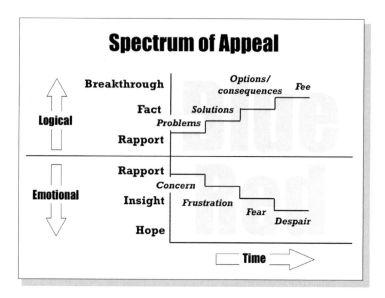

As the dentist explains the problems in the patient's mouth, the patient feels concern. Too often, instead of acknowledging and supporting the concern, the dentist presses on and outlines the solutions, which can frustrate the patient because he doesn't feel heard and doesn't understand the vocabulary. Following that, the dentist details the consequences of not treating the dental problems—tooth loss, heart disease, dentures, etc.— which can bring on fear. And just when the patient is feeling worse, at the lowest point in the level of appeal, the dentist quotes the fee! Because the patient has accumulated unacknowledged negative feelings, the fee can represent an insurmountable emotional wall; instead of experiencing hope, the patient feels despair.

Do you want your right-side patients to experience fear and despair when they hear your fee? What will patients remember best: your great treatment plan, or the despair they felt when they heard the fee? What do you think they'll tell their friends about their trip to the dentist?

Figure 4-20 illustrates a more successful spectral pattern of presenting care.

FIGURE 4-20

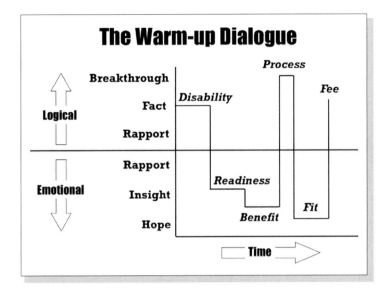

This is the pattern for the Warm-up Dialogue, CD-4. It's a 20/80 pattern (20 percent logic, 80 percent emotion). I'll get into greater detail regarding the Warm-up Dialogue in a later chapter. For now, though, I'll give an overview of this process.

You begin the presentation in the blue spectrum by stating what you know about the patient's **disability**—how her dental problems are affecting her life—*"Michelle, I know that you're embarrassed about the appearance of your front teeth."*

Then you shift into the red spectrum with a **readiness** statement—the appropriateness of the timing of her care—*"When you're back from your business trip to Italy..."*

Now you deepen the emotional appeal by stating a specific, strong **benefit**—*"After studying your case, I feel really good that we can completely restore the confidence you have in your appearance."*

Shift back to the blue spectrum and give the patient an easy-to-understand idea of the **process** of fixing her teeth—*"We'll replace the dark and* *chipped enamel from your front teeth with a new enamel-like material."*

Return to a deep level of emotional appeal by stating your willingness to *fit* the cost and time factors of restoring her teeth into the realities of her life circumstance. Fit issues are very red spectrum for the patient and give the patient hope and demonstrate that you're her advocate. This is a very powerful, positive moment for the patient and it's presented immediately prior to quoting the blue spectrum *fee*. When presenting fees, the best emotional state for the patient to be in is that of feeling hope.

This case presentation model is *not* designed to provide informed consent. It's designed to create an appealing process for presenting care that inspires hope and opens the conversation about how to fit the dentistry the patient needs into the circumstance of her life. You'll read much more about this model in later chapters.

Designing Brochures and Promotions

The Spectrum of Appeal applies to written material as well. Design your brochures and promotional materials using a 20/80 ratio (20 percent logic, and 80 percent emotion). Other than consent and financial documents, the 20/80 ratio is good for patient-targeted literature and promotional materials. While your right-side patients are processing their decision to accept your care, your 20/80 printed material will support them and reinforce the attitude of your office.

The 20/80 ratio is true for everything patients see on the walls of your office. What would have greater appeal to a patient: a close-up technical photograph, with lips retracted, showing a before-and-after cosmetic result; or a full-face photograph of a happy patient with a great letter of appreciation? And how about that poster that shows the progression of periodontal disease from a healthy mouth to advanced periodontitis, including close-up photographs of very nasty teeth and gums. How much appeal does this have? It's time to take down all the photographs and illustrations that showcase disease. I'm very glad some dentists I know don't practice urology!

Beyond "Yes"

Whether you use an 80/20 or 20/80 style, the goal is the same: you want your patients to say "Yes" to your treatment recommendations. We can argue that if you can get to "Yes" by either style, what difference does it make? The difference is apparent in what happens after the coveted "Yes." The only thing 80/20 and 20/80 have in common is that you can get a positive response from either method. But that's where the similarity ends.

Beyond "Yes," the 20/80 style brings you and your team a better relationship with the patient. This relationship enhances all of the positive responses occurring during and after treatment is complete (see **Figure 4-11**). The 20/80 style helps you with:

1. **Commitment**: Patients are motivated to follow through with treatment or return if they postpone treatment.
2. **Clinical management**: Reduces stress and creates a more therapeutic atmosphere.
3. **Collections**: People who like you, pay you.
4. **Insurance**: Patients adopt your opinion, not the insurance company's.
5. **Recall**: Patients are willing to follow your instructions.
6. **Referral**: People who like you tell their friends about you.
7. **Management of failures**: Retreatment issues are less stressful.
8. **Medical/legal**: Patients who like you are less likely to sue you.
9. **Profitability**: You'll make more money and experience less stress when treating cooperative complete care patients.

The Lesson

Study the patterns discussed in this chapter and notice how most of what we do in case presentation is in the blue spectrum. Nearly every dentist I work with uses an 80/20 structure for case presentation. A very clear relationship exists between 80/20 blue spectrum, case acceptance patterns and left-side, high-volume, stressful, tooth dentistry. The traditional case presentation model predominantly uses blue spectrum activities (a sales model) and focuses on quality, patient education, a show-and-tell technical approach to communication, and dealing with the limitations of dental insurance. The dentists who use this model typically ask me to help them with the same issues: They want to do more dentistry on fewer patients, reduce their stress, and make more money. In every case where dentists learn a 20/80 red spectrum approach, they see an increase in complete right-side care, lower-volume and lower-stress dentistry, and an increase in profit.

Blue spectrum 80/20 case presentation patterns are not wrong. Rather, they are incomplete in terms of appeal. In our country, we enjoy the highest standard of care in the world. Blue spectrum case presentation techniques are responsible for the overwhelming majority of the dentistry done in our country. However, when I look at the dentists who are consistently doing the right-side complete care cases, I always see strong 20/80 leadership patterns in the dentist, the staff, or both.

Dr. Carl Misch, although he uses abundant logic in his presentations to dentists, takes an opposite approach with patients. He says:

"I never get into the deep technical details of the case–how many implants, their angulations, bone density–none of that. The patient wants to know that I've done it before, that I feel comfortable that I can do it for them, and once they have that feeling, then it's my job to get them there. I create a sense of hope in the patient that the result can be theirs."

"When I'm in Europe and in another dentist's office, my acceptance rate is higher than the host dentists. This is amazing that I can often not speak the patient's language fluently yet be able to communicate to them an overwhelming passion that I can take care of them. My general presence, eye contact, confidence tone of voice, and facial expressions have an enormous impact on case acceptance."

"It's not the amount of time you spend with the patient; it's the amount of impact. I often walk into an operating room getting ready to do a hip bone graph and realized that I've only spent a few minutes with this patient in conversation, and yet there is a significant level of trust and bond that's formed between us."

The lesson is simple. If you want to do more right-side complete care cases, learn red spectrum skills. But it's human nature to resist change, and I've had clients ask if I could help them sell bigger cases without using that "warm, fuzzy red spectrum stuff." The answer is "Yes," but to do it you have to create a marketing machine that produces a parade of new patients for your practice. Then, once they're in your chair, use your 80/20 blue spectrum, drive-by style, show-and-tell case presentation pattern, and sell one out of fifty complete care cases. When they seek my services, most of my clients are running their practices that way, and now they want to learn a new approach.

When clients want to bypass the "warm fuzzy" approach, I just tell them that they'll hear "No" more often, make even less money, and have much more stress. So, if you want to practice right-side dentistry and live to tell about it, you'll need to learn red spectrum skills. If you are reading this book because you want to get to the "next level," then you've got to stop trying to sell things to people and start building relationships.

In a Nutshell
Chapter Four—The Spectrum of Appeal

- There is consistent agreement among experts that influence is a combination of logical and emotional appeal. To be influential means weaving logical and emotional appeal into your communication style.

- The Spectrum of Appeal is a visual representation of blending logical and emotional appeal. It is an illustration that depicts logical appeal a blue and emotional appeal as red. Maximum total appeal is created when blue and red elements are combined.

- Just about everything we touch and see in the dental office, along with most of our conversations, are based in logical appeal. We use an abundant number of blue spectrum tools. Most of our dental school and continuing education is blue spectrum, so it's easy to see why dentists and staff use blue spectrum tools almost exclusively and are the most comfortable with them.

- To increase our appeal, we need to recognize, develop, and use more red spectrum tools; these include humor, storytelling, colorful comparison, metaphors, attitude, visual language, and tone of voice.

- Broad appeal is when we combine blue and red appeal. In the presence of broad appeal, asking the listener for action sounds and feels like you're offering great advice. In the absence of broad appeal, asking for action sounds like you've got something to sell.

- The key to answering questions and comments using the Spectrum of Appeal is to give your answer in the same spectrum as the question. If you hear a blue spectrum question, *"When is my appointment?"* reply in the blue spectrum: *"Your appointment is tomorrow."* If you hear a red spectrum question or remark, *"I'm afraid it will hurt,"* reply in the red spectrum: *"It's normal to feel afraid, and many of my patients are afraid. We make sure everyone is comfortable and safe in our office. We'll do the same for you."* Answer questions and objections in the spectrum in which they originated. If your answer doesn't work, change spectrums.

Chapter Five
Great Relationships Begin on the Telephone
The Identity Dialogue

I have a love/hate relationship with the telephone. I hate it when I'm on work overload and I've got one nerve left... and it's the telephone that usually gets on it. There are times, though, when I love it—especially when I'm stuck in some godforsaken airport and my cell phone rings because my lovely daughter, Kristen, is calling to remind me to take care of myself or to update me on my first grandson, Joseph Paul.

Some of my best business opportunities and relationships have started over the telephone. Some of yours have, too. Every month new patients call your office hoping to start a great relationship. This chapter on the Identity Dialogue is about making the most out of the initial telephone call between your office and the new patient. The Identity Dialogue is important because it sets the stage for giving the new patient an excellent initial experience with your office.

The Identity Dialogue is important because it sets the stage for giving the new patient an excellent initial experience with your office.

Right-Side Patient Initial Appointment

The process for complete dentistry starts with the Identity Dialogue, CD-1. This dialogue takes place over the telephone between the new patient and the scheduler. The intention of the identity dialogue is to identify whether the caller is a left- or a right-side patient and, once identified, to correctly appoint the patient into the schedule. Left- and right-side patients receive different types of initial appointments. In this chapter we'll discuss the right-side patient.

I like early-in-the-week appointments for new right-side patients because they're not yet dealing with the hassles of the entire week and still have the energy and focus to make good healthcare decisions. Of course, the same is true for you and your staff—everyone has more energy early in the week.

Most dentists block out hours in their schedule for production and have specific days and times they prefer to reserve for these appointments. I recommend that you also block out hours for new right-side patient experiences, examinations, and consultations. Typically the first appointments in the morning and afternoon are best for right-side patients. Look at **Figure 5-1** to see an example of correct right-side scheduling. You'll notice in the diagram that heavy production appointments follow the new right-side initial appointment.

FIGURE 5-1

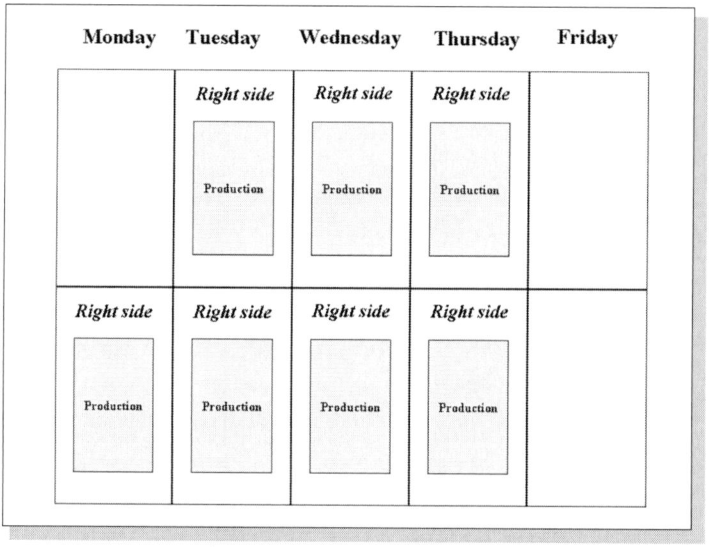

Monday	Tuesday	Wednesday	Thursday	Friday
	Right side Production	*Right side* Production	*Right side* Production	
Right side Production	*Right side* Production	*Right side* Production	*Right side* Production	

By having the first appointments, the probability is high that these patients will be seen on time. Devote at least a full hour for the initial appointment for the right-side patient without any other patients on your schedule at that time. When you meet new patients and are not burdened with running back into an operatory to perform a clinical procedure, your interpersonal skills are sharper, you stay on time more easily, and you'll demonstrate a better attitude because you're less stressed.

FIGURE 5-2

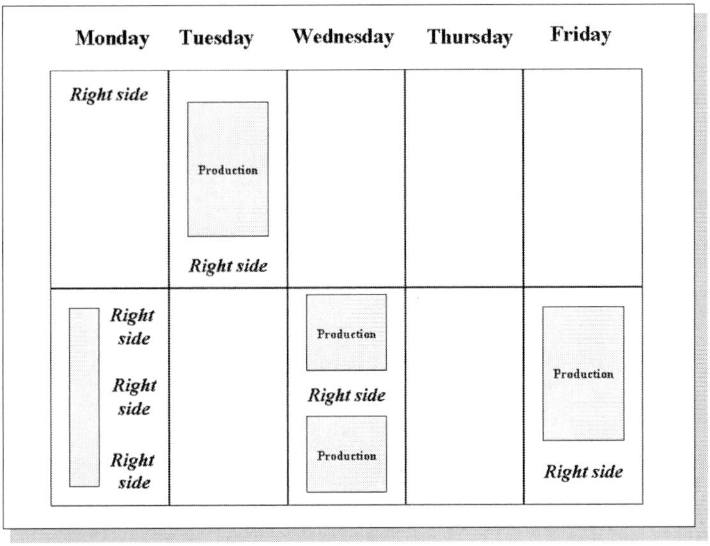

Monday	Tuesday	Wednesday	Thursday	Friday
Right side	Production			
	Right side			
Right side / Right side / Right side		Production / Right side / Production		Production / Right side

Figure 5-2 shows an incorrect way of scheduling the right-side patient. I never saw new right-side patients on Monday morning, because sometimes a few of my team members needed time to recover from their weekends! However, Monday morning might be fine for you. I used Monday mornings for team meetings and getting things in order for the week. (Keep in mind that the concept of scheduling new right-side patients first thing in the morning and in the afternoon also applies to right-side consultations and right-side emergency appointments.)

Monday afternoon has *stress* written all over it, with you running in and out of treatment scenarios while trying to stay on time and trying to be pleasant for the new patient. Tuesday morning is tough, too, because you and your team are tired after the long appointment and might be running late. Worse yet, you could miss lunch—again! Wednesday afternoon is the classic mistake. The first patient runs long and the second production patient comes in early and runs laps around your reception area, driving your receptionist nuts, while your new patient feels the stress pouring out of everyone. And Friday afternoon is the worst scenario yet for the new right-side patient. By Friday, everyone—including the patient, your team, and you—is stressed-out and tired; not a good time for making good first impressions and important decisions. In fact, my personal opinion is that nothing good happens in a dental office after Wednesday!

Now that you understand how to schedule the right-side patient, let's look at how to identify the right-side patient during the initial telephone call.

Identifying Right-Side Patients

The section on leadership discussed the concept of "right side" versus "left side." Remember, a right-side patient has significant dental break-down; a left-side patient has relatively little. The right- and left-side distinctions have nothing to do with their income level, readiness for care, or dental IQ.

Patients, of course, aren't going to tell you whether they're right or left side, but a few questions over the telephone can clear it up.

Patients, of course, aren't going to tell you whether they're right or left side, but a few questions over the telephone can clear it up. Figure 5-3 and the text that follows provide some questions you can ask during the initial telephone call to help you identify whether your new patient has significant dental breakdown (right side). Some of these questions don't directly relate to the level of dental breakdown; rather, they give you greater insights into patients' lifestyle issues and attitudes that are used in other areas of building good relationships with patients.

FIGURE 5-3

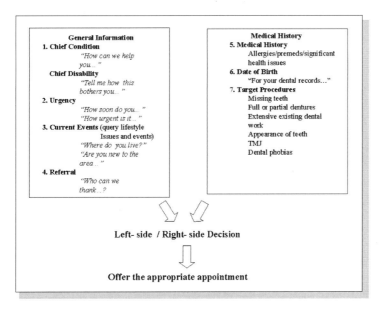

Think of the questions asked in the Identity Dialogue as ingredients in a recipe for a great telephone conversation. These questions are presented in numbered order only for the sake of organization; this sequence is not necessarily how they will be introduced into the conversation. For example, the patient might start talking about the appearance of his teeth (question #7), then talk about where he lives (question #3). Let the conversation flow and, when necessary, guide it to any remaining unanswered questions. Here are more details on the questions and their relevance to the left- versus right-side distinction.

1. Start with **why** the patient wants to make an appointment. A good rule to follow with all the dialogues is to state the intention of the dialogue within the dialogue: *"I'd like to **identify** how we can best meet your needs. How can we help you today?"* Listen for their **chief condition** (what's wrong), and their **chief disability** (how the condition is affecting them).

The chief condition is an excellent indication of the left- versus right-side distinction. Comments like *"I hate the appearance of my teeth"* or *"I can't eat with my dentures"* are clear indicators that significant conditions exist.

An experienced administrative team member can easily get   people to talk about their condition and reveal enough information to determine left- or right-side status.

Be curious about the disability—how the condition is affecting the patient's life. Ask open-ended questions such as, *"When did you first notice this problem?"* or *"Does this bother you more at work or at home?"* or *"Tell me about when this condition bothers you the most."* Questions like these often lead to the patient telling you a story about her disability, which is great for gaining a deeper understanding of how her teeth are affecting her life.

2. Get an idea how **urgent** the situation is by asking questions such as, *"Is there any important event coming up that you need your dentistry completed by?"* or *"How urgent is this situation for you?"*

3. What **current events** (issues that affect time, money, stress) are occurring in the person's life? Find out what we need to fit our dentistry into by engaging in "fit-chat." "Fit-chat" is like chitchat, except with "fit-chat" we're listening for and being curious about issues in the patient's life that we need to fit our dentistry into. These issues can include things like:
- new home
- new job
- family issues
- significant health issues
- special events (wedding, vacation, etc.).

You're not looking for the patient's life story here. If the patient is not a talker you might not hear anything related to life events or circumstances. That's OK (other people will talk you to death and give you everything you need to know). Remember that it's important to keep patient confidentiality, as mandated by the Health Insurance Portability and Accountability Act (HIPAA) of 1996. According to Certified Environmental Compliance Manager Deborah Hammaker, *"Be careful not to repeat out loud anything that could identify the person you are talking to others in the practice who don't have a need to know."*

4. How did this patient **find out about you**? Was he/she referred by a right-side patient? The relevance of the referral source is that if your new

patient is referred by a known right-side patient, the chances are good the caller also is a right-side patient.

5. Shift the conversation to the **medical record** and ask about medications and significant health issues. Transition from the general information questions to medical questions by asking, *"If you have a few more minutes, may I ask you some questions about your health history?"* (According to Ms. Hammaker, *"It is important to ask 'May I?' because then the patient is granting permission to discuss this kind of information over the phone, where someone could possible overhear."*)

Medical history issues are generally more prevalent in right-side patients because they tend to be older. Think about medical history issues as more than just indications and contraindications for care and postoperative management. Significant medical history issues like upcoming hip replacement surgery, chemotherapy, or physical therapy all have time and budget fit issues attached to them. You have to take into consideration how the medical history affects their lifestyle as well as your therapeutic approach.

6. Ask for **date of birth**. The relevance of age to right- and left-side distinction is that right-side patients tend to be over fifty, although not always.

7. Ask about **target conditions**—conditions you're especially interested in treating, and whether these conditions are related to their chief condition or disability. A "Yes" response to whether your caller has any of the following conditions is a strong indication that he or she is a right-side patient:
- missing teeth
- full or partial dentures
- poor appearance
- TMJ problems
- significant existing dentistry
- dental phobias.

(A brief note on significant existing dentistry: Patients who have existing reconstructive dentistry should be thought of as right-side patients. As we all know, existing restorative dentistry, over time, can require retreatment.)

The answers to the issues discussed in 1 through 7 above will reveal whether your new patient caller is a right-side or left-side patient. Only *after* you've identified right- or left-side status should you do the following:
- Offer the appropriate appointment. Here's a good way to communicate to right-side patients who call the right dental office: *"Karen, it sounds like you're a perfect fit for our dental practice. We reserve time in our schedule especially for patients like you. I'd like to schedule you either first thing in the morning or in the afternoon. That way we'll be able to seat you immediately and get right to helping you with your concerns."*
- Schedule for impact.
- Finish the conversation by addressing any other issues, such as directions to your office, insurance, parking issues, etc.

The goal of the Identity Dialogue is to schedule the right-side patients appropriately so that it's easy for you and your team to create an environment where patients feel good about their decision to choose you as their dentist. In other words, *make it easy for new patients to feel better about themselves when they're with you.* You can't do this unless you identify them on the telephone and schedule them when you have enough time to give them a great experience. During a right-side patient's initial appointment, be prepared to do a variety of things to make them happy, ranging from a complete examination, an extraction, partial denture repair, a bite adjustment, and so forth. Flexibility in the new patient process allows you to do any of these procedures and stay on time, without any added stress!

Make the Right-Side Patient Happy; Make it Easy
Notice that in the Identity Dialogue we did not indicate that the first appointment with the right-side patient is an examination appointment. Our goal at the first appointment is to make the right-side patient happy. When there's a chief condition that's causing a significant disability, it's best to treat that condition to the best of your ability within the standard of care. Obviously it's best to initiate complete care with a complete

examination. At times though, it's better leadership (helping patients feel better about themselves when they're with you) to first make them comfortable, then suggest a complete examination. If patients aren't ready for a complete examination, forcing them to go through one will make them less likely, not more likely, to eventually accept compete care.

Twenty-Four Ways to Begin Care for a Right-Side Patient

The traditional sequence of the process of complete patient care is as follows:

1. complete examination
2. consultation
3. treatment
4. referral.

Let's label this sequence using the numerals 1, 2, 3, 4. This textbook approach is logical but, as with many processes involving human behavior, logic doesn't always rule. Often the process through which right-side patients enter our practice and receive care is influenced more by patient preferences and fit issues than by our preferences for what we want patients to do, which is consent to complete examinations and treatment plans.

Most dentists have been taught that their role is to modify patients' behavior and direct them into the textbook model of 1, 2, 3, 4. What most dentists discover, however, is that the energy, stress, and time needed to change patient behavior create conflicts between patients and the dental office and among dental team members.

Adopt a more flexible attitude about how patients start care in your office. Remember, our destination is complete care. How we start that journey—treating a chief condition, prophylaxis, extraction—really doesn't matter as long as we keep making progress toward the destination.

An easier way to process patients that creates far greater patient satisfaction and eliminates the stress and conflicts among patients, dentists, and staff is to change our view that patient care must proceed following the rigid 1, 2, 3, 4 model.

Take the sequence 1, 2, 3, 4. Now scramble the numbers in any order and you'll end up with twenty-four different combinations:

| 1, 3, 2, 4 | 1, 4, 2, 3 | 1, 2, 4, 3 |
| 2, 1, 3, 4 | 2, 3, 1, 4 | etc. |

Pick any combination at random and you've picked a sequence that reflects how some right-side patients would prefer to be treated.

For example, here's a scenario for sequence 3, 4, 1, 2: Mrs. Humbert (a right-side patient) comes in for an emergency appointment and you treat her chief condition (3). She loves you and your team and the next day she refers you to her best friend (4). Two months later Mrs. Humbert returns for a complete examination (1) and one week later she has her consultation (2).

Here's an example of sequence 4, 3, 2, 1: Mr. Adams works with your spouse, knows you're a dentist, and refers his brother to you (4). His brother reports back to Mr. Adams that he had a wonderful experience. A month later Mr. Adams has an emergency and you take great care of him (3). While he is still in the chair, he asks you about complete care. You have some time so you give him a good overview of what is possible for him (2). He likes what he hears and returns a week later for a complete examination to start complete care (1).

The twenty-four combinations of patient sequencing work best with right-side patients. If you get too far away from the traditional 1, 2, 3, 4 model for left-side patients, then your practice can get chaotic. For most general dentists, right-side patients are easily identified over the telephone and sequencing is established based on what patients feel are their most pressing concerns. Make them happy early in your relationship, and when they're ready for complete care, they'll choose you.

Case Study: Michelle

This case study will help you understand how to identify and schedule the right-side patient (Identity Dialogue, CD-1), and also maintain patient confidentiality. We'll use this case study throughout the book.

Michelle is forty-three years old, well educated, owns a prestigious local art gallery, and is single. At her last dental appointment, three years ago, she had her teeth cleaned and a filling replaced. She is remodeling her gallery and getting ready for her big annual black-tie art show in three months. Michelle has been referred by Janet, a right-side patient of yours. You restored most of Janet's teeth and she loves them.

Here's the Identity Dialogue, showing how being curious, listening for clues, and asking the right questions reveal Michelle as a right-side patient.

Ginger: *"Hello, this is Ginger at Dr. Homoly's office. How can I help you?"*
Michelle: *"Hi, my name is Michelle Adams and I'd like to make an appointment to see Dr. Homoly."*
Ginger: *"Thanks for calling. Michelle, I'd like to identify how we can best meet your needs. What would you like Dr. Homoly to help you with?"*
(Says Ms. Hammaker, *"Always refer to a new patient by first name only, until you've established permission to use her last name, which could be overheard or seen."*)
Michelle: *"I hate the way my upper front teeth look. They're starting to look really bad."* **(Chief condition)**
Ginger: *"When did you first notice this problem?"*
Michelle: *"The other day I had an important art dealer in my studio—a cute guy, too—and when I was talking to him I noticed he was looking at my teeth! It's not the first time this has happened. It's come to the point that I'm embarrassed when talking to customers, and I'm beginning to feel very self-conscious about my appearance."* **(Chief disability)**
Ginger: *"I can understand why you'd be discouraged about that. Michelle, let me ask you, how urgent is this problem for you? Is this something that's important for you to get solved right away?"*
Michelle: *"Yes, it is. In three months I'm hosting my big annual art show. A lot of dealers, artists, the general public, and the media will be there. I need to look great by then."* **(Urgency)**
Ginger: *"Sounds like you've got your hands full. I'm curious, what do you do for a living? Sounds like you're an artist."*
Michelle: *"I own the Kaleidoscope art gallery on York Road in Oakbrook. We deal in sculpture, oils, and fine-art photography."*
Ginger: *"Tell me more about your art show."*

(Adds Ms. Hammaker, "*Don't repeat the name of the patient's business out loud–it may be overheard and could then identify the patient.*")

Michelle: "*It's really a big deal for me. I do a lot of business during and after the show. This year will be the biggest turnout ever. I've got builders, interior designers, and sawdust everywhere and it's becoming nerve-racking for me. I've hired two new full-time staff members and I'm trying to get them up to speed on displays and inventory. Plus I'm traveling more now, looking for good pieces to sell.*" (**Current events**)

Ginger: "*Michelle, how did you find out about us? May we thank that person for referring you?*"(Ms. Hammaker states, "*Unless you phrase it this way, you might end up thanking Janet when Michelle really didn't want Janet to know she became a patient and is having work done.*")

Michelle: "*Janet Bamber is a friend of mine and Dr. Homoly did some cosmetic dentistry for her and she looks great.*" (**Referral**)

(Ms. Hammaker adds, "*This is where you might want to mention that you are going to thank Janet, giving Michelle the opportunity to say 'Okay, but don't use my name.'*")

Ginger: "*If you have a few more minutes I'd like to ask you a few questions about your health history–would it be alright with you to do that over the phone? Do you have any allergies?*"

("*Wait for the patient's permission to discuss health history over the phone,*" Ms. Hammaker stresses.)

Michelle: "*No.*"

Ginger: "*Are you taking medications, or do you have any medical conditions that we need to be aware of?*"

Michelle: "*No, I'm a very healthy person. And when this art show is over, I'll feel even better!*" (**Medical history**)

Ginger: "*For your health history, could I have your date of birth?*"

Michelle: "*September 16, 1961.*" (**Date of birth**)

Ginger: "*Michelle, do you have any missing teeth? Do you wear full or partial dentures or have they ever been recommended to you?*"

Michelle: "*I have two missing upper back teeth, but they don't bother me because you can't see them when I talk or smile.*" (**Missing teeth**)

Ginger: "*Is there anything else we need to know about you or your dental condition before we see you?*"

(Adds Ms. Hammaker, "*It's important to note here that Ginger didn't repeat any of Michelle's health history out loud.*")

Michelle: "*Lately, I've noticed I'm having trouble chewing and some pain that I think is on the lower right side. Sometimes I swear it's the lower and other days it feels like it's coming from the upper.* (**Condition**) *I don't know what it is but it worries me, too.*" (**Disability**)

Ginger: "*Michelle, it sounds like you are a perfect fit for our dental practice. We reserve time in our schedule especially for patients like you. I'd like to schedule you either first thing in the morning or in the afternoon. That way, we'll be able to seat you immediately and get right to helping you with your concerns. Does this Tuesday at 8 a.m. work for you?*" (**Schedule for impact**)

Michelle: "*That's perfect.*"

Ginger: "*I'll put in the mail your medical history questionnaire, a map to our office, patient registration information, and our Notice of Privacy Practices so you can fill it out before you come in. That will save you time. You can visit our Web site, www.paulhomoly.com, and learn more about us and how we help lots of people like you.*"

(Ms Hammaker stresses, "*The Web site must now include your 'Notice of Privacy Practices,' usually as a link at the bottom.*")

Ginger: "*Michelle, at your first visit with us, you and Dr. Homoly will decide the best thing for you to do. He's good about offering choices. You may decide to do a compete examination or if there's something of more of an immediate nature, he'll take care of it right then. The fee for our complete examination is $125 and if he does anything else, we'll be sure to discuss the fee beforehand.*"

Michelle: "*This sounds like exactly what I'm looking for. Thanks so much.*"

Ginger: "*Thanks for calling, Michelle. We'll take great care of you.*"

Telephone Slip

Figure 5-4 shows a telephone slip to help document and guide your team in the new patient telephone conversation. You can easily adapt the steps for identifying a right-side patient to your own telephone slip.

FIGURE 5-4

Identity Dialogue Telephone Slip

Name:

Scheduled on:

1. Condition: *How can we help you today?*
How can we best help you at your first appointment with us?

Disability: *How does this affect you...*
Is this more of a problem at home or work...

2. Urgency: *How soon do we need to get you in?*
Do we need to see you right away?
Is there something coming up that you need this done by...

3. Current events (prompt for lifestyle issues concerning time, money, and stress that will impact how dentistry will **fit** into their lives):
Where do you live? Where do you work? Have you lived in the area long? Where are you from?

4. Referral: *How did you hear about our office?*
Who can we thank for sending you to us?

5. Medical History:

Need for premedication prior to dental work

Allergies and significant medical history conditions

6. Date of Birth:

For your dental record may I ask your date of birth (age)

7. Target conditions:

Missing teeth
Full or partial dentures
Concerns about appearance of teeth
Jaw joint pain
Severe fear
Extensive existing dentistry

Right-Side or Left-Side Patient:

Appointment Preferences:
Last Dental Visit:
X-rays:
Previous Dentist:
Address:
Phone: Home   Work
E-mail/Fax
Works For:
Dental Insurance:
Mailed NP Packet:
HIPPA materials:

Acknowledgment

My thanks to Deborah Hammaker for her help with the information related to patient confidentiality/HIPAA contained in this chapter. Ms. Hammaker is a Risk Management/Safety Coordinator at Benco Dental Company in Mechanicsburg, Pennsylvania.

In a Nutshell
Chapter Five—The Identity Dialogue

- The Identity Dialogue, Critical Dialogue Number One (CD-1), takes place over the telephone between the new patient and the scheduler. The intention of the Identity Dialogue is to identify whether the caller is a left- or a right-side patient and, once this is identified, to correctly schedule the patient.

- It's important to keep patient confidentiality, as mandated by the Health Insurance Portability and Accountability Act (HIPAA) of 1996.

- Typically the first appointments in the morning and afternoon are best for right-side patients. Devote at least a full hour for the initial appointment for the right-side patient without any other patients on your schedule at that time. When you meet new patients and are not burdened with running back into an operatory to perform a clinical procedure, your interpersonal skills are sharper, you stay on time more easily, and you'll demonstrate a better attitude because you're less stressed.

- Identify right-side patients during the initial telephone call by being curious about their chief concerns, urgency, current events of their life, referral source, medical history, age, and their overall dental conditions.

- Be flexible in your approach as to how patients begin care in your practice. Don't keep too rigidly to the traditional sequence of complete examination, consultation, treatment, and referral. Make it easy for right-side patients to accept care.

Chapter Six
Making A Great First Impression:
The New Patient Interview

Have you ever met someone you've immediately liked or disliked? I know you have. When people first meet you, what sort of experience do they have? Do they immediately like or dislike you, or do they come away on the fence, without a strong feeling either way? This chapter is about meeting the new right-side patient for the first time and your critical first conversation. This conversation begins the process of you and your patient learning about each other and provides evidence to your patient that she has made a good choice in selecting you as her dentist. Solid relationships and excellent first impressions start with a great conversation.

To "See" One Another

The word *interview* comes from the French *entrevoir*, "to see one another." I like this definition; it means that each person in the interview learns something about the other. However, that's not what usually takes place in the traditional new patient interview. The interview is usually one-way—we learn a lot about patients; they learn very little about us. We learn their medical and dental histories and their dental concerns, and if we have time in our schedule, we may learn a little about what they do for a living and some bits of family information. However, in the traditional interview process the patient may learn nothing about us. Is it important for the patient to get to know us? It is if you want to do sophisticated right-side dentistry.

When conducting the new patient interview, think of it as a *conversation*, one where there is an exchange of ideas, opinions, and experiences, where you and your patient come away understanding and trusting each other more, crafting the underpinnings for a good relationship that leads to good healthcare decisions.

The new patient conversation should be a sharing of stories. Within the patients' stories, you'll learn what they're concerned about, what they'd like done about it, what their dental health has been, how they make healthcare decisions, the facts about their medical history and previous dental experiences (good and bad), and how they would like their dental health to be in the future. From your story, your patients learn whether they're in the right dental office that can meet their needs and if you've treated other people like them. Most importantly, your patients want to feel good about their decision to come to you.

> *Most importantly, your patients want to feel*
> *good about their decision to come to you.*

In terms of interview content, spend the majority of time getting patients to talk about themselves. The interview is not the time for long statements from you about quality, excellence, or mission statements. Think of using 90 percent of the interview time listening to them and 10 percent of the time letting them get to know you.

To facilitate this conversation you need to have the right environment, keen communication skills, and a structured process.

The Right Environment
The new patient conversation with a right-side patient is best held in a quiet, confidential area. I like a private consultation room. Many right-side patients have significant disabilities (intimacy issues, abuse, low self-esteem) that often are embarrassing to talk about. Open-bay operatories are not the place to have confidential conversations. Make your consultation room cozy and comfortable. I've seen many excellent ones that incorporate fruit juice dispensers, libraries, and beautiful artwork. The best ones I've seen conceal all clinical items. Large full-face photographs of your patients showing off their smiles are great to showcase your work. Use track lighting and imagine your consultation room is an art gallery of your best dentistry.

> *An important part of the environment is the people*
> *who are present during the new patient conversation.*

An important part of the environment is the people who are present during the new patient conversation. You have a few choices: the dentist and patient; the dentist, assistant, and patient; or the assistant and patient. I've seen all combinations work. My first choice is dentist and patient; with dentist, assistant, and patient a close second. The advantage of the dentist-and-patient combination is that there is complete privacy in the conversation. I treated severely disabled patients for twenty years and conversations often took very important turns that I believe never would have happened if anyone else had been in the room. The disadvantage is that it's hard to have a meaningful conversation and document it in the record at the same time. It can be useful to have an assistant document the conversation while it's happening, as well as to provide a second set of ears. My advice would be to use common sense to decide whether the assistant will help or hinder the quality of the conversation.

Many dentists have a team member engage in the new patient conversation without the dentist present, then report her findings to the dentist. The advantage of this is efficiency; the dentist can be producing income while the team member is conversing. Another advantage of this method is that if the dentist is a weak communicator, it makes sense to instead use someone who is a good conversationalist. The greatest disadvantage to this method is that a team member, no matter how skilled, does not have the authority and credibility of the dentist. Patients feel respected when they have the opportunity to speak directly to the dentist to express their concerns.

Communication Skills

The second issue affecting an excellent new patient conversation is superb communication skills, the leading one of which I call *authentic presence*. Authentic presence is a characteristic of leaders who, when they communicate (both by speaking and listening), help others feel better about themselves. When patients feel better about themselves, they start the process of looking for reasons to trust you. If your new patients want to find reasons to like and trust you, they'll find them in your tone of voice, your team, your facility, etc. If your new patients want to find reasons not to trust you, they'll find those, too. Patients see what they want to see. It's human nature to find what you're looking for. Let's look at each of the parts of authentic presence—speaking and listening.

Speaking

We send messages to others by what we say, how we say it, and how we look. The oft-quoted Dr. Albert Moravian's study at Yale University showed that when a conversation has ambiguous and confusing aspects (as do many dentist/patient conversations), listeners tend to be influenced more by what they see and the tone of the speaker's voice than by the meaning of the speaker's words. What this means is that we need to be very aware of our total communication "package"—how we look, how we sound, and what we say. There are three specific things that would benefit most dentists in terms of speaking: eye connection, storytelling, and response management.

Eye connection. "Eye connection" means paying attention to your patients as you're talking and as *they're* talking. You don't look away or make only fleeting eye contact. You can tell if someone understands and trusts you; and you can sense their likes, dislikes, and fears, by the look in their eye. Connecting with patients gives them the opportunity to look into your eyes, too. Patients can tell a lot about you by the expression in your eyes. If you're distracted, nervous, or tired, they can sense it. They also can sense if you're accepting, interested, kind, and patient.

Many dentists don't connect in this way. Instead, they make brief eye contact and talk while they're looking at a file or off into space. Many team members do the same. There are too many distractions in the dental office. Pay attention to your patients as you speak and listen to them. It's an important part of them understanding more about you and, consequently, trusting you. With complex care, patients don't understand all that you're saying. A big part of how they make their decision to receive care is by getting a good glimpse into who you are. Connection gives them the opportunity to say "yes" to you, and when they do, the dentistry follows.

Storytelling. In my second book, *Isn't It Wonderful When Patients Say "Yes,"* I devote an entire chapter to the topic of storytelling. Storytelling is a great way to get to know people and let them know you. It's also a great way to offer advice without making people mad or defensive. The process of StorySelling® I developed years ago uses stories and story-like devices—metaphors, similes, other comparisons—to "sell" your ideas in story form. In January 2005, the *Harvard Business Review* published an article called "What's Your Story?" by Herminia Ibara and Kent Lineback. The authors discuss the power of personal stories, noting that to know a person well is to know their story—the experiences that have shaped them. Likewise, when we want someone to know us, we share stories of our childhood, our family, our life. Storytelling is an important part of authentic presence and is worthy of your study.

In the context of the new patient conversation, it's important that you and your patient share your stories (remember, do more listening than talking). Patient stories can sound like this:

"Doctor, my problems started when I was a child; my parents brought me to a dentist and he said I had soft teeth. Then when I became pregnant with my first child, I lost all the calcium from my teeth. Since then I've had nothing but problems with..."

You've heard many patient stories before but may not have thought of them as stories (dentists call stories "health histories"). If you think of them as stories, then it gives you permission to share one of yours with your patient. This is a powerful form of disclosure and gives patients insight and confidence in you. Do you have a story that discloses who you are? For example, many of my new patients would tell me stories about their long history of dental care, going from one dentist to another over their lifetime. I often would respond to their story with a story of my own dental history, including orthognathic surgery, orthodontics, restorative dentistry, and periodontal care. Your stories reveal your humanity to your patients. Dentists are seen as professionals and many patients may see us as "superior" to them; in subtle ways this may diminish how they feel about themselves when they're with us. Stories about your fears, frustrations, and your human condition can help your patient not only hear what you have to say, but they also can feel it. Right-side patients need to know how you feel, and stories are the best way to do that.

Listening

The other half of "authentic presence" is listening, and for most of us this is the more difficult half. According to *Listening: The Forgotten Skill*, by Madelyn Burley-Allen, adults in business situations spend 70 percent of their time in the communication process—speaking, listening, writing, and reading. Within those four categories, 40 percent of the time is spent listening, 35 percent talking, 16 percent reading, and 9 percent writing. Here's the amazing part: most adults, when their listening skills are tested, listen only at 25 percent efficiency. It's no wonder that patients, team members, and dentists at times have trouble communicating and getting along!

It's hard for dentists and team members to listen for several reasons. Most of us have never studied listening skills and our listening habits are just that—habits, good or bad, that we've picked up. The dental office environment often runs at high speed: checking patients in and out, answering telephones, and staying on schedule. I believe that listening is difficult because we have to do so much of it. Everyone around the dentist has their hooks into him/her—hygiene checks, emergencies, calls to the lab, consultations, etc. After a while we put up filters and let in only what we're listening for—chief complaints, clinical information—and all the rest bounces off us. Listening through filters protects us from overload. However, when doing right-side dentistry where deep disabilities and significant fit issues exist, you need to listen to it all.

Response management. "Response management" means becoming aware of how you typically respond in the new patient interview and which response categories best serve you and your patient.

According to *Listening: The Forgotten Skill*, there typically are four types of responses people make as a result of listening. First is the "advice response" when, after hearing what was said, the listener offers advice. For example, during the new patient conversation Michelle says, *"I hate the way my front teeth look!"* An advice response from you might sound like, *"We can make your smile look great by using veneers on your front teeth. The way we'd do it is by..."* The next response is the "curiosity response" and the request for more information. Again Michelle says, *"I hate the way* my front teeth look!" A curiosity response might sound like, "Tell me more about what you don't like. Is it the color, the shape..." The next response is the "empathetic response;" this lets listeners know that you understand how they feel and that they've been heard. An empathetic response to Michelle might sound like, "I know it's embarrassing when you don't feel confident in your appearance. We see a lot of patients who..." The last response is the "critical response," in which you're disapproving or unsympathetic. A critical response to Michelle might sound like, "Michelle, if you practiced better home care of brushing and flossing, your teeth wouldn't be in this condition."

Of the four response categories, which do you use the most during the new patient conversation? My experience is that most dentists and team members launch into advice responses the most. Treatment recommendations during the new patient conversation are a form of the advice response. The advice response can stop the dialogue between doctor and patient and result in a technical lesson that does not serve the purpose of the new patient conversation.

In addition, it's common for critical responses to surface. Unintentionally we say things that sound fine to us, but to the patient our responses can sting. For example, preaching about home care, or neglect, or low dental IQ can be perceived by our patients as criticism. Remember that a big part of the objective of the new patient conversation is to help patients feel better about themselves when they're with you. Criticism and unsympathetic remarks don't help people feel better about themselves.

During the new patient conversation, the curiosity and empathetic responses work best to keep the conversation flowing. Become aware of your response management. For the most part you've heard many of the complaints and concerns that patients have. Practice curiosity and empathetic responses to common patient scenarios with your team. Do this well and your patients will sense in you greater compassion and interest in them.

The New Patient Interview Process

Having great conversations is like dancing: the process brings out expression. Here's the process of the new patient interview—it's loose enough that it allows the conversation to go where it needs to and bring out discoveries, and is sufficiently constructed so that all parties say what they need to say, and are heard. The process is:

1. Discovering the current conditions/disabilities
2. Patient's story
3. Your story
4. Next step.

Discovering the Current Conditions/Disabilities

Start your new patient conversation with discovering why the patient has come to you. Chances are excellent that if your administrative team did a good job with the Identity Dialogue, they've documented on side one of the Discovery Guide™ your patient's chief condition, chief disability, its associated conditions, and information about the current events of her life (see Chapter Twelve for an in-depth discussion of the Discovery Guide). Review this information before the new right-side patient's appointment.

> *Start your new patient conversation with*
> *discovering why the patient has come to you.*

If you already have a good sense of her dental and life issues, begin the conversation demonstrating your knowledge of and interest in her. For example, in Michelle's case a good way to start the new patient conversation is to let her know what you already know about her.

"*Hello, Michelle, I'm Paul Homoly–welcome to our practice. I was talking to Ginger, my receptionist, who spoke to you on the phone, and she shared with me that you're not happy with the appearance of your front teeth. Tell me more about that.*"

If you don't know much about the patient, invite her to tell you why she's come to see you.

"*Michelle, welcome to our practice. I'm Paul Homoly. How can I help you today?*"

With this invitation, most patients will tell you what's bothering them. Listen for the link between what they say is wrong in their mouths (their conditions) and how they affect their lives (their disabilities). Conditions are in the mouth, i.e., broken teeth, loose dentures, dark teeth, pain.

Conditions are biological, aesthetic, functional, and phonetic issues. Disabilities usually are emotional issues—embarrassment, fear, concern, anxiety. Disabilities are in their lives.

Be curious about how the disability is affecting the patient's life. Ask open-ended questions such as, *"When did you first notice this problem?"* or *"Does this bother you more at work or at home?"* or *"Tell me about a time when this condition bothers you the most."* Questions like these often lead to the patient telling you a story about her disability, which is great for gaining a deeper understanding of how her teeth are affecting her life. **Figure 6-1** shows side one of the Discovery Guide. Notice that the section on disability offers topics—work, home, health, etc.—to lead the conversation toward the most significant aspect of the disability.

FIGURE 6-1

Disabilities / Fit and Readiness issues

Conditions: Unattractive front teeth, pain right side

Disabilities: How is their dental condition affecting their life? Be curious.
Work, Home, Health, Activities, Family, Hobbies, Confidence, Fear, Shame, Inconvenience, Intimacy, Energy, Concentration, Anger, Worry

Michelle hates the appearance of her upper front teeth. She says customers are staring at them. She owns a local art gallery and is loosing confidence with customers because of the appearance of her teeth. She's annoyed by pain on her right side.

Fit & Readiness Issues
Money, Time, Events, Stress, Health, Emotions, Energy/attention

She has a big art show and black tie event in three months and wants to look great by then. She's very busy remodeling her gallery, training new employees, and doing a lot of travel. She's worried that she won't have the time to get everything done.

Dr. John Gordon, of Kansas City, Kansas, has an effective process for discovering the patient's disability at its most significant level. I observed him in his office during a new patient interview with an Asian woman in her mid-thirties. The conversation went like this:

"Sue, how can I help you today?"

"Dr. Gordon, I really don't like the appearance of my front teeth. They look ugly."

"Which front teeth are you concerned about, the uppers, the lowers, or both?"

"It's mainly the uppers."

"What is it that you don't like about them?"

"I don't like the chips in the edges, and see how they overlap in front and how these two are crooked?"

"I see, and how does this bother you? When does it bother you the most?"

"Mostly at work. My husband doesn't even notice."

"Tell me how they bother you at work."

"Well, I can tell that people notice my teeth. Every so often I catch some one staring at them."

"It sounds like you're embarrassed about your appearance at work."

"Yes, I am. I have an important job as a data base manager and I talk to people all day long, and there's times when I feel awful."

"Tell me more about that. What happens?"

"Well, the other day I was working when a few people who were standing near my desk started laughing, and it seemed like they were laughing at me. I felt so bad. I'm so ashamed of the way I look."

"We can help you with how you feel about your teeth."

This conversation first disclosed her chief condition—chipped and crowded front teeth. Dr. Gordon then guided the conversation to discover the most significant level of her disability—her embarrassment at her appearance at work. Which is a stronger platform for John to build value for his dentistry, veneering her front teeth or relieving her shame? Relieving her shame is why she will accept treatment of her front teeth. Discovering the chief condition and the most significant level of the disability early in the new patient conversation is critical to keeping the conversation relevant from the patient's point of view.

Dr. Betsy Bakeman, of Grand Rapids, Michigan, talks about getting patients to discuss what relieving the disability and enjoying the benefit would mean to them:

> *"Often a patient has never verbalized what having better dental health would mean to them in specific terms. It's common for it to become an emotional moment for patients when they get in touch with how they really feel about getting their teeth fixed. As they state their reasons and what it means to them, I listen very closely and make sure that their reasons play a dominant role in my future conversations with them about their care."*

The early part of the new patient interview is also a good time to review medical history. In addition to its impact on treatment decisions, medical history can provide insight into fit and readiness issues. Patients who are considering future surgery or who have recently been ill may or may not be ready for dentistry now.

A good thing to keep in mind on this first part of the new patient interview is to not offer treatment recommendations or get into technical conversations. When the conversation gets into the technical aspects of care, the dialogue dies because the communication becomes one-way, from the dentist to the patient. If Dr. Gordon had launched into a show-and-tell about veneers too early in his conversation with Sue, he may have never learned about her deeper disability.

Patient's Story

The next step in the interview process is to encourage patients to tell their story. You may have already heard part of their story in the discussion about conditions and disabilities.

Stories have a structure that we're all familiar with. Typical story structure is:

- Past events—*"Once upon a time..."*
- Crisis/turning point—*"Then one day..."*
- New events/future—*"... and they lived happily ever after."*

Story form is a natural way for people to talk to one another and is a good guide for us in the new patient conversation. Stories also provide a chronology and dental history of your new patient. To encourage new patients to tell you their story, ask questions in a way that gives them permission to tell their story. Everyone has one and loves to tell it.

Stories start in the past—*"Once upon a time..."* Ask your new patient to tell you about her early memories about her dental health and experiences with other dentists. With some right-side patients, brace yourself for some incredible stories about their dental history. On many occasions I've heard stories of abuse, humiliation, and mutilations that make it a miracle that some people return to the dental office.

Stories have a crisis or turning point—*"Then one day..."* As you hear the story, listen for this crisis or turning point. ("Crisis/turning point" means a life-changing event, good or bad, that causes patients to take action, change their beliefs, or become ready for a change.) A major emphasis of this book is the concept of readiness: how to discover it, how it rarely occurs in the dental office, and how to listen to and respect patients when they're not ready. My experience is that when you become aware of the concept of readiness, you'll see evidence of it (or the lack of it) in every patient. Crisis statements in your patients' stories sound like these:

"When I saw my mother without her dentures in and how old she looked, I knew right then I needed to do something about my teeth."

"My front tooth on my partial popped out in the ladies' room at my high school reunion and I wanted to die."

"Now that my kids have graduated and on their own, it's time to take care of me."

"I just got promoted and my new job puts me in front of a lot of people and I have to look good."

Not all patients reveal their crisis/turning point, however. In situations like these, simply ask them. For example:

"Sue, you've told me you haven't been to the dentist for many years. What brings you here now?"

"Tamara, tell me what's happened to make you interested in fixing your teeth now?"

It's important to listen for the crisis/turning point because it discloses to you what's important to patients and how they became ready for care. Knowing what's important to them is at the heart of the benefits statements you'll make in the consultation appointment.

Knowing the crisis/turning point adds to your inventory of examples for conversations with other patients who may have had similar circumstances. When you're able to tell your patient that you've treated other patients with similar situations, it increases their confidence in you.

After patients disclose their past crisis/turning point, they often will bring their story back into the present and acknowledge the reason for their visit. When they do, encourage them to continue their story and ask them to imagine how the story of their dental history will end.

Stories have endings with new events and future focus – *"... and they lived happily ever after."* Some good questions that encourage patients to tell you what they'd like for themselves and their dental health in the future are:

"If you could wave a magic wand and have anything you want in terms of your dental health, what would it be?"

"Tell me how you'd like your dental health to be years from now?"

"How do you see your dental health in the future?"

A few cautions about future-oriented questions during the new patient conversation. These questions can easily take the conversation down the path of treatment recommendations and stifle the intention of the new patient conversation. Future-oriented questions to a patient who is not ready may feel like sales pressure. Future-oriented questions often are safer after the patient has had an opportunity to get to know you and your team. Give patients time to form an opinion of you, your care, and your team before you ask them to trust you. In Chapter Eight, in the Choice Dialogue, you'll see how future-oriented questions are easier for patients to answer when positioned after an examination and post-examination discussion.

Your Story

After you've heard the patient's story, it may be helpful for you to tell her yours. It's important during the new patient interview that patients learn about you and hear your story. Your story might be about a life crisis/turning point that is similar to what your patient told you about, or a story about something you have in common—home of origin, a hobby, or people.

The most important story to tell illustrates why you practice dentistry. If you're a staff member, the most important story to tell illustrates why you work for your particular dentist. Its impact results from the fact that it discloses your beliefs, experiences, and attitudes.

I used my story for twenty years. My own dental history is dramatic. I developed a slanting open bite with a full-centimeter anterior open bite. As an adult the only teeth that made contact were my second molars. My speech and chewing were difficult. In 1975, I endured extractions, ortho-dontics, palatal expansion, vertical pull chin cup, head gear, and a sagittal split osteotomy. I know what it's like to have bad teeth and I know what it's like to get them fixed. I use my story to let patients know I'm not per-fect and I know what it's like to be in their shoes. This brings us closer.

For example, Nanette, a new right-side patient, was discouraged about all the dentistry she thought she needed. I answered her by telling her a short version of my story:

> "Nanette, twenty-five years ago I had teeth that were in bad shape. I was a junior in dental school when I decided to get them fixed. Now I get compliments all the time about my teeth and I feel good about them. I'm glad I had them fixed. I hope you'll be glad, too."

You may not have a dramatic dental history to share, but you can tell your patients how you feel about dentistry and how you enjoy seeing great results. You can talk about how you love helping people and why you want to make a difference in people's lives. Then shift your belief to the patient: *"You'll see great results, too," "I'll enjoy helping you," "This dentistry will make a difference in your life."*

Notice that the story I shared with Nanette consists of only five sentences. Most stories can be told in just a few sentences. Work on them until you have them down to the simplest language with the fewest words. Good short stories are more persuasive and memorable than long, boring ones.

Team Members' Stories

Your team members need to tell patients why they work for you. For example, your patient Guy tells your assistant Sally that he's worried about costs. She then says:

"Guy, I've been a dental assistant for eight years and I've worked in three other offices. I love my work and wanted to find an office that appreciated me. I've been here now for five years and I feel great about working here. They take good care of people here and they'll take great care of you, too."

The best story I've heard from a team member was told by a hygienist in the office of Dr. John Hopp in Gillette, Wyoming. I asked her to role-play with me as if I were a patient and to tell me a story that gives me insight into their practice or dentist, or a story that would help if I was hesitant about periodontal care. She didn't hesitate a second. She said:

"Paul, you remind me of my father. My mom and dad became patients in this practice fifteen years ago. They both had dental problems like you do—loose teeth and infected gums. My mom went through treatment and today she has all her teeth. My dad didn't and today he wears dentures. What would you like to do?"

I recommend that you read/reread the chapter in my book *Isn't It Wonderful When Patients Say "Yes"* on storytelling. Stories have powerful influence. Learn to tell them in short, conversational language. Stories help you acknowledge the toughest issues and emotions, and the success stories help to define your practice. Stories disclose your humanity and allow patients to know you beyond your role as a dentist or team member. Right-side patients need to know you and what's inside you, and your stories allow them to learn this.

Sandy Roth, an internationally known communications expert and co-founder of ProSynergy Dental Communications, says this about the new patient interview and stories:

> "Every patient has a story. Your first job is to learn each patient's story as
> completely and clearly as possible. To do anything less will deny you an
> understanding of this patient, how he thinks, what he wants, the barriers
> and limitations that govern his choices, and a myriad of other things that
> will influence this patient's choices in your practice. Each patient wants
> you to know his story and, given the right opportunity, will convey what
> is important for you to know and understand. While this information can
> be forthcoming without prompting, some patients are more timid in
> revealing their stories. Creating a safe environment for both types of
> patients is essential. A constant curiosity and excellent open-ended
> questions will serve you and your staff well when beginning to learn about
> your patient. A quiet, private place with no interruptions will encourage
> fuller disclosure. An unhurried demeanor and excellent listening skills
> will ensure that patients go beyond surface comments to those issues more
> deeply important to them. While many dental teams believe they must
> first "educate" their patients, this thinking will get in the way of their
> being properly educated by their patients."

The Next Step

When you reach a point in the conversation where you sense that you and your patient understand each other, it's time to recommend the next step. For most right-side patients, their next step is a limited examination to discover the condition responsible for their disability, or a complete examination if no urgent condition or disability exists. This is the simplest aspect of the new patient interview and it signals that the conversation, for now, is finished and you're moving forward together. For example:

> "Michelle, I understand how you feel about your teeth and you've given
> me some good insights into what's important to you. Let me make this
> recommendation. Let me take a look in your mouth and examine you so
> I can better understand your conditions. After the examination, we'll
> return to this conversation and together we'll decide the best way to
> proceed. How does this sound to you?"

A key point deserves repeating here. During the new patient interview, avoid specific treatment recommendations. That's not to say you should avoid telling success stories of other patients with similar conditions or avoid referring to your clinical experiences. Rather, resist the urge to educate and make treatment recommendations. When the new patient conversation turns to treatment recommendations, its purpose of discovery and disclosure is lost and replaced with a one-sided show-and-tell, often leading you and your patient into a superficial dialogue, which benefits no one.

In a Nutshell
Chapter Six—The New Patient Interview

- When conducting the new patient interview, think of it as a new patient conversation, where there is an exchange of ideas, opinions, and experiences.

- The new patient conversation is a sharing of stories. Within patients' stories you'll learn their conditions, disabilities, the benefits they want, medical and dental history, fit and readiness issues, and how they see themselves in the future.

- Within your story is disclosure of who you are, what you have in common with your patient, why you love dentistry, and evidence to your patients that they made a good decision to see you.

- Listen much more than you talk. Stay conversational and avoid treatment recommendations and patient education.

Chapter Seven
When The Patient Is Ready The Dentist Will Appear:
Readiness And The Right-Side Patient

You're excited—you just performed a complete examination on a right-side patient and you can hardly wait to start treatment. During the exam you did it all: intraoral and full-face photographs, full-mouth radiographs, study models, facebow, TMJ examination, Doppler auscultation (analysis). One week later the patient returns for her consultation. You've spent an hour-and-a-half working the case up, talking to specialists and the lab. But after you spend forty-five minutes presenting her treatment plan she looks at you and says, stunned, *"I didn't know I had this much wrong with my mouth. How much does all this cost?"*

"Your fee is nineteen thousand five hundred dollars," you say, as you squint at your shoes.

"Nineteen thousand five hundred dollars!" she exclaims. *"I had no idea it would cost that much. That's more than I paid for my car! All I really wanted you to do is fix this dark front tooth. How much does that cost?"*

Want to run away? Many dentists who invest huge amounts of time and effort into patients who aren't ready want to do just that. Presenting big treatment plans to patients who aren't ready or can't afford them hurts the patient, too. The disappointment, embarrassment, and/or anger it causes can prevent them from receiving complete care and trusting dentists, and can discourage them from seeking care in the future.

How do you decide what level of care is appropriate for patients? How do you know what patients think is the appropriate amount of treatment for them? Do you treatment plan based on existing conditions, or on what you think they can afford? Lots of questions, the biggest one being,

How do you discover what the patient is ready for? This chapter addresses the concept of "readiness."

Discovering readiness is one of the most important acts of leadership for the complete-care dentist when treating right-side patients. Without understanding right-side patients' readiness, you risk over-/under-treating patients, wasting a lot of time (yours and patients'), and adding needless stress to everyone's life. With an understanding of readiness, you can offer treatment plans with no stress and with complete confidence in the suitability of your treatment recommendations.

Readiness

Readiness is the patient's inclination to accept complete-care treatment recommendations now. Some patients are more ready than others. Many different things affect readiness, but two have the greatest impact: their fit issues and their decision-making process.

A major component of readiness is fit issues—patients' life circumstances that relate to their budget, work schedule, current events. Patients will not be ready for care if a treatment plan will not fit into their budgets or other important aspects of their lives.

Another component of readiness is deeper emotional issues that relate to patients' decision-making processes. Some patients aren't rapid decision makers, or good decision makers, or just don't handle change very well. Complete full-mouth dentistry represents big change for patients, along with big risks. Many patients, especially older ones, don't like assuming big risks. Even if some patients are unhappy with their present oral conditions and can afford the dentistry, in their mind there are no risks associated with staying just the way they are; the status quo feels safe to them.

Dr. John Kois, Founder and Director of Creating Restorative Excellence® Center for Advanced Dental Learning, in Seattle, Washington, understands patient readiness and what influences it. He says:

"Sometimes when a patient comes in to see me they are in crisis,
(emergency). When they're in crisis it's pretty obvious that they're not

ready for complete care. They're being forced to do something, and it never feels right. Even if they have the money, if they're restoring their mouth because they're having a crisis, it never feels right. When they're actually ready it's a joy, an absolute joy."

Most Right-Side Patients Aren't Ready... Today

Most right-side patients aren't ready the first time they hear a complete treatment plan. They need time to sort out the significant lifestyle and financial issues affecting their decision. Dr. Bruce Quolette of West Palm Beach, Florida, says, *"Respecting readiness is a form of choice; we can treat you now or later. Choice combined with readiness gives patients control and a sense of involvement in their treatment, and they love it."*

Most general dentists I know tell me that less than two to three percent of patients to whom they quote a fee of greater than $10,000 are ready for a complete treatment plan. Additionally, most dentists report that the biggest cases they do are for patients who've been in their practice for more than a year. Everything I've heard from hundreds of dentists supports this conclusion: it's human nature for right-side patients to take time to get ready for complete care, and when they become ready, they choose the dentist they already have a good relationship with to do their dentistry.

Based on that conclusion, it makes perfect sense to adopt a case acceptance process that is in tune with human nature and issues by acknowledging and accommodating right-side patients who aren't ready. By maintaining a good relationship with them while they're in their "incubation" process, when they become ready they choose you to provide their care. This is exactly what the Making It Easy approach is all about.

In sharp contrast to this is the traditional approach to case acceptance, which emphasizes making patients ready. Although making patients ready may not be a conscious action, it is exactly what we are doing when we overeducate our patients, push "hot" buttons, create urgency, overcome objections, or use sales techniques to "close" the sale. To us these activities may feel like the right things to do, but to patients who aren't ready, they feel like sales pressure. The traditional approach implies that if patients have dental conditions, they should treat them as soon as possible. What this does not take into account is that the patient's life circumstances may dictate that complete dentistry is not be their next best step.

Take Kelly, for example, who is struggling with her weight. She's been depressed over it and it's been hard on her relationship with her husband. She's seriously considering bariatric surgery and is worried about the costs not covered by her medical insurance. Kelly also has a poorly fitting partial denture, with the typical associated problems that brings. What's Kelly's next best step: treating her weight problem or her teeth? The Making It Easy approach will help you to guide Kelly to her next best step. It may not be her dentistry. But later on, when she's ready, she'll appreciate the fact that you recognized that, and she'll choose you to do it.

You Don't Need the Right-Side Patient to Say "Yes"... Today

A big part of my assumption when writing this book is that your practice is profitable and that you enjoy doing left-side dentistry. In fact, most dentists get far into their careers practicing on the left side. If most dentists changed nothing about their practices, they'd still be doing comparatively well. The left side pays the bills and funds the retirement. It's the right side that, in addition to boosting income, provides the sense of professional accomplishment and the satisfaction that comes from growth. We don't need the right side to eat; we need it to enjoy our careers more. With this in mind, don't get impatient if a right-side patient isn't ready for complete care. It's not financial life-or-death for you. In fact, most right-side patients are not ready for care in the first year they're in your practice. The biggest cases most general practitioners do are for patients who have been in the practice for a year or more, sometimes for several years—this at the heart of the philosophy supporting the processes described in this book. It is human nature and perfectly natural for right-side patients to take their time to decide on care. Consequently, the best strategy is for you to adopt a case acceptance system that manages and leads right-side patients who *aren't* ready. And when they become ready, they are already in your practice and the decision that feels the best for them is to choose you to restore their mouths. The processes described in this book will show you how to have hundreds of right-side patients who are not yet ready, but are happy, in your practice. And over time, the inevitability of continued dental breakdown combined with the twists and turns of life circumstances help make right-side patients ready. If you have hundreds of happy but not-ready right-side patients in your recall system, I guarantee that you eventually will have at least one or two of these patients showing up at your door *every* month saying, *"I'm ready!"*

The best strategy is for you to adopt a case acceptance system that manages and leads right-side patients who aren't ready.

Dental IQ

There is a cornerstone principle in dentistry that educating a patient about the details of their conditions and their consequences; and the benefits, risks, and alternatives of treatment creates a greater likelihood for treatment acceptance. This process has been labeled "raising the dental IQ." The question I'd have you think about is: Has it been your experience that raising patients' dental IQ predictably improves case acceptance for right-side dentistry? I strongly doubt it. It's time dentistry looked at the efficacy of the concept of raising patients' dental IQ.

In the last decade, patient education has reached new heights through the use of multimedia simulations to help patients understand what's wrong with their mouths and how we can help them. I'm not against using the latest technology, but I am against the belief that having intra-oral cameras and television monitors in every operatory guarantees case acceptance. I've seen many dentists and team members go overboard in their thinking, believing that all they need to do is educate patients to get them to say "Yes." In many ways, we're trying to educate our patients into being ready. Once you believe you can educate a patient into being ready, you get caught up in the Dental IQ Trap.

Dental IQ Trap

The Dental IQ Trap (**Figure 7-1**) is the corner we paint ourselves into by believing that a thorough diagnosis, combined with abundant patient education, leads to treatment acceptance.

FIGURE 7-1

The Dental IQ Trap

Diagnosis

Patient education

Treatment acceptance

The Dental IQ Trap is so ingrained in the culture of dentistry that it's hard to imagine it not being true—diagnosis plus patient education must lead to treatment acceptance! When dentists, caught in the Dental IQ Trap, experience a right-side patient saying "No" to treatment, they assume it's due to inadequate patient education, that they didn't communicate well enough. So they increase the time and effort they put into patient education (**Figure 7-2**).

FIGURE 7-2

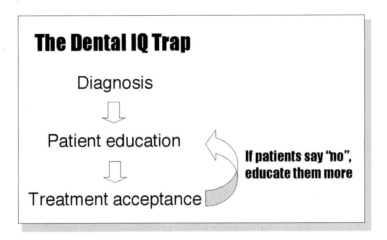

When *that* doesn't work, they look at the step before patient education: diagnosis. Dentists caught in the "trap" boost their efforts in diagnosis, leading many of them into more elaborate and time-consuming examinations and diagnostic procedures (**Figure 7-3**).

FIGURE 7-3

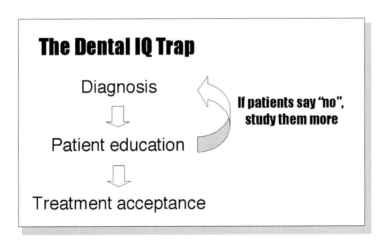

Look at your own situation. If you doubled your efforts in patient education and diagnosis, would you double the number of right-side patients who say "Yes?" I'll bet that you'd probably *decrease* case acceptance. The way out of the Dental IQ Trap is to understand that you can't educate a patient into readiness.

> *The way out of the Dental IQ Trap is to understand*
> *that you can't educate a patient into readiness.*

Readiness Does Not Occur in the Dental Office

It's crucial to recognize that readiness does not occur in the dental office. Rather, it's life circumstances—weddings, new jobs, high school reunions—that make patients ready for complete care. Yes, you can plant the seeds of ideas to help patients visualize how they may look or feel once they have their teeth restored, but the actual moment of readiness doesn't happen in your chair. You have little control over making patients ready.

For example, Jan is married to Hank. Jan's had bad teeth her entire life, but has never been ready to fix them. Hank has been an S.O.B. all his life. One day Hank drops dead. Now, Jan's ready!

Another example is Stanley, who drives a forklift. He has a mouth full of problems, but he has better things to do with his money than make his teeth look pretty. One day his boss says, *"Stanley, you're a good man. You know more about this business than the owners do. I'm promoting you to the front office. It means more money and time off, but you're gonna have to fix your teeth."* Now, Stanley's ready!

At some point, all of us become ready for something. Maybe it's to lose weight, get married, get divorced, have a baby, or change jobs. Think back to a time when you knew what to do but weren't ready to do it. Then one day, you became ready, probably for a variety of reasons, some of which had nothing to do with the act itself. Patients are just like you.

Patients may understand the clinical reasons to get their teeth fixed, you can use all the logic in the world; but if they're not ready, the boat isn't going to leave the dock.

(Im)patient Education

When I teach the concept of readiness at a seminar, it always ignites controversy. I'll hear participants say, *"Yes, but isn't that what patient education is all about–helping people become ready? If we don't educate patients about what's possible, they'll never know that they can be helped. Besides, it's the educated patient–patients with a high dental IQ–who really appreciates their teeth; they're the ones who'll opt for complete care."*

I don't oppose influencing patients and helping them to understand and accept comprehensive care. But there is a line between influencing and nagging that I see many dentists cross. *Influencing* is offering complete care. It's having the right attitude and giving patients hope. It's being willing to work within a patient's budget. It's modeling you and your staff's excellent dental health. It's having new patients talk with happy, already-treated patients. Influencing is planting seeds for complex-care dentistry.

On the other hand, *nagging* is forcing patients to undergo long, expensive examinations and consultations when that isn't what they want. It's criticizing them for poor dental health. It's making subtle threats about the consequences of delayed treatment. It's showing your disapproval of their financial limitations. Nagging is asking manipulative closing questions and using your position of authority to intimidate.

Where I differ significantly from many dentists who have an evangelistic attitude about dental health, is that I make it clear that it's OK for someone with dental problems not to do anything about them right now. Patients should never be made to feel that their decisions about care are wrong. I've found that if I don't make patients feel that they're wrong, they return when they are ready. (In addition, I don't make myself crazy wishing that patients would change!)

> *Patients should never be made to feel that their*
> *decisions about care are wrong.*

Speak "Horse"

When we focus on raising patients' dental IQ, we usually end up doing all the talking. We show them patient education videos and teach them the fundamentals and vocabulary of dentistry—plaque, hygiene, occlusion, veneers. In many ways, we try to teach them to speak dentistry.

When my daughter Kristen was young she rode horses, she would perch on the back of her fourteen-hundred-pound horse and launch it over jumps that were three feet high and up. One time I asked her, *"How do you train the horse to jump?"* She replied, *"You don't train the horse, you train the rider."* In other words, the rider must learn to speak "horse," must learn to communicate with the horse in a way the horse understands (leg pressure, rein tightness, etc.). What else can you do—raise the horse's "jumping IQ" by showing it a videotape? Or by teaching it to understand English? Of course not.

Don't try to teach your patients to speak dentistry. Instead, you should learn to speak their language; communicate with your patients in a way they understand. The Critical Dialogues and the tools you'll learn in this book are all about speaking the patient's language.

In a Nutshell
Chapter Seven—Readiness and the Right-Side Patient

- Discovering readiness is one of the most important acts of leadership for the complete-care dentist when treating right-side patients.

- Without understanding right-side patients' levels of readiness, you risk over/under treating patients, wasting a lot of time (yours and the patients') and adding needless stress to everyone's life. With an understanding of readiness, you can offer treatment plans with no stress and with complete confidence in the suitability of your treatment recommendations.

- A major component of readiness is fit issues—patients' life circumstances that relate to their budget, work schedule, current events. Patients will not be ready for care if a treatment plan will not fit into their budgets or lives.

- Adopt a case acceptance process that coincides with human nature by acknowledging and accommodating right-side patients who aren't ready, and by maintaining a good relationship with them while they're in their "incubation" process so when they become ready they choose you to provide their care.

- The Dental IQ Trap is the corner we paint ourselves into by thinking: *"A thorough diagnosis combined with abundant patient education leads to treatment acceptance."*

- Readiness does not occur in the dental office. Life circumstances—weddings, new jobs, high school reunions—are the things that make patients ready for complete care. Yes, you can plant the seeds of ideas to help patients visualize how they may look or feel once they have their teeth restored, but the actual moment of readiness does not happen in your chair.

Chapter Eight
Discovering Patient Readiness:
The Choice Dialogue

Have you noticed that some patients are more ready than others for complete care? A good example of a patient who is not ready is my mother, Wanda. She's a wonderful woman and I love her dearly. She's eighty-one years old and was raised during the Depression in a tough Polish-Italian neighborhood in Cicero, Illinois. My mom's dental health is far from ideal. Very early in my career I got her to sit in my dental chair. I restored her, but over time, her condition has worsened. Even though I've encouraged my mom many times, she's satisfied with her dental health. I'm the one her dental health bothers.

No one can restore my mother's teeth, because she's not ready and she'll never be ready. Guess what? My mom is in your practice, too—my mom is everywhere.

In the previous chapter I discussed readiness as being one of the most important acts of leadership for the complete care dentist when treating right-side patients. This chapter is about discovering readiness.

The Limited Examination

After you've completed the initial interview, the next step is a limited initial examination (oral cancer screening, periodontal screening, panoral radiograph, and simple tooth charting Code #D0140. The goal of the limited examination is to get better insight into the patient's conditions (and associated disabilities), meet the standard of care, move through the clinical aspect of the new patient experience, and return to the communication/relationship aspect. You can do a limited examination in ten minutes.

In Michelle's case, during the limited examination you want to get a

better idea of what's going on with her front teeth and a general understanding of her overall dental health. I would introduce the idea of the
limited examination by saying something like, *"Michelle, let's start things by
letting me do a simple examination for you. Suzette, my assistant, will take an
x-ray. After that I'll examine you, and then we'll talk about things. Is that all
right with you?"*

Understand the Nature of the Disability

In the limited initial examination, you should gain enough clinical
information to discover what conditions are responsible for the patient's
disability (how a particular dental condition impacts a patient's life).
For example, Michelle's disability is that she hates the way her front
teeth look and they make her self-conscious at work. During the simple
examination you notice several clinical conditions responsible for her self-
consciousness: discolored fillings in her front teeth, uneven incisal edges,
and open contacts. It's obvious why she's unhappy with her front teeth.
You understand the clinical aspects of her disability.

During the limited examination, you notice other conditions in her
mouth that she may or may not be aware of. Make note of these on the
examination form. The patient is not complaining about them, yet they
may be significant contributors to the chief problem and/or the source of
future problems. The Making It Easy process deals with conditions the
patient is not aware of and/or not complaining about. You'll learn more
about that in Chapter Twelve, in the Discovery Guide™.

Keep the limited examination short. Remember, at this point we may
not know the patient's level of readiness for care. Return to the communi-
cation/relationship aspect of the initial appointment as soon as you have
a good idea of her general dental health and the nature of the conditions
responsible for her disability.

The Post-Limited Examination Discussion

Immediately after the limited examination is the post-limited examination discussion. Be sure the patient is sitting up in the dental chair and
remove your gloves, mask, and protective eyewear. The goals of this
discussion are to:

- make the patient "right" by letting her know you understand her concerns
- give the patient hope that she's in good hands
- begin to discover her level of readiness for complete care.

Make the Patient Right

Make the patients right by confirming that you understand why they feel the way they do about their teeth. The following are some examples of making patients right:

"Michelle, I can see why you're not happy with the appearance of your front teeth. They have large dark fillings in them and the edges of the teeth are uneven."

"Mindy, I can see why you're in pain and losing sleep. You have some deep decay in your wisdom teeth."

"Tom, I sure can understand why you have trouble eating. Your dentures don't fit very well and I'm surprised you do as well as you do."

I emphasize making the patient right immediately after the examination because many dentists have the habit of making patients "wrong." Here are some examples of making patients wrong:

"Michelle, I'm not surprised you're unhappy with the appearance of your front teeth. If you had more frequent cleanings, these filling wouldn't be nearly as dark as they are."

"Mindy, I can see why you're in pain and losing sleep. You've got deep tooth decay in your wisdom tooth because you're not brushing and flossing this area very well."

"Tom, I can understand why you're having trouble eating because your dentures don't fit well. You should have gotten these dentures relined years ago."

The blaming attitude in these statements make the patients feel wrong.

Yes, the statements are true, but do they make anyone happy? You can talk about more frequent cleanings, home care, and relines in a positive light. Start your post-limited examination discussion on a positive note by making your patients right about how they feel. Resist getting into solutions, recommendations, reprimands, or mission statements. This experience is about the patient, not you.

Give the Patient Hope

Next, give patients hope. Let them know they've come to the right place and that you've successfully treated many patients just like them. Here's an important point about giving patients hope—refer to how you've helped other patients with similar circumstances. For example:

"Andy, I've treated many patients like you. We have a lot of experience treating gum problems."

"Casey, about one-third of the patients I see have concerns about the appearance of their teeth and we do a great job for them."

"Kathy, we see a lot of patients like you who have problems with the comfort of their bite, and we get very satisfying results for them."

Notice that in the above examples I didn't tell the patients how they can be helped. Instead, I referred to how I've helped other people with similar problems. The concept illustrated here is called social proof. Social proof is a strong influencing principle that calls attention to your ability and history of helping others, implying that you can help the patient you're currently with. Social proof signals to patients that they are in the right place—*"if they helped others like me, they can help me, too."*

Be careful not to recommend treatment at this point. Treatment recommendations usher in a whole host of questions and concerns (insurance, fees, pain) that you don't want to deal with for the time being. Making patients aware that their situation can be helped by referring to similar situations is much more powerful than launching into a show-and-tell about crowns and veneers. Here are some examples of recommending treatment too soon and not building social proof and offering hope.

"Andy, you've got gum disease and need four quadrants of root planing."

"Casey, your front teeth have tetracycline stains and need crowns."

"Michael, your occlusion is causing your teeth to break. You need an equilibration and a nightguard."

Each one of these statements will instigate a conversation that takes us off-track. The track we need to stay on is providing a sense of hope to the right-side patient that they can be helped.

Right-side patients need hope more than patient education. Many of the rehabilitative cases we do are remakes of previous rehabilitative care. Patients like these need to feel hopeful that they're in the right dental office. So would you.

> ### Right-side patients need hope more than patient education.

A good rule to follow is to offer hope before you offer care. Dr. Betsy Bakeman offers a great insight on this:

> *"Every patient seems to have a different threshold for despair, which we as clinicians need to gauge, if we are to be successful in case presentation. For some patients, the fact that they have a cavity sends them spiraling downward into the depths of despair. When I was young, we were happy if we only had one cavity! I have a mental color analogy for desperation and hope. If I see that a patient is not feeling hopeful, a 'red light' goes on to warn me that it is not the time to move forward with treatment options and fees. Instead I spend time building hope, and when I see the patient feel more hopeful, I know the patient is ready to go, and it's like a 'green light' with treatment options and fees. This one thing has made an amazing difference in my case presentations."*

Discover Level of Readiness With the Choice Dialogue

After you've made patients right and given them hope, you've helped them to get into a positive frame of mind and can now begin to discover their level of readiness for complete care. Plus, you haven't offered up a lot of treatment recommendations that may confuse or scare the patient.

Now is an excellent time to begin learning how much dentistry he or she is ready for. One of the best ways to discover patient readiness is to offer a choice. One of the best choices you can offer is between treating the chief condition/disability or, in addition to that, developing a plan for treating all the conditions in the mouth. This choice is called the Choice Dialogue—Critical Dialogue Number Two. The Choice Dialogue is begun immediately after making patients right and offering them hope, and is designed to discover the patient level of readiness for complete care. The intent of the Choice Dialogue is to offer the patient a choice relative to the level of care to be received. That choice reveals the patient's readiness for complete care.

> **One of the best ways to discover patient
> readiness is to offer a choice.**

The generic structure of the Choice Dialogue looks like this:

"(Patient name,) before we decide on anything, let me offer you a choice. We can focus on (relieving disability), or in addition to that, we can (comprehensively treatment plan you). What's best for you today (now, at this appointment)?"

Let's look at some examples of the post-limited examination discussion and the Choice Dialogue with right-side patients.

Case Study: Michelle—Clinical Findings from Limited Examination

Michelle has a normal jaw relationship and tooth positions. She has large discolored mesial and distal composites in ##6–11 along with minor incisal edge wear and uneven incisal edge positions. Teeth #28 and #29 have large fractured amalgam restorations. Teeth #3 and #14 are missing, with slight adjacent tooth drift into the edentulous areas. Adjacent teeth have large amalgam restorations. No significant supraeruption has occurred in the opposing arch.

Michelle has moderate subgingival calculus, bleeding in most posterior areas, 4- and 5-millimeter soft tissue pocketing, and minimal tooth mobility.

Your preliminary treatment plan includes restoring her maxillary anterior teeth with all-porcelain crowns, two three-unit maxillary posterior bridges, crowns on #28 and #29, and four quadrants of root planing and appropriate medications. The ballpark fee is $17,000, with treatment duration estimated at two months.

Post-Examination Discussion

Make the patient right. *"Michelle, I understand why you're not happy with the appearance of your front teeth. During my exam, I noticed several large dark fillings in the front teeth, and the teeth have worn-down edges and gaps between them."*

Give the patient hope. *"I must see three to five patients a week who have similar concerns as you. More and more people are interested in having their teeth look as good as possible. We do a lot of this kind of dentistry and really enjoy it."*

Offer the patient a choice. *"Before we decide on what to do for your front teeth, let me offer you a choice. We can focus on getting you more confident with the appearance of your front teeth, or in addition to that, we can look at all the conditions in your mouth and put together a plan to help you keep all your teeth. What's best for you today?"*

Here's another scenario for the post-limited examination discussion, during which we make the patient right, give the patient hope, and offer the patient a choice.

Case Study: Jack—Clinical Findings from Limited Examination

Jack is an attorney and has many business meals with clients. He's been wearing a removable mandibular partial denture for years, and it fits poorly. His chief disability is that while he eats, food packs under it, so he must excuse himself from the table during meals to clean it.

The results from his limited examination reveal a loose mandibular partial denture replacing teeth ##19–21. The abutment teeth show minor mobility. Teeth opposing the partial denture show slight supraeruption. There is a significant discrepancy between centric relation and centric occlusion, and gingival bleeding and minor pocketing are present.

Your preliminary treatment plan includes four quadrants of root plan-ing, equilibration and nightguard therapy, and implant-supported crowns replacing ##19–21. The ballpark fee is $15,000–$17,000, with treatment duration estimated at eight months.

Post-Examination Discussion

Make the patient right. *"Jack, I can see why you're not enjoying your lower partial denture. During the exam, I noticed that it's very loose. It looks like while you're eating it lifts off the teeth and gums that support it, allowing food to pack under it."*

Give the patient hope. *"Patients who wear partial dentures like yours often find that they need adjustments from time to time. I treat many patients like you who have missing teeth and we have good results with them."*

Offer the patient a choice. *"Jack, there's a couple of things we can do for you, but before we do anything, let me offer you a choice. Would you like for me just to address the partial denture and see what we can do to help keep food from packing in under it? Or, in addition to that, would today be good time for us to look at all the conditions in your mouth and put together a plan to help keep you from losing more teeth? What's best for you now?"*

Dr. Steven Davidson of Libby, Montana, uses an interesting variation on the Choice Dialogue. He and his team say, *"We're glad to go ahead right now and take care of your (disability) <u>or, in addition to that</u>, many of our patients prefer that we look at all the conditions in their mouth and give them an idea of a lifetime plan for dental health. What's best for you now?"*

Notice that the choice is an inclusive one—*"We're glad to go ahead right now and take care of your (disability) or, in addition to that, many of our patients prefer..."* The phrase *"in addition to that"* tells the patient there are three choices: Treat the chief condition only, examine all conditions in the mouth and plan for complete care, or both.

Don't offer the Choice Dialogue as an either/or decision. It can force some patients into a difficult situation—*"We can focus on getting you more confident with the appearance of your front teeth, or, we can look at all the con-ditions in your mouth..."* Make the choice in the Choice Dialogue an easy one to make.

Accept the Answer

The toughest part about the Choice Dialogue is accepting the patient's choice. We want patients to pursue complete care, but if they're not ready for it, it's in everyone's best interest that they don't pursue it. The Choice Dialogue guides us to the most suitable path of care for the patient; demonstrates our willingness to provide great service; and reduces our frustration and wasted time by eliminating any long, complete examinations and consultations for patients who aren't interested or aren't ready. The Choice Dialogue reveals patients' readiness for care—a little or a lot.

> *The toughest part about the Choice Dialogue*
> *is accepting the patient's choice.*

A Fork in the Road

The Choice Dialogue marks a fork in the road to complete dentistry. To this point in the relationship, our sequence is linear. However, once the choice is offered, then we lose control of the sequence and give control to the patient (**Figure 8-1**).

FIGURE 8-1

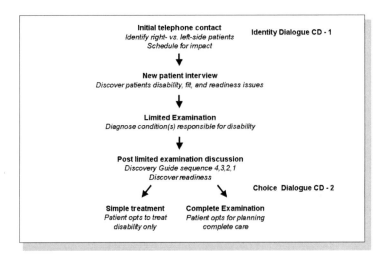

Remember, the choice is *theirs*. If your patient simply wants to have a disability relieved, and you can do it within the standard of care, then do it quickly, painlessly, and without whining. It's more important that you make right-side patients happy on their first visit than it is to gather all the diagnostic data. The other choice the patient can make is to pursue complete care. If that's the choice, then most of the time the next best step is a complete examination, which you would start immediately.

Relieve the Disability

If the patient chooses for you to take care of the disability, and you see an obvious problem related to aesthetics, phonetics, infection, or pain, it's good dentistry, and good business, too, to take care of the immediate problem first. There are two examinations going on: yours and the patient's. To pass the patient's examination and prove yourself, taking care of an immediate problem is a great way to build trust. It always makes good sense to let patients experience your care, your touch, and your attitude before you ask them to make major decisions about their dental health.

If your patient wants to have his disability relieved and you don't have the time, reschedule him ASAP. It's especially important that you know if your patient is from out of town, information you gather in Critical Dialogue One. Give yourself time to fix the disability so this patient won't have to make the return trip.

After the condition is treated and the disability is relieved, restate your offer to develop a lifetime strategy. In the example of Jack, the attorney, he chose to have you treat the condition of the loose partial denture. You adjusted the clasps and did an in-office reline and he was pleased. Because the patient is happy that his disability has been relieved, you can re-offer the complete-care option:

> *"Jack, now that we have you comfortable, let me re-visit my suggestion that we look at all the conditions in your mouth and put together a plan to help you keep your teeth for a lifetime. You have conditions in your mouth now that, if left untreated, can give you problems later."*

Offer Jack an appointment for a complete examination. If he still isn't ready to pursue complete care, document in the treatment record that he was informed of existing conditions and an examination was offered. How Jack is managed now varies. You may want to put him on recall and re-offer lifetime planning at his hygiene visit (see Chapter 17, Hygiene Dialogues). Or you may tell Jack that his next visit with you will be an examination, and not offer other choices. I prefer getting the patient through the complete examination, then testing for readiness after the examination (see Chapter 10, The Advocacy Dialogue). If the patient still is not ready for complete care following a complete examination, put him in hygiene recall and let time and Mother Nature help him become ready. Then, at all of his recall appointments, let your hygienists test for readiness for complete care (see Chapter 17, Hygiene Dialogues).

Supervised Versus Unsupervised Neglect

Every time I teach this part of the process, I'm accused of practicing supervised neglect. Apparently, my accusers feel I should do more to get patients to accept complete care, like giving more thorough and lengthy patient education sessions; or having them sign a release forms underscoring the importance of my recommendations; or asking them to leave my practice. Do any of these tactics work? I haven't seen much evidence that they do. The concept of supervised neglect is part of the traditional model that focuses on changing patients' behavior to coincide with healthy outcomes. Dentists with this mind-set believe that if patients aren't ready for care and if they don't aggressively oppose it, then they become a party to the neglect.

As you can guess, I don't buy into the concept of supervised neglect. Let's look at Michelle. If she isn't ready for complete care, is this an indication that she's neglectful? Mightn't her lack of readiness be due to issues outside her control, like aging parents who need her financial support, or a child who's in crisis, or any number of issues that we may be completely unaware of?

And so what if Michelle isn't ready? Is she not better served by maintaining a relationship with a dental office that can at least provide her with routine cleanings, screenings, and palliative care? I would much rather that her "neglect" be supervised (seen in the recall system on a regular basis) than unsupervised (kicked out of the practice). If she becomes a disruptive, habitual emergency patient, then it may be time for her to leave. But if she respects your schedule and appreciates your relationship, then hold on to her as long as she wants, and one day when she becomes ready for complete care, she'll ask you to do it.

Complete Dentistry

If, as a result of the Choice Dialogue, the patient chooses to pursue complete care, typically your next best step is to perform a complete examination. Once the complete examination is done you'll enter into the post-complete examination discussion and the Advocacy Dialogue (Chapter 10).

Choice Dialogue Tips

Here are some tips when delivering the Choice Dialogue:

Make Your Intention Obvious

State the intention of the dialogue within the dialogue—"*Michelle, today you have a choice. We can focus on...*" *Choice* is a trigger word, in that it triggers your listener's attention to what you are about to say. It's helpful to state the intention of the Critical Dialogues within each of the Critical Dialogues, making them clear as possible.

Keep the Choice Simple

Keep your choice simple and easy to understand. For example, here's a simple choice to understand. "*Nicole, we can focus on helping you with your bleeding gums or, in addition to that, we can look at all your teeth and help you keep them for a lifetime.*"

Here's the same situation, but the choice is much more difficult to understand. "*Nicole, the reason you have periodontal disease and bleeding gums is that bacteria have colonized in the sulcular epithelium and as result of that they create ... [blah, blah, blah]. Now we can we can treat the periodontal diseases with root planing and intrasulcular antibiotic, but you'd have to be really good with your home care. Or, in addition to that, we can perform a complete intraoral and extraoral examination that will help me diagnose and treatment plan the other conditions that I see in your mouth."*

Notice that when I introduce treatment rationale and recommendations into the Choice Dialogue, it begins to sound like a case presentation and is far more difficult to understand.

Keep the Choice Unbiased

Don't make the complete-care option sound far more appealing than the option of relieving the disability—keep the choice unbiased. If your bias for complete care is obvious to the patient, you run the risk of sounding like a salesperson; and, more important, defeat the intention of the Choice Dialogue, which is to determine readiness. Here's a biased Choice Dialogue. *"Ashley, you have a choice. We can just fix this one tooth for you or, in addition to that, we could really help you by doing a very thorough examination where we'd be able to see everything that could cause you problems in the future and keep your smile looking really good. Would you like that?"*

In the Choice Dialogue, as in every dialogue, don't think that there is a specific word order, as in a rigid sales script, that must be followed. Don't focus on saying the words just right; focus on conveying the intention of the dialogue. When you keep the intention in mind, your own words will come naturally.

Use Positive Framing

It's important to tell patients what's healthy and good about their dental condition; this is called *positive framing*. For example, when using positive framing for Michelle in the post-examination discussion it may sound like this:

"Michelle, I see why you're unhappy with the appearance of your front teeth. They have large discolored fillings in them and have spaces in between them. But even though their appearance is not what you'd like, the good news is that they are very healthy in the sense that they have good gum and bone foundation, and their position relative to your bite is excellent."

The focus of our education has been to tell and show people what's wrong with their dental health and not often mention what's right. I call that *negative framing*. Consequently a patient, negatively framed, who needs just a few restorations and minor periodontal care, may come away from your post-examination discussion feeling overwhelmed by her negative perceptions of the severity of her dental health. For example:

"Michelle, I see why you're unhappy with the appearance of your front teeth. They have large discolored fillings in them and have spaces in between them. The size of the fillings concern me in that if they are too close to the nerve then you'll probably need root canals and posts before we can restore them. Also, the papillae between the front teeth show inflammation and before we can do anything with the front teeth, we'll need to resolve this inflammation before it causes bone loss."

Some dentists tell me that they have patients with so many overwhelming negative findings that they have a hard time finding good things to say. If you find yourself in this position, try taking a broader perspective. Look at the overall bone support beyond the alveolar bone, the health of the salivary flow, the overall jaw relationships, the muscles of mastication and facial expression, etc. Remember, with end-stage dental disease, issues of blood supply, innervations, muscle attachments, saliva flow, soft tissue health not associated with the teeth (palate, floor of mouth) are critical to implant, bone-grafting, and orthognathic   procedures.

For example, here's a dialogue using positive framing for a patient with severe conditions—end-stage periodontal disease, missing teeth, endodontic abscesses, and mutilated occlusion. She knows she has a lot of dental problems and is in your office because she broke a front tooth. You've done a limited examination and you realize she'll probably lose all her teeth and, at her young age, at some point might want to consider implant replacements.

"Colleen, I understand why you're disappointed in the appearance of your broken front tooth. I see how this can make you feel self-conscious. You mentioned earlier that you have some severe problems with your teeth. I treat many folks just like you and what they often don't realize is all the good things about their teeth. It's true that you have some problems; but, Colleen, you also have some very good things going for you. The overall bone structure of your jaws is excellent. The relationship between your upper and lower jaw is excellent. I know a lot of patients who would love to have the remaining healthy bone you have.

Your sinuses look healthy, your saliva flow is excellent, the overall health of the gums not associated with the teeth is good, and your jaw joint appears to be healthy. Plus, you're relatively young and healthy. Those are all good things. Yes, you have problems, but you also have key areas that are healthy."

"Before we decide what to do for you, let me offer you a choice. Are you interested in only fixing the broken front tooth or, in addition to that, are you interested in talking about how we can help you with your overall dental health? What's best for you today?"

Positive framing does not mean sugar-coating your patients' clinical findings. Positive framing is presenting a balanced appraisal of their dental health. Get into the habit of telling patients positive findings along with negative findings. When you use positive framing, your patient comes away knowing what's wrong with her mouth, but also has a good perspective on what's right.

Get into the habit of telling patients positive findings along with negative findings.

Positive framing is an excellent leadership communication tool. In Chapter One, I discussed the idea that case acceptance is a form of leadership—helping people feel better about themselves in your presence. Positive framing definitely helps patients feel better about themselves when they're with you... and when they're at home making their dental healthcare decisions. That's powerful medicine for case acceptance.

The following is an e-mail I received from Dr. James Spitzer of Green Bay, Wisconsin. I believe it's a great way to end this chapter on the power of choice.

November 23, 2004

Dear Dr. Homoly:

We were fortunate to have a very "right-side" patient come into our practice soon after our staff and I attended your workshop. After discussing a team approach to handling this patient, we were amazed at the results of using the dialogues learned at your workshop. This patient had not been to a dentist in 25 years because the last dentist had said she would have to lose all her teeth and have dentures. She decided to hang onto what she had as long as possible.

When she came to see us, "positive framing" brought her to tears because she was expecting to hear the worst. My staff did such a beautiful job of recognizing that she needed to be treated differently than most of our patients. The information I had about her disabilities (embarrassment of smiling, toothaches, and infections) allowed me to be very effective in talking to her about what she wanted to hear first. By making her right, giving her hope, and giving her a choice I opened the door to win her trust. She had two brown incisors with deep lingual decay and apical cysts. She would put white gum behind them to lighten them in public.

In my 27 years in practice, this was the first time I did two quick direct composite veneers even before the endo or a complete work-up was done. She was so happy that she sent our office a beautiful plant in gratitude. We discovered at an early stage a budget she could live with, which was $10,000–$15,000/yr. I would never have gotten a chance to do a case of this magnitude if you hadn't guided us with the correct approach. We were very grateful for your additional help when we called you for another lesson.

Our appointments are in early stages and they all end with hugs. What a great feeling!

Thank you,

Dr. Spitzer and Team

In a Nutshell
Chapter Eight—Discovering Readiness

- Immediately after the limited examination make the patient right by letting her know you understand her concerns, give the patient hope that she's in good hands, and offer her a choice to begin discovering her level of readiness for complete care

- The generic structure of the Choice Dialogue looks like this: "(Patient name) before we decide on anything, let me offer you a choice. We can focus on (relieving disability), or in addition to that, we can (comprehensively treatment plan you). What's best for you today (now, at this appointment)?"

- Positive framing gives patients the good news of their dental health versus the bad news of what we see as needing care. It's important that patients know what's healthy and good about their dental health.

Chapter Nine
All Patients Come With "Baggage:"
The Concept of "Fit"

Dentists who are smart leaders take the time to learn what's going on in the lives of their patients, especially the ones who are considering rehabilitative dental care. Knowing how your recommendations for complete-care dentistry fit into the current—or foreseeable—events and circumstances of your patient's life is a mandatory leadership skill for practicing complete-care dentistry. Major fit issues include finances, work schedules, special current events, travel, stressors, health factors, significant emotional issues; in short, any issues that dominate the patient's energy/attention.

I used to think that people were motivated to get their teeth fixed by what was going on in their mouth, but I've come to realize that what alters their motivation to get their teeth fixed is not what's in their mouth, but what's in their hands. And you know what patients have in their hands? Their "baggage," their "stuff," the stuff of their life. That baggage includes—but certainly is not limited to—issues involving their kids, marriage, health, job, bills, etc. Any issue that affects a patient's time, money, demands a lot of their attention, causes stress, etc. is "baggage." (And realize that good things—a wedding, pregnancy, a new baby, vacations, a new job—cause stress, too.) Do patients leave their baggage outside on the sidewalk before they step into the dental office? No, they bring it right in and sit in the chair with it! Then you lay a $10,000 treatment plan on them. *Now* they've got $10,000 worth of more baggage!

This chapter is about discovering what's in your patients' baggage and finding a way to fit their dental needs into their life, either now or later.

Don't "Rip the Zipper"
When you present rehabilitative dentistry, it's got to fit into the patient's

baggage without ripping the zipper. Think about it. If you offer most people a $10,000 treatment plan, something in their baggage has to come out, or something has to "give," right? People need to wait to get their tax refund, wait for a child to graduate from college, get more settled in their new job, or take a much-needed vacation.

Fit issues are not so critical with patients needing only simple care. With an $800 treatment plan, for example, insurance will pick up most of the cost or the patient can put that amount on their credit card. But $10,000—that's got to fit into their life. Without "fit," there's no case acceptance, regardless of the level of dental IQ or your zeal for patient education.

> **Without "fit," there's no case acceptance, regardless**
> **of the level of dental IQ or your zeal for patient education.**

Who's Going "Kayaking?"

Imagine that you're a 46-year-old father, and your 14-year-old son comes to you with an outdoors magazine, shouting, "Dad—this is so cool!" He's pointing to an ad for a whitewater kayaking trip: six days on the river, camping, a guide, the works. *"Dad, this is so great! We need to do this! You-said-that-if-I-did-well-in-school-we-could-do-something-special-and-we-really-need-to-do-this!!"* And you're thinking, *"Whitewater kayaking—what're you, nuts?!"* Then you look at the boy, he's down on one knee, he's got a magnifying glass and he's burning a hole in a piece of wood, and you're thinking *"Wow, I don't know..."* *"How much is it?"* you ask cautiously. *"$6,500,"* he replies. $6,500! You've got estimated taxes due, your wife's car needs a new transmission... then you look at your boy's face, shining with excitement, and you think, *"He's 14—in two years he'll be a complete idiot!"* *"OK, let's do it,"* you say. He jumps up, thrilled, and bam! you're $6,500 poorer.

The next day you bite down hard and break off the cusp on tooth #30 and a sharp edge is cutting your tongue. Now, you're a normal person, you haven't been to the dentist in about five years, so you ask your wife, *"Honey, where should I go to the dentist?"* She says *"Go to Dr. O'Malley, that's where I take the kids."* So you go to Dr. O'Malley. Well, Dr. O'Malley's just been to the "Institute of the Milky Way" and he's all jazzed up. You

walk in his office and the first thing they do is read you their mission statement, give you a tour of the office, and have you soak in the hot tub. And
then they start the complete examination. They start taking a mouthful
of radiographs and you protest, trying to tell them that you just want your
broken tooth fixed. They counter your objections with some reasons that
make no sense at all and when you leave their office to go home, your
tooth is still broken and the hole in your tongue is deeper... but they've
given you a nice flower.

So you go back a week later for the case presentation, and it's magnifi-
cent. There's a big color monitor up in the consultation area with the
"before-and-after" photographs and models, and patient testimonials, and
it's wonderful and you sit down, and the dentist goes into a tooth-by-tooth
description and does a smile analysis, and he's all excited, and finally you
say, *"Doc, how much does this cost?"* and he says *"$6,500."* Now let me ask
you, what's going to win—the dentist or the kayak trip? One hint... it's not
the dentistry!

Here's the question you need to ask when practicing rehabilitative dentistry: *"How many of my patients are going kayaking?"* What's the answer?
They all are. From their point of view, patients have much better things
to do than give their time and money to you. Consequently, we need to
know what those better things are so we can suggest ways of fitting our
dentistry into their lives. Educating them that they need to fit their lives
into our dentistry doesn't work. How do I know? You've proven it, haven't
you?

Discovering What's Going on in Your Patients' Lives

Your team knows what's going on in the patient's life. How do they
know? They talk, they chit-chat with the patients. You're back in the
operatory fixing a tooth and there's Ginger at the front desk with patients,
"chit-chat, chit-chat." At times I'd think, *"Get back to work and stop the mind-
less chatter."* Over time, however, I realized that chit-chat is some of the
best work when it's done on purpose. The purpose of chit-chat is to learn
about those fit issues in your patients lives that will impact their treatment
decision. When chit-chat is done on purpose, I call it fit-chat—an indirect
way of discovering patient fit issues.

When you *fit-chat*, be curious and listen more than talk. Listen for how they're spending their time, what's creating stress in their life—money issues, health issues, family issues. If they mention an issue you believe may influence a treatment decision, be curious about it and get them talking more about it. Through indirect fit-chat, you're going to discover what's going on in a patient's life.

> **Listen for how they're spending their time, what's creating stress in their life—money issues, health issues, family issues.**

Some right-side patients don't *fit-chat* well. They're simply not talkers. I'm that way. When I get my hair cut, the last thing I want is a chatty experience. When you have a rehabilitative patient who won't *fit-chat*, you can try a more direct approach to discovering fit issues.

Here's an example of a direct approach:

> *"Kevin, I know from the line of work you're in that you're busy. I also know that you're aggravated by food trapping around your lower partial denture. Next time we're together why don't we talk about your choices and how we can best fit your dentistry into what's going on in your life. Is now a good time to talk about that?"*

Here's another example of a direct approach:

> *"Kevin, most people like you are busy, on-the-go, and have lots of irons in the fire. I need to know if any of these irons are affecting how much stress you're under, how much time you can spend here with us, or if there are any financial issues that I need to take into consideration in planning your care. I want to reassure you that I'm very good at helping patients fit their dentistry into what's going on in their life."*

Whether you're using an indirect *fit-chat* approach or a direct approach to discovering fit issues, an absolute prerequisite to having a comfortable conversation is for you to have a connected communication style. This means that you hold good eye contact, your tone of voice is conversational, and your speaking rate is relaxed and you pause long enough to let what you're saying sink in. If you attempt to use a direct approach to fit issues but have a disconnected style (don't look the patient in the eye, speak too quickly, etc.), your conversation may be perceived as being inappropriate, unprofessional, and a slimy way of trying to diagnose their pocketbook.

Personal Fit Issues

At times, there may be a single issue in the patient's life that is the dominating factor that affects all other decisions. This is called the Personal Fit issue. Examples of Personal Fit issues are divorce, marriage, graduation, home purchases, new jobs, losing a job, significant health issues, moving, births, and deaths. Patients will be sensitive about Personal Fit issues. If one of your team members discovers one, be sure she asks the patient's permission to share it with you: *"Kevin, I'm sorry you're going through a divorce. With your permission I'd like to mention this to Dr. Borchert. He's very good at helping patients fit their dental needs into their life circumstances."*

Personal Fit issues are not necessarily negative things in our patients' lives. Any issue, positive or negative, that consumes the patient's energy, stress, time, money, attention, or emotions is a Personal Fit issue. Personal Fit issues always impact rehabilitative care. They may keep patients from accepting complete dentistry, or may be the reason why they're ready to do it *now*.

For example, during your initial conversations with Kevin he mentions he's in the middle of a custody battle for his children. Obviously this is a fit issue that is consuming an enormous amount of Kevin's energy, focus, time, money, and stress. It may be that having his teeth fixed is exactly the thing Kevin needs to boost his morale and do something nice for himself. Or, if you ignore this significant fit issue in his life and recommend a full-mouth rehabilitation, it might make Kevin leave your practice.

Our role is to acknowledge his Personal Fit issue and help him decide how to best proceed with his care. When possible, mention the Personal Fit issue in treatment conversations. Acknowledging fit issues is not inviting the patient to postpone care. (I've been accused more than once during a seminar by some irate dentist, *"Hey Homoly, aren't you just reminding patients of their problems and just begging them to put things off?"*) Patients aren't "reminded" of their problems—they're already well aware of them!

Acknowledging their Personal Fit issue in the treatment plan demonstrates to the patient that you have an tremendous level of awareness, empathy, and common sense.

Dr. John Fish, an advanced restorative and implant dentist from Hildebran, North Carolina, says: *"Addressing the patient's concerns about the cost of dental care early in the relationship has been a breakthrough for us. I've been using this process for many years now. It's been the cornerstone that I've built my complex care case acceptance process on. If patients don't have the resources for complex care, we find that out early and don't put them or us in a position of unrealistic expectations. It's saved us a lot of time and the patients never feel pressured that we're trying to sell them something they're not ready for."*

Go Home and Think About It

If the patient has a Personal Fit issue and you're unaware of it (or are aware of it but don't mention it) and recommend a significant amount of dentistry, chances are great that the patient will "go home and think about it." How many times do patients who need care and seem to be interested in it, postpone or cancel their appointments? How many times have you chalked off their behavior to their low dental IQ, insurance dependence, or inadequate appreciation of quality care? If you're not looking for and discussing the Personal Fit issues with complete-care candidates, maybe it's time for you to "go home and think about it!"

Inside-out Versus *Outside-in*

The traditional method of case acceptance is an "inside-out" process; that is, we begin by studying the *inside* of the patient's mouth (examination, diagnosis, treatment plan). Then after we go through the consultation process, we learn about what's happening *outside* the patient's mouth (their budget, work schedule, time, etc.), and usually it's these fit and readiness issues that determine the course of our treatment plan (**Figure 9-1**).

FIGURE 9-1

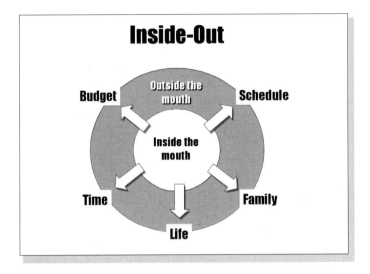

The Making It Easy approach to case acceptance, however, is an "outside-in" process; that is, we start by understanding what's happening outside the patient's mouth (their fit and readiness issues). Only after we have an understanding of how complex dentistry might fit into their life do we begin to discuss details about the inside of their mouth (**Figure 9-2**).

FIGURE 9-2

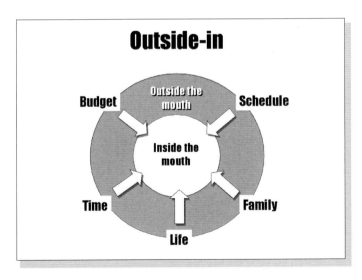

An excellent example of an outside-in sales process is the purchase of a home. Imagine you and your honey decide to buy a new house. You go to a realtor and, just a few minutes into the conversation, you're talking about price range, neighborhood, schools, proximity to work, financing, and down payment. These are all "big picture" outside-the-home issues. Once you settled on the broad outside-the-home issues, then—and only then—does it make sense to begin discussing the detailed inside-the-home issues such as room size, carpet and tile   selection, lighting, etc.

Now imagine that you and your sweetie go to the realtor, but this time she's a former dentist. As soon as you sit down the realtor begins discussing inside-the-house issues and shows you photographs of tile samples. What would you think? You'd think about finding another realtor! How many of your patients, after they experienced your inside-out process, found another dentist?

Right-side dentistry is an outside-in process. Get the big picture of what makes sense for your patients first, and then get into the appropriate details. You'll save an incredible amount of time, both for you and your patient, and you won't blow patients out of the water—and out of your practice anymore.

In a Nutshell
Chapter Nine—The Concept of "Fit"

- Knowing how your recommendations for complete-care dentistry fit into the current—or foreseeable—events and circumstances of your patient's life is a mandatory leadership skill for practicing complete-care dentistry. Major fit issues include finances, work schedules, special current events, travel, stressors, health factors, significant emotional issues.

- From their point of view, patients have much better things to do than give their time and money to *you*. Consequently, we need to know what those better things are so we can suggest ways of fitting our dentistry into their lives. Educating them that they need to fit their lives into our dentistry doesn't work.

- The purpose of chit-chat is to learn about those fit issues in your patient's life that will impact their treatment decision. When chit-chat is done on purpose it's called *fit-chat*—an indirect way of discovering patient fit issues.

- Whether you're using an indirect *fit-chat* approach or a direct approach to discovering fit issues, an absolute prerequisite to having a comfortable conversation is for you to have a connected communication style.

- A Personal Fit issue is when there is a single issue in the patient's life that is the dominating factor that affects all other decisions. These issues may keep patients from accepting complete dentistry, or may be the reason why they're ready to do it now.

- The traditional method of case acceptance is an "inside-out" process (we begin by studying the *inside* of the patient's mouth—examination, diagnosis, treatment plan). The Making It Easy approach to case acceptance, however, is an "outside-in" process (we start by understanding what's happening *outside* the patient's mouth—their fit and readiness issues). It's usually these fit and readiness issues that will determine the course of our treatment plan.

Chapter Ten
The Heart of Case Acceptance:
The Advocacy Dialogue

It's the middle of what's been a tough week. On Monday you were slammed—emergency patients, broken temporaries, staff members out sick. Now, two days later, you're sitting on your hands, fuming over a last-minute cancellation of a two-hour appointment that's left your whole afternoon a bust. Then, out of the blue, in walks Mrs. McBucks, the lady with rings on every finger, to whom you presented a mouth full of dentistry a year-and-a-half ago. She had told you she needed to "think about it," then disappeared from your practice. Now in she walks, waving your treatment plan and saying, "*I'm ready now!*" and you think, "*Thank you, God!*"

Has this scenario happened to you? I'll bet it has. Why do patients who've been gone for many months, sometimes years, come back to you when they're ready? They do because in some way they see you as their advocate—someone who is one their side. Creating an advocacy relationship with the patient is at the heart of case acceptance for complex care and a cornerstone in the leadership issues surrounding case acceptance. Having a patient return to your practice after a long absence is not accidental or random. In fact, a patient returning to your office for complete care when they're ready can be a predictable event. This chapter shows you how.

> *Having a patient return to your practice after*
> *a long absence is not accidental or random.*

Advocacy

The word *advocate* comes from the Latin word *advocatus*, meaning "to call" as a witness or advisor. The modern meaning of the word (outside the legal realm) is, "one who acts as a supporter or one who encourages."

Think of advocacy as the experience patients have when they realize you're on their side. Another way of thinking about it is that when you and your team adopt an attitude of advocacy, it communicates to your patient that treatment acceptance is not a condition of your continuing good relationship, and that treatment can proceed when she's ready. It's easy to be a patient advocate when the person is ready for care. I hope to convince you that it's even more important to be one when the person is *not* ready.

> *It's easy to be a patient advocate when the person is ready for care...*
> *it's even more important to be one when the person is not ready.*

Advocate Versus Provider

We have two roles in our relationships with patients: *advocate* and *provider*. The advocate is the advisor, the one who guides, supports, and encourages. The provider is the clinician, the one who performs dentistry and directs clinical services. Our fee for being the advocate is paid by the patient for the examination and consulting services. Our fee for being the provider is paid by the patient for clinical services. It's important to keep these two roles separate in your mind. Because of the economic pressures of profitably operating a dental practice, there is a potential for conflicts of interest if the roles of advocate and provider are inappropriately linked. For example, if you take advantage of your advocate role and recommend complex care (benefiting your provider role) when simpler care would meet a patient's needs, you have violated your advocate role, along with dental ethics and standard of care issues. It is this potential for conflicts of interest that mandates dentistry be licensed and regulated to ensure that advocate and provider roles don't get confused.

Outcomes Versus Inputs

You'll discover that when you present care from your advocacy role that your consultations with the patient take on more leader-like qualities. Advocates talk in terms of *outcomes—comfort, confidence, peace of mind*, etc. Providers talk in terms of *inputs—crowns, bridges, implants*. For right-side dentistry, presenting care from the perspective of preferred outcomes far outperforms presenting care from the perspective of inputs. Outcomes are far easier for the patient to understand and help them to see the light at the end of their tunnel. Talking in terms of outcomes provides a positive resonant energy patients need to endure the rigors of right-side dentistry.

A good comparison to the dual roles of dentists is the two roles that some fee-based (non-commissioned) financial advisors have. For example, let's say you hired a financial advisor to help you plan your overall financial needs: home purchase, insurance issues, college expenses for your children, investments, and retirement. She does her "examination" and assesses your past and current financial situation, creates a "diagnosis" of your current conditions, and presents to you a "treatment plan" or financial plan to help you meet your lifetime goals. At this point you are referred to products specialists who provide you with insurance, write your will, manage your money, etc. The fee-based financial planner earns no fees or commissions from your product purchases; she simply advises and helps you find ways to create financial health. If you want a nice house and have trouble understanding how you can afford it, she helps you find the way to make it happen now, or later; or she may recommend that you consider a smaller home. She doesn't build the house, she helps you make smart decisions.

This is what your role as advocate is—to help your patients make smart dental healthcare decisions and help them understand how they can fit complete dentistry into their lives. You guide them to find a way to make it happen now, or later; or you recommend alternative treatment plans. Your foremost role as an advocate is to help your patients make healthcare decisions regardless of the impact of those decisions on the provider role clinical fees. The more you keep your advocate role clear in your own mind and obvious to the patient, the more your patient will trust the clinical recommendations that will benefit your provider role. The Advocacy Dialogue makes your advocate role obvious to the patient.

> *Your foremost role as an advocate is to help your*
> *patients make healthcare decisions regardless of the*
> *impact of those decisions on the provider role clinical fees.*

The Advocacy Dialogue

A few years ago Dr. Phil Potter of San Clemente, California, and I were teaching together on the topic of case acceptance. Dr. Potter told our audience of dentists, *"Be the patient's advocate, not adversary, when presenting care."* I really liked this distinction and since then the spirit of his statement has evolved into an important leadership dialogue within the case acceptance process: The Advocacy Dialogue, CD-3.

Structure

The intention of the Advocacy Dialogue is to reassure that patient that we'll look to find a way to fit our treatment recommendations into their life circumstances. This dialogue opens the conversation about whether some, all, or none of your treatment recommendations will fit into their lives now.

The Advocacy Dialogue links what's going on in the patient's mouth to what's going on in the patient's life. This dialogue typically occurs immediately after a complete examination, but can be delivered at any time during the initial appointment by the dentist or any team member.

To understand the Advocacy Dialogue, you'll need to understand a few other concepts. The first concept is that of "fit." Briefly, fit is the suitability of complex dental care relative to the patient's life circumstances (budget, work schedule, family issues, current events, etc.). Complex treatment **must** fit into patients' lives.

Another concept integral to the Advocacy Dialogue is that of "disability." Briefly, disability is how the patient's dental conditions affect her life (embarrassment, worry, lack of confidence, etc.).

The generic structure of the Advocacy Dialogue looks like this:
"(Patient name), I know you're concerned about (fit issues) and I also know that you're concerned about (your disability). At our next appointment we'll talk about your choices, and let's find the best way to fit fixing your teeth into what's going on in your life. Is now a good time to talk about this?"

Notice that the Advocacy Dialogue ends with a question: *"Is now a good time to talk about this?"* This question opens a conversation about how best to fit complex dental care into the fit issues of the patient's life. This is the conversation you want to have before you treatment plan your patient. You want the patient to go home and think about financial issues after the initial appointment, not the consultation appointment.

Addressing the Patient's Inner Dialogue

Do you remember watching cartoons when you were a kid, and the character in the cartoon would have the angel and the devil on each shoulder, whispering good and bad things in each ear? Well, patients are listening to "little voices," too. Patients walk into your office with their own inner dialogues going on. For example, your new patient, Jack, has two children starting college this fall. Jack's inner dialogue is whispering in one ear, "*Two kids in college, two kids in college, two kids in college.*" Whispering in his other ear is you: "*Golden proportion blahblahblah, centric relation blahblahblah.*" Think about it: "*Two kids in college*" versus "*Centric relation... golden proportion.*" You have to address the patient's inner voice first. Patients have a hard time listening to you unless you acknowledge and address their inner dialogues first. The intention of the Advocacy Dialogue is to reassure patients that their fit issues will be respected. This soothes their inner dialogues.

Ultimately, the conversation that results from the Advocacy Dialogue addresses the inner dialogues and answers the patient's questions:
- What is the big picture of my clinical needs?
- What is the ballpark fee and total time in treatment?
- How can I pay for it?
- How much does my insurance help?
- How much do this dentist and team care about me?

The Advocacy Dialogue and the resultant conversation also answer your questions:
- Is this patient interested in the overall treatment recommendations?
- Is this patient comfortable with the ballpark fees, time estimates, and financial/insurance arrangements?
- Is this patient ready for complete care now?

In the absence of The Advocacy Dialogue, the above questions for the patient and dentist are usually answered only *after* you've presented the treatment at the consultation appointment. Often, the treatment plan is presented without regard to the fit/readiness issues, ignoring whether the care is suitable for the patient. Too often, after the patient learns the fee and other details of her care, the dentist and/or treatment coordinator have to pick apart the dentistry and figure out which parts fit, which ones don't, or if anything fits at all. This process is highly stressful and embarrassing, creates anger, wastes time, devalues the relationships, and is regarded as the low point by most dentists, team members, and patients. To avoid this, use the Advocacy Dialogue and get the fit/readiness issues out on the table before you treatment plan and present care.

Case Study: Michelle—The Advocacy Dialogue

Michelle, during her initial telephone call and preclinical interview, was very clear about her chief disability: embarrassment over the appearance of her front teeth and some discomfort on her right side. From your team's conversation with her, you learned many of Michelle's fit issues—she owns a busy art gallery, she's in the middle of a remodeling project, she's training new staff members, she wants to look great for a black-tie affair she's hosting in three months, she's traveling a lot on business.

During the examination, you noted the clinical conditions (large discolored composites and open contacts) responsible for her disability. During the post-examination discussion, you introduce the Advocacy Dialogue. Personalizing it for Michelle, it sounds like this:

"Michelle, I know you've got a lot going on at your gallery right now. You've got carpenters remodeling your gallery, you're in the middle of training new staff members, and are on the road a lot this season. I also know that you're embarrassed about the appearance of your front teeth and aggravated by some pain on your right side. At our next appointment we'll talk about your choices, and let's find the best way to fit fixing your teeth into what's going on in your life. Is now a good time to talk about this?"

If you were Michelle, what would your most likely response be to *"Is now a good time to talk about this?"* I'd bet some of the top nonclinical questions would be along the lines of how much will this cost, how long will it take, how much time will I have to spend here, and will my insurance help?

Let's look at these questions and think through some best responses.

Best Responses

You already know the number one question most complex patients have about complete care: *"How much does it cost?"* In the context of the Advocacy Dialogue, you want to give a ballpark estimate with about a $5,000 range, preferably on the high side. Along with the ballpark fee estimate, give estimates of total time in care, number of appointments, and the most affordable payment options all in the same answer:

"Michelle, I'd say a good ballpark estimate of your care would be fifteen to twenty thousand dollars. A case like yours typically takes us about two months to complete with about six appointments. Many of our patients enjoy starting care with no initial payments, and then make payments over time. I'd estimate monthly payments for you to be about $500 a month. Is this comfortable for you?"

(Note: Make the monthly payment options available through a patient financial services provider such as CareCredit.)

The question, *"Is this comfortable for you?"* starts the negotiation process you'd normally have following case presentation at the consultation appointment. The big difference here is that you haven't yet invested hours of time and work treatment planning and presenting the case. Once you've asked the question, just listen. This is a great time for your treatment coordinator to be with you and your patient. Remember, the intention of the Advocacy Dialogue is to reassure the patient that you'll find a way to fit her dentistry into her life. Maybe she's comfortable with the ballpark fee estimates and can go ahead with complete care. If so, set her consultation appointment and look forward to starting her case.

If she's not OK with your ballpark estimates, guide her through some good options for implementing complete care—patient financing, segmented treatments plans, holding plans, alternative plans, or maybe no treatment at this time. (I realize that there is no formal treatment plan at this time. My assumption here is that you're able to base your estimates on a quick visualization of the scope of her treatment plan.)

Keep in mind that your role here is one of an advocate, not a salesman. The big distinction between the two is that with an attitude of advocacy, the patient senses that her treatment acceptance is not a condition of your continuing good relationship. Help the patient find a way to fit her dentistry into her life—now or later, a little or a lot, all or none. Your attitude that drives "...*let's find a way*..." is what answers the patient's unasked question, "*How much do this dentist and team care about me?*"

Advocacy and the Advocacy Dialogue are everyone's responsibility. If you and your team do this well, chances are excellent that you will demonstrate to your patients an incredible amount of leadership, empathy and common sense. They'll sense that they're welcome in your practice regardless of their level of treatment acceptance. This type of experience often is the very first one of its kind that the patient has had in any dental or medical office. And as a result, patients will bond with you; and even after they've moved out of your area, will oftentimes travel many miles to return to your office for care.

In a Nutshell
Chapter Ten—The Advocacy Dialogue

- The attitude of advocacy communicates to your patient that treatment acceptance is not a condition of your continuing good relationship, and that treatment can proceed when she's ready.

- Creating an advocacy relationship with the patient is at the heart of case acceptance for complex care and a cornerstone in the leadership issues surrounding case acceptance.

- As dentists we have two roles: advocate and provider. The advocate is the advisor, the one who guides, supports, and encourages. The provider is the clinician, the one who performs dentistry and directs clinical services.

- Advocates present treatment in terms of outcomes—comfort, confidence, peace of mind, etc. Providers present treatment in terms of inputs (crowns, bridges, implants, etc.).

- The more you keep your advocate role clear in your own mind and obvious to the patient, the more your patient will trust the clinical recommendations that will benefit your provider role.

- The Advocacy Dialogue links what's going on in the patient's mouth to what's going on in the patient's life. This dialogue typically occurs immediately after a complete examination, but can be delivered at any time during the initial appointment by the dentist or any team member.

- The Advocacy Dialogue and gets the fit/readiness issues out on the table before you treatment plan and present care.

Chapter Eleven
Doing It Your Way:
Alternative Approach to Case Acceptance

Everybody has their own way of doing things. If you've practiced dentistry for more than a few years, I know, as you read this book, you've been thinking, *"Yeah, but what if instead of doing what Homoly says, I think it would be better if I did it like...."*

If you're thinking like that, then you'll like this chapter. It's about other ways the Making It Easy approach is done successfully by dentists just like you who've taken my workshops and have modified the processes to fit their style and their team's ability, experience, and aptitude.

Offering the Choice Dialogue During the Initial Telephone Call
One of the best alternative approaches to the process you've been reading about here is to combine the Identity and Choice Dialogues during the initial telephone call. Doing so eliminates the need for the limited examination and the limited-examination discussion. **Figure 11-1** shows how it looks.

FIGURE 11-1

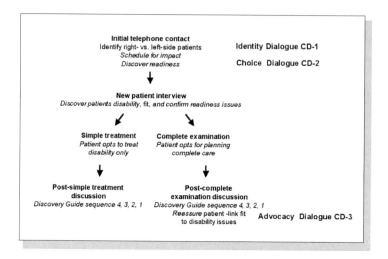

Benefits

When you can determine readiness for complete care over the telephone (Choice Dialogue), you can more accurately schedule the initial appointment. If the patient is clear about being interested in treating a chief disability, having a complete examination, or both, then you can set aside the appropriate amount of time and anticipate the room set-up.

The Choice Dialogue is a great way to build rapport. In the context of "choice," the patient and your scheduler can begin forming a relationship, and the scheduler can set the stage for making an excellent first impression at the initial appointment.

The Choice Dialogue is an excellent process for discovering conditions and their associated disabilities. The more you know about your patient's disability, the better. The sooner you discover the patient's disability, the sooner the patient realizes that you're listening and are interested, and that he or she is in the right dental office.

Discovering readiness over the telephone eliminates the need for the limited examination and the post-limited examination discussion. Remember, the objective of the limited examination is to understand the condition responsible for the disability. If you already are aware of this through telephone dialogues, there's no need for the limited examination.

Risks

The choice you're asking the patient to make and the resulting conversation may get lengthy and complex, during which it's common for patients to want detailed information about treatment options, fees, and insurance. I am not against having this level of conversation on the telephone *if* it's being handled by a savvy, experienced, empathetic, and intelligent team member who truly understands the Making It Easy process. If your team member is not skilled and/or comfortable with this conversation, it will come across poorly to that patient and you're off to a bad start.

Many practices have team members who are so busy processing left-side patients in and out, collecting fees, and setting appointments that they can't slow down and engage in a substantial telephone call with a right-side patient. During my workshops, one of the most common comments I hear from team members is that they don't have time to connect with right-side patients over the telephone because they're too busy with everything else (i.e., left-side patients).

If handled poorly, the Choice Dialogue during the initial telephone call may sound to the patient like you're trying to up-sell to complete dentistry (i.e., *"Would you like fries with your hamburger?"*) Remember, most patients have never experienced the Making It Easy process, but they have been up-sold many times. Unskilled telephone team members may phrase the Choice Dialogue in a way that destroys its intention—determining readiness for complete care. The Choice Dialogue is not a sales pitch for complete care. For example, your team member says, *"Kristen, I want you to know that you have a choice when you come in. We can just fix your broken tooth or it's probably a better idea for you to have us do a complete set of x-rays and an examination so we can really understand all your dental problems so we can give you the smile you'll love. Would you like to schedule the examination?"* Ouch!

The telephone can be a tricky tool for doing business and building relationships. Because you have no visual context, your intention and impact are largely determined by tone of voice. It's been estimated that tone of voice accounts for up to 85 percent of the impact you have on the telephone. When you're under stress, one of its first manifestations is in your tone of voice. I call many dental offices every day, and I'd say over half of the team members I talk to have a recognizable level of stress in their voice. If the Identity and Choice Dialogues are delivered with discernible stress in the voice, it becomes immediately apparent and lowers the confidence your patients have in you.

> **When you're under stress, one of its first manifestations is in your tone of voice.**

One of the ways around the problem of having time to make the right impression during a right-side telephone call and dealing with the reality of a busy left-side practice is to have a dedicated telephone line and number for new patients only. List this number in your yellow pages and all marketing materials so when this line rings and lights up, chances are good that it's a new patient calling. Many offices will hand off a new patient call to a team member who enjoys the new patient call and has a keen aptitude for it.

Case Study: Michelle

Here's an example of how the Choice Dialogue is offered during the initial telephone call. I'll use an excerpt from the telephone dialogue from Chapter Five, on the Identity Dialogue. We'll join the conversation just after Michelle has explained why she's very unhappy with her front teeth.

Ginger: *"Is there anything else we need to know about you or your dental condition before we see you?"*

Michelle: *"Lately, I've noticed I'm having trouble chewing and some pain that I think is on the lower right side. Sometimes I swear it's the lower and other days it feels like it's coming from the upper. I don't know what it is, but it bothers me too, but not as much as the front teeth."*

Ginger: *"Michelle, it sounds like you are a perfect fit for our dental practice. We reserve time in our schedule especially for patients like you. (Choice Dialogue) Before I schedule you, I want you to know that you have a choice at your first appointment with us. We can focus on your main concern, which seems to be your front teeth, or in addition to that, Dr. Homoly can look at all your teeth and help you develop a plan to help you keep your teeth healthy for a lifetime. What would be best for you at your first appointment?"*

Michelle: *"If he can do both, that would be great."*

Ginger: *"Yes, he'll be glad to help you with any immediate need and get you started toward great dental health. I'd like to appoint you either first thing in the morning or in the afternoon. That way we'll be able to seat you immediately and get right to helping you with your concerns. Does this Tuesday at 8 a.m. work for you?"*

Michelle: *"That's perfect. This sounds like exactly what I'm looking for. Thanks so much."*

Offering the Choice and Advocacy Dialogues During the Interview

Another alternative is to offer the Choice Dialogue and/or Advocacy Dialogues during the initial interview (**Figure 11-2**). Under the right circumstances the initial interview can provide a rich source of disclosure relative to your patients comfort zones, preferences, and insights into her life circumstances. These topics are perfect segues into the Choice and Advocacy Dialogues.

FIGURE 11-2

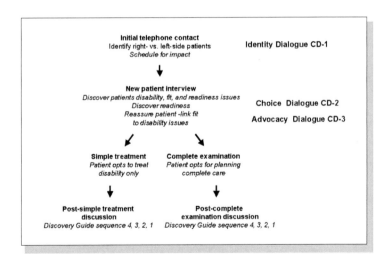

Benefits

The benefits of offering these dialogues during the interview are that they may fit perfectly into the context of the conversation. For example, Joseph reveals during the interview that he has discomfort in the back of his mouth. He says he knows he probably has other problems, too, but he's been too busy to get to the dentist because of his new business he started last year. Here's a sample dialogue employing the Choice and Advocacy Dialogues in the initial interview. You've already started the interview and are a few minutes into it...

Joseph: *"The pain in my lower left side started on and off over a year ago. At times it's worse than others. Just when I get ready to make a dental appointment, the pain goes away. I'm so busy with my new business that it's tough to find the time."*

You: *"You're not alone, this happens to a lot of people. Tell me more about your new business."*

Joseph: *"My brother and I sold our furniture business two years ago and now we're building a construction and real estate business specializing in furniture retailers. We got a few good breaks early and things are going well, but in this business you never know. We have our fingers crossed. Plus my wife and I just had our first child last February and that's another whole set of priorities that takes time."*

You: *"I know, I went through that a few years ago myself.* (Choice Dialogue) *You know, Joseph, you have a choice. I can focus on the problem area on your lower left and see what I can do to make you comfortable. Or, in addition to that, we could spend some time looking at all your teeth and help you understand what your overall dental health is like and what you need to do to keep from having other problem areas come up. What's best for you today?"*

Joseph: *"For sure, let's take a look at this lower left area. I know something is wrong there. As far as my other teeth are concerned I know that I need a cleaning and I lost some teeth when I was in the Army. I'd like for you to give me an idea of what else might be wrong, but I need to be careful about how much it all costs. My wife tells me our dental insurance only covers $1,200 a year."*

You: (Advocacy Dialogue) *"Joseph, I understand why you need to be careful about your budget with your new business and new baby. You've also told me you've got some pain now and are concerned about problems in other areas. I'm really good about helping patients find ways to fit their dentistry into what's going on in their lives. Is now a good time for us to talk about how we need to fit your care into your budget?"*

Joseph: *"Yeah, it is. Do you have an idea what all this will cost and how much insurance covers?"*

You: *"The best thing I can do for you now is to take a look in your mouth and see where the best place to start is. Before we do anything, let's revis it this conversation about fitting your care into your budget. Does that sound OK?"*

Joseph: *"Let's do it, Doc."*

In this example, I introduced the Advocacy Dialogue into the interview, but I couldn't follow through on giving the patient any ballpark estimates on costs or time in treatment. Now, following the examination and/or simple treatment of Joseph's lower left side, I'd revisit the advocacy conversation and offer ballpark estimates (**Figure 11-3**).

FIGURE 11-3

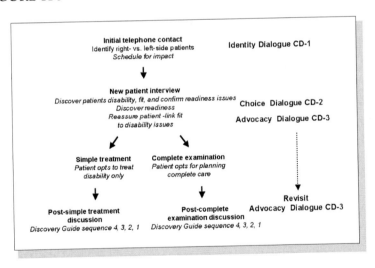

Risks

There are risks to offering the Choice and/or Advocacy Dialogues during the initial interview. The biggest risk is that when a right-side patient has many conditions accompanied by low awareness and/or minimal disabilities, the Choice and Advocacy Dialogues may force the patient's decision-making process beyond the comfort zone. Additionally, you may not be familiar enough with the patient and his or her disabilities to deliver the dialogues and manage the resulting conversations well.

> **If you're not a good conversationalist or have poor interview skills, offering the Choice and Advocacy Dialogues may sound like a sales pitch to your patient.**

If you're not a good conversationalist or have poor interview skills, offering the Choice and Advocacy Dialogues may sound like a sales pitch to your patient. These dialogues, although powerful when delivered well and at the right time, can be destructive when delivered poorly or with the wrong intentions, or delivered with an absence of common sense. One of the worst examples of this was when a dentist called me a few days after he completed my case acceptance workshop. Here's what I remember of the telephone conversation:

Mad Client: *"Hey, Homoly, I used that* [expletive deleted] *Advocacy-Budget thing you said I should do and the patient walked out even before I could do the exam. This* [expletive deleted] *stuff doesn't work in my area."*

Me: *"What did you say to the patient?"* [expletive thought, but not spoken]

Mad Client: *"I said that I needed to know how much they could spend before I told them what they needed, just like you said I should."*

Me: *"No, I never said that. I told you to ask, 'Is now a good time to talk about how your dentistry can fit into your life?'"*

Mad Client: *"What's the* [expletive deleted] *difference?"*

If you don't know the difference, it may be time for you to put this book down and take a course in common sense. So much of the Making It Easy process is about common sense. The most frequent comment I hear from dentists and team members following a workshop is that this process is just common sense that's well-packaged and well-labeled. I had one dentist tell me, *"I do a lot of this already, but you've given me "permission" to use common sense."* I had a group of team members tell me, *"This stuff makes so much sense. It would be the way we'd do things if we never took all those courses on practice management and just used our intuition and good sense."*

So much of the Making It Easy process is about common sense.

"Bundle"—Don't Skip

Notice that the alternatives I've offered "bundle" the dialogues, and don't skip or rearrange them. Keep them in chronological order (Identity, Choice, Advocacy). It's a big mistake to start talking budget (Advocacy) before you determine readiness (Choice). As you work more with the dialogues, you'll find that they can be used at various stages of the patient's experience with you. Think of it as if you're sprinkling the attitude and words of choice and advocacy throughout the new patient experience. At times, you may find yourself using the Warm-up Dialogue, CD-4, and the Financial Options Dialogue, CD-5, during the first appointment. The dialogues are designed to lead, not sell, patients toward complete care. Keep their sequence intact and you'll find they are highly versatile and predictable in their outcome. In fact, there are times when I've used all five dialogues at the initial appointment if I knew we had a special relationship with the patient.

For example, my new right-side patient, Karen, is married to Clark for whom we had provided reconstructive care two years ago. I'd previously met Karen when she, Clark, and I had several conversations about Clark's care. Now it was Karen's turn to get her teeth fixed. Karen had a disability similar to Clark's and was completely familiar with our financial arrangements and the way we handle dental insurance.

For many patients like Karen, at the end of the new patient interview I'd say, "Karen, I believe I have a good general understanding of what your dental problem is. I'm also confident that I can help you. I've helped many patients just like you in the last fifteen years. The thing that I need to know is, is now a good time for you to get your teeth fixed?"

Notice that the intention of this question (to discover readiness) is the same as the Choice Dialogue. The answer usually leads to an advocacy discussion about fee and financial arrangements, even though, in this case, the patient already knows what rehabilitative care costs.

Karen may respond, *"Yes, I think I'm ready. I know what Clark went through and this is a good time for me because I won't start teaching again until fall. How much do you think my case will cost?"*

Whenever costs come up in the conversation, it's usually a good strategy to enter into the Advocacy Dialogue. In Karen's case, I have not looked in her mouth yet, so my ballpark is based on my experience with cases like hers.

> *"Karen, complex dentistry usually costs about $15,000 per jaw and if you have most of your teeth, it can take us about four to six months to complete. Can this level of expense and time commitment fit into your life right now?"* (Advocacy Dialogue)

Assuming the cost and time commitment was OK with Karen, I'd do a complete examination. After the examination I'd go through the Discovery Guide dialogues. For the post-complete examination discussion, I'd do the Warm-up Dialogue, CD-4. We'll discuss this dialogue, but here's a preview. After the examination, I'd say:

> *"Karen, now that I've had a chance to examine you, I can see you're dis appointed in your partial dentures. They're very bulky and loose and I can see the sore spots you mentioned and how they can handicap your speech. I know that's important to you as a teacher."*

> *"When you're ready, we can make it feel as if you have natural teeth when you speak, and with nothing removable or bulky in your mouth."*

> *"The way we'd do this is by replacing your missing teeth with teeth that you brush right in your mouth, just like we did for Clark."*

> *"Of course, let's look at your summer schedule and see when it makes the most sense for you to start. What questions do you have for me?"*

Typically, the conversation would go to fees and financial arrangements and if I'd be able to treatment plan her case now, we'd go into the Financial Options Dialogue, CD-5. If her care required me to study it before I made a diagnosis and treatment plan, I'd reinforce my ballpark estimates and reschedule her for a consultation appointment.

Karen's example demonstrates the flexibility of the dialogues. Again, I don't recommend you alter their sequence: Identity, Choice, Advocacy, Warm-up, and Financial Options. You can however, under the right circumstances, deliver them when the conversational opportunities present themselves, regardless of where you are in the treatment process. For example, when you or the patient is unsure how much dentistry is appropriate at the time, use the Choice Dialogue. If the patient is concerned about finances, enter into an Advocacy Dialogue.

How you alter the structure of the Making It Easy process is up to you. My experience and the experience of hundreds of dentists and teams is that when you keep the sequence of the Critical Dialogues intact and clearly communicictable way of making it easy for patients to say "Yes."

In a Nutshell
Chapter Eleven—Alternative Approaches to Case Acceptance

- One of the best alternative approaches is to combine the Identity and Choice Dialogues during the initial telephone call. Doing so eliminates the need for the limited examination and the limited-examination discussion.

- Another alternative is to offer the Choice and/or Advocacy Dialogues during the initial interview. Under the right circumstances, the initial interview can provide a rich source of disclosure relative to your patient's comfort zones, preferences, and insights into her life circumstances. These topics are perfect segues into the Choice and Advocacy Dialogues.

- There are risks to offering the Choice and/or Advocacy Dialogues during the initial interview. The biggest risk is that when a right-side patient has many conditions accompanied by low awareness and/or minimal disabilities, the Choice and Advocacy Dialogues may force the patient's decision-making process beyond the comfort zone and level of readiness.

- The alternatives described here bundle the dialogues, and don't skip or rearrange them. Keep them in chronological order. It's a big mistake to start talking budget (Advocacy) before you determine readiness (Choice). As you work more with the dialogues, you'll find that they can be used at various stages of the patient's experience with you.

Chapter Twelve
Determine Concern Before You Recommend Care:
The Discovery Guide™

I love the classic 1973 movie *Young Frankenstein*. Near the beginning of the movie Dr. Frankenstein (Gene Wilder) travels to Transylvania to study the work of his late grandfather, who was reputed to have "reanimated life from the dead." Arriving at the Transylvania train station one foggy night, he's met by Igor (Marty Feldman), the humpbacked caretaker of his grandfather's castle.

Noticing Igor's large humpback, Dr. Frankenstein offers, *"I'm a rather brilliant surgeon and I don't mean to be rude, but I can help you with that hump."*

Igor replies, *"What hump?"* leaving Dr. Frankenstein speechless.

"What hump?" is a good leadership lesson for us. How many times do we look in patients' mouths, see something that concerns us but the patient is unaware of, recommend treatment, and the patient says, *"What hump?"* Recommending treatment before you determine concern is a mistake and a fast way to confuse, embarrass and/or create resistance in patients. This chapter on the Discovery Guide™ keeps you from making that mistake. The Discovery Guide is equally valuable for left- and right-side patients, and as you read this chapter, keep in mind it applies to every patient in your practice.

The Lesson
The lesson for us in *Young Frankenstein* is this: Speak first about what interests your listener, speak second about what interests you. Otherwise you lose the listener's attention and your message goes unheard. Another way of thinking about the lesson is this: Understand their level of concern *before* you recommend care. Steven Covey says this in yet another way in

his book *Seven Habits of Highly Successful People*: "Seek first to understand, then to be understood."

> ***Speak first about what interests your listener,***
> ***speak second about what interests you.***

Most dentists, however, do the opposite — they seek first to be understood. You have a choice when you speak to patients. You can communicate like a clinician and tell them everything they need to know and do very little listening. Or you can communicate like a leader and learn what concerns your patients (lots of listening), address that first, and address your issues next. To which do you think patients will respond better—your communicating like a clinician, or like a leader?

Knowing what your listener's/follower's/patient's interests are and paying attention to that *before* you express your interests is at the heart of communicating like a leader.

Dental "Humps"

Let's take the lesson learned from *"What hump?"* and apply it to communicating like a leader to patients. Dentists are good at finding "humps" in patients' mouths (conditions patients are unaware of and not bothered by) and recommending treatment for them.

You say, *"Ginnie, you've got periodontal disease and I'm going to recommend root planing, rigorous home care, an equilibration, and a night guard."*

Ginnie says, *"What periodontal disease? I'm not having any problems!"* and now you're stuck, not only trying to defend your recommendations but also trying to keep a good relationship with your patient.

Confronting patients with a list of all the things wrong with their mouths, followed by a detailed description of how to fix them *without first understanding what's important to them* is a great way to confuse patients, overwhelm them with too much information, and motivate them to leave your practice. Instead, communicate like a leader and learn the language of disabilities and conditions and help them make good decisions about their dentistry.

Conditions Versus Disabilities

Here is a simple distinction that every dentist and team member must become expert at making:

A *condition* is a clinical finding that is outside of normal/healthy limits (i.e., pathology, esthetic, phonetic, or functional disorders). Fractured cusps, abscesses, TMJ pathology, caries, and periodontal disease are a few of the many conditions that may exist in our patients' mouths. Remember, these may or may not be associated with a disability. A *disability* is what the patient is experiencing in his or her life as a result of a dental condition. *"I **hate** the way my teeth look and have **no confidence** when I teach my classes,"* or *"Every time I eat I **worry** that I may **choke** on my food,"* or *"My jaw joint **hurts** me twenty-four hours a day and makes it **impossible for me to concentrate**"* are good examples of how dental problems affect people's lives.

Conditions are *clinical* in nature, disabilities are *emotional.*

Disabilities bother the patient; their conditions bother us. Disabilities occur outside the mouth; conditions are inside the mouth or related to the mouth. Patients respond to talking about relieving their disabilities, while we get excited about the process of fixing their conditions. Patients usually spend just a few minutes telling us about their disabilities, while we spend much longer telling them about how we can fix their conditions.

Conditions With and Without Disabilities

Important distinctions must be made between two types of conditions:
- Conditions *with* disabilities that have created significant, unwanted effects in patients' lives
- Conditions *without* disabilities—patients with dental problems they may or not be aware of and/or conditions that don't affect their lives.

It's this second situation—patients with conditions but no disabilities—that is a common finding among your patients. It also presents the most difficult and frustrating challenge for dentists and team members who are trying to motivate them to undergo complete care dentistry.

Communicating to patients with disabilities requires a different approach than communicating to those without disabilities. To challenge us further, patients often have several conditions, some that are associated with disabilities and some that are not. To communicate in a way that is clear, confident, and appealing, we must adapt our communication style based on their level of *disability* and *awareness* of their condition. The Discovery Guide™ helps us do that.

The Discovery Guide™

The Discovery Guide™ is a leadership communication tool. It helps your patients understand their conditions and helps you and your team understand the patients' disabilities. It also guides us in our discussions with patients when we present care.

FIGURE 12-1

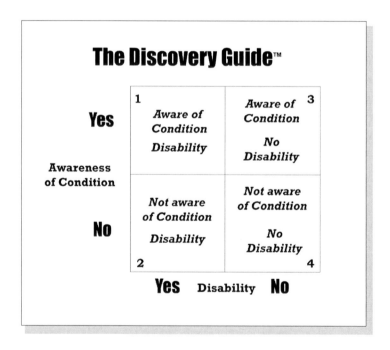

The horizontal axis of the Discovery Guide as shown in **Figure 12-1** relates to disability: either patients are experiencing a disability or they're not. The vertical axis relates to awareness of condition: either they are aware of a dental condition or not. The Guide is divided into four quadrants, each representing a situation that is a combination of awareness of condition and disability. Keep in mind that patients may have all four situations in their mouths.

Quadrant One—Compelling

In quadrant one (**Figure 12-2**), the patient has a distinct disability and is aware of what's causing it. Good examples of this are the embarrassment associated with discolored/chipped front teeth, inability to enjoy food caused by a loose mandibular denture, or slurred speech associated with a sore tongue rubbed raw by a broken filling. Situations in quadrant one mean the patients are very clear about why they are in the dental office. These situations are *compelling* and patients usually are very interested in treating the condition responsible for their disability.

Quadrant Two— Aggravating

In quadrant two (**Figure 12-2**), the patient is experiencing symptoms that are affecting her life (a disability) but she is unaware of what's causing it. Typical examples of this include loss of sleep from a toothache of unknown origin, embarrassment from chronic bad breath, or the inability to concentrate brought on by jaw joint pain and headaches. Situations in quadrant two are *aggravating* the patient, but she doesn't know what's causing them, and usually wants something done about them.

Quadrant Three—Apathetic

In quadrant three (**Figure 12-2**), patients are aware they have a dental problem. They know something is not right, but it doesn't significantly affect their lives (no disability). They are *apathetic* to the situation and unmotivated to do anything about it now. Posterior missing teeth, bleeding gums, and jaw joint noises can be typical examples of quadrant three situations.

Quadrant Four—Clueless

In quadrant four (**Figure 12-2**), patients aren't experiencing any disability and are not aware of any condition; they are clueless about the situation. For example, patients with periodontal disease, periapical abscesses, or dysfunctional occlusions may be completely without symptoms (no disability) and completely unaware (clueless) that anything is "wrong" in their mouths. (Note: Remember that the quadrant labels describe the situation in the patients' mouths, not the patients themselves. A patient may be clueless to a dental situation, yet be an intelligent person.)

FIGURE 12-2

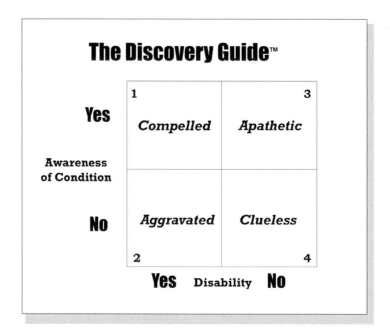

The Sequence of Conversation

The Discovery Guide™ can be used as a guide to the sequence of conversation. Earlier in this chapter I introduced a leadership principle: Speak first about what interests your listener, speak second about what interests you. Otherwise you lose the listener's attention and your message goes unheard. Patients listen best and are influenced most when you discuss what's important to them first and important to you next. So when you're talking to a patient following any examination, discuss situations in quadrant one first, quadrant thwo second, quadrant three third, and quadrant four last (**Figure 12-3**).

Patients listen best and are influenced most when you discuss what's important to them first and important to you next.

FIGURE 12-3

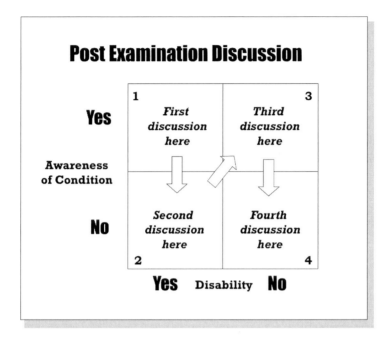

Let me be quick to add, the discussion sequence is *not* the same as the treatment sequence. The *treatment sequence* is governed by the therapeutic decisions; the *discussion sequence* is determined by what the patient is most ready to listen to. It's likely that you're in the habit of presenting dentistry in the *treatment sequence* as a result of your training. Save treatment sequence for the informed consent process and use the *discussion sequence* to make it easy for patients to listen to you.

Case Study Using The Discovery Guide™

Michelle is forty-three years old and during her preclinical interview she says:

> "I hate the way my upper front teeth look. It's come to the point that I'm embarrassed when talking to customers and I'm beginning to feel very self-conscious about my appearance. I know I'm missing some upper back teeth, but they don't show when I smile so I'm not concerned about them."

Just before your discussion ends, Michelle adds:

> "Lately, I've noticed I'm having trouble chewing and some pain that I think is on the lower right side. Sometimes I swear it's the lower and

other days it feels like it's coming from the upper. I don't know what it is but it worries me, too."

When asked about any other conditions she's concerned about she says, *"No, other than the front teeth and the problem with the discomfort that I think is on the lower right, I'm OK!"*

Clinical findings. Michelle has large, discolored mesial and distal composites in ##6–11 along with minor incisal edge wear and uneven incisal edge positions. Teeth #28 and #29 have large fractured amalgam restorations. Teeth #3 and #14 are missing with slight adjacent tooth drift into the edentulous areas. Michelle has moderate subgingival calculus, bleeding in most posterior areas, 4- and 5-mm soft tissue pocketing, and minimal tooth mobility. Michelle has gum disease and is not aware of it.

Figure 12-4 shows how the Discovery Guide for Michelle looks after her examination.

FIGURE 12-4

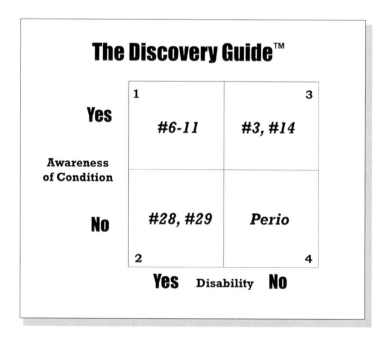

To best hold her attention, the sequence of discussing her   con-
ditions—speaking like a *leader*—is shown in **Figure 12-5**:
- First—##6-11
- Second—#28, #29
- Third—#3 and #14
- Last—periodontal disease.

FIGURE 12-5

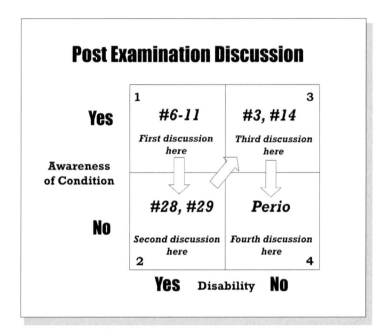

Typically, most clinicians would discuss Michelle's conditions in the
sequence of how they would be treated—speaking like a clinician. This
sequence would most likely look like this:
- First—periodontal disease
- Second—#28, #29
- Third—#6-11
- Last—#3 and #14.

Which way of discussing Michelle's conditions—speaking like a clinician or speaking like a leader—will have the greater positive impact on

Michelle? You'll discover that when you speak like a leader—discussing what's important to the patient first and what's important to you second—patients will listen better and ultimately be more open to your treatment recommendations.

Creating Awareness and Establishing Concern

The goals of the Discovery Guide™ are to:

1. Create patient awareness of their conditions in a way that makes it easy for them to listen to and understand.

2. Make it easy for us to understand patients' disabilities and their readiness to treat them.

3. Set the stage for treatment recommendations — understand patient's level of concern *prior* to making our treatment recommendations.

Looking back at **Figure 12-2,** which quadrant is the patient most ready to treat? Quadrant one (Compelled). Wouldn't it be nice if there was a way we could take the conditions in the other Discovery Guide™ quadrants and "click and drag" them into quadrant four? In other words, would case acceptance be easier for you if patients were aware and concerned about all their conditions? Of course. Our next step using the Discovery Guide™ is to create awareness and determine concern, and hopefully, move all conditions into quadrant four. The first step in creating awareness and determining concerns is to know where the conditions fall relative to the awareness and disability lines.

Awareness and Disability Lines

The horizontal line through the middle of the Discovery Guide™ (**Figure 12-6**) is the Awareness of Condition line (the patient is aware of any condition above this line). The vertical line through the middle of the Discovery Guide™ (**Figure 12-7**) is the Disability line (conditions to the right of this line are bothering the patient).

FIGURE 12-6

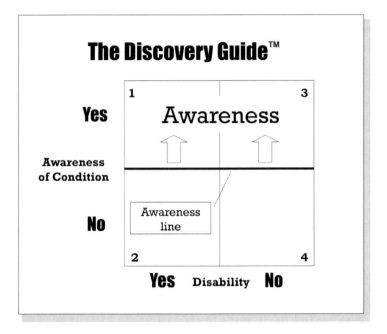

FIGURE 12-7

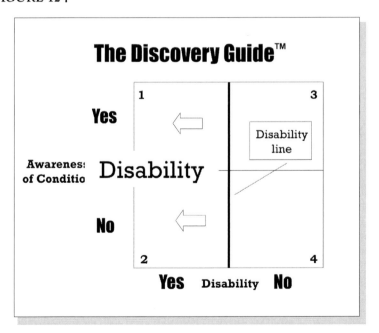

It's important to be aware of these lines and where the condition/disability you're discussing exists relative to these lines. Generally speaking, patients are more open to listening to you speak about conditions that are to the left of the Disability line and above the Awareness of Condition line. Additionally, patients are more ready to treat conditions to the left of the Disability line than conditions to the right of the line. Patients are willing to pay for dentistry to the left of the Disability line. Patients want the insurance company to pay for dentistry to the right of the line.

This is human nature—people are more open to discussing and taking action on conditions they're aware of and that are bothering them. Conversely, in the absence of a disability, most of our patient education and treatment recommendations fall on deaf ears.

> *People are more open to discussing and taking action*
> *on conditions they're aware of and that are bothering them.*

To accomplish the first goal—creating patient awareness about their conditions—means moving all the conditions above the Awareness of Condition line (**Figure 12-8**). This means moving quadrant two conditions into quadrant one and all quadrant four conditions into quadrant three. We do this best by asking specific questions and offering illustrations and information (the Curiosity and Illustration Dialogues).

FIGURE 12-8

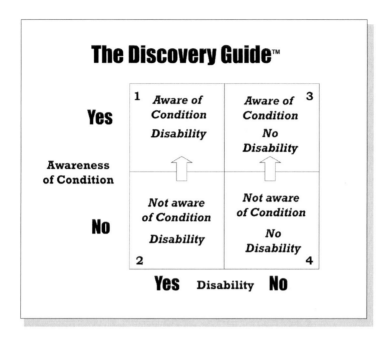

To accomplish the second goal (discover patients' concerns and their readiness to treat those concerns) means asking questions about their concerns. This is done by offering examples of the consequences of these untreated conditions from patients with similar conditions, then asking the patient whether the consequences of not treating these conditions are a concern (the Consequences and Concern Dialogues) (**Figure 12-9**).

FIGURE 12-9

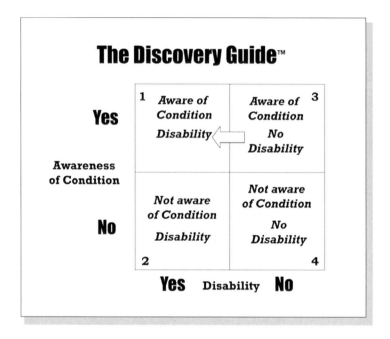

Discovery Guide™ Dialogues

There are four Discovery Guide™ dialogues that help move conditions among the quadrants. These dialogues are generally used in this sequence:

A. Curiosity. A question that determines whether the patient is aware of an existing condition *without* judgment, agenda, or treatment recommendations

"Adam, are you aware that you have a few cracked fillings in your lower molars?"

Not:

- *"Adam, how long have you had these bad fillings?"*
- *"Adam, if I can show you a way to replace these discolored, faulty fillings, would you be interested?"*
- *"Adam, we can replace your cracked silver fillings with tooth-colored fillings."*

B. Illustration. A comparison, metaphor, or simile that helps patients understand the nature of their condition (an intraoral photograph or study model often helps illustrate a condition).

"Cracked fillings are like bricks in a home foundation that have crumbled over time from the weight of the house. Here's a close-up picture of your cracked fillings."

C. Consequences. A comparison of the patient's conditions to other patients (social proof) with similar conditions and foreshadowing the most likely associated disability if the condition remains untreated.

"Adam, for many of my patients with cracked fillings, if they leave them untreated it leads to fractured teeth and tooth loss."

D. Concern. A determination of the level of concern the patients have for the most likely future disability and their readiness to avoid it. Concern/worry is a disability.

"Adam, does the thought of losing teeth sometime in the future concern you?"

Here's how to use the four dialogues: Dialogues A and B (Curiosity and Illustration) are used in quadrants two and four (**Figure 12-10**). These dialogues create awareness of the condition and illustrate it, moving each situation above the awareness line into quadrants one and three.

FIGURE 12-10

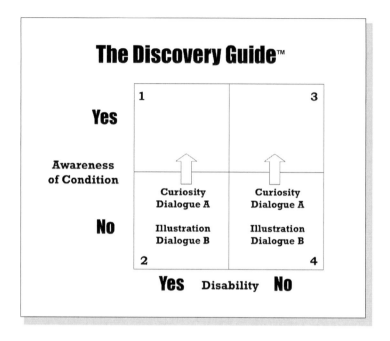

For those conditions that were in quadrant four and are now in quadrant three, we use Dialogues C and D (Consequence and Concern) (**Figure 12-11**). These dialogues foreshadow the most likely future disability and determine patients' concerns about avoiding the disability. If patients express concern/worry, the conditions are now in quadrant one because concern/worry is a major form of disability. If the patient is not concerned, then the condition remains in quadrant three.

FIGURE 12-11

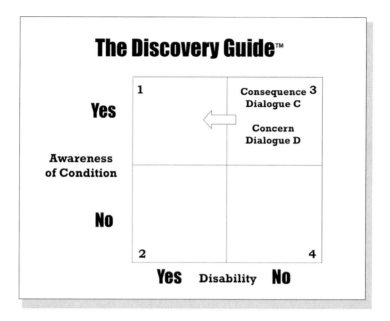

Let's look at each Discovery Guide dialogue in detail. Assume we're discussing a situation in quadrant four. A good example of this is periodontal disease. The patient has it, it's causing no effect on her life, and she is completely unaware of it.

Discovery Guide Dialogue A: Curiosity. A question that determines whether the patient is aware of an existing condition, without judgment, agenda, or treatment recommendations.

When we realize that a patient has a quadrant four condition, the first step is to ask a simple question about the condition, getting curious about the patient's awareness of the condition. Curiosity can take many forms; consequently, the Curiosity Dialogue can have many forms. Here are some examples:

"Did you know that you have some infection in your gums around your back teeth?"

"Have you noticed any bleeding, discomfort, or redness in your gums?"

"Have you had a problem with bad breath or a bad taste in your mouth?"

"Has a dentist ever mentioned to you that you have some infection in your gums?"

"Does anyone in your family have gum disease?"

The intention of the Curiosity Dialogue is to start a conversation, the substance of which gives you insight into the patient's awareness of and attention to their own health. Avoid any direct or negative statements about quadrant one conditions, such as:

"You have gum disease."

"You have bone loss and bleeding gums."

"You have loose teeth and a bad bite."

Such statements can lead to defensiveness and minimize interaction, and don't support the intention of curiosity.

The Curiosity Dialogue draws a response from the patient. For quadrant one conditions, this response is usually in the form of surprise and/or curiosity.

"No, doc, I didn't know I had gum problems."

"Gum infection, nobody ever told me about that."

"No, I've never noticed anything wrong with my gums."

"What do you mean by gum disease?"

"How much of a problem is that?"

"Is it serious?"

Once the patient acknowledges that he is now aware of his condition, you can proceed to Dialogue B.

Discovery Guide Dialogue B: Illustration. The Illustration Dialogue helps patients understand the nature of their condition by comparing it to something they're familiar with, using a metaphor, simile, and comparisons. For example, an illustration for discolored front teeth is: *"Teeth discolor over time like the inside of a coffee cup."*

A distinction between *illustration* and *education* is necessary here. Unlike *illustration*, *education* is teaching the patient something new. For example, educating a patient about discolored front teeth sounds like this: *"The enamel matrix on the labial surface of the maxillary incisors is porous and tends to absorb oral fluids."*

Which is easier to understand (hence, more influential), illustrations or education? Most people agree that illustrations are more easily understood. You can support your illustrations with visual aids (models, photographs, pictures). The most persuasive visual aid is an intraoral photograph of the patient's mouth that demonstrates your verbal illustration.

Here are some examples of illustrations for typical quadrant four conditions:

Periodontal disease: *"Michelle, gum infection is like an infection you have in other areas of your body. It's like you had a sliver in your arm; it would turn red and swollen and sometimes cause pain. Gum infection can also cause the bone to dissolve."*

Fractured amalgam restoration: *"John, the silver fillings in your mouth are beginning to crumble like old brick foundations you see on older homes. The bricks crumble from the weight of the house, and your fillings can crumble from the force of your bite."*

Traumatic occlusion: *"Adam, the way your teeth fit together is causing them to break and wear out. It's like stripped gears in a transmission."*

Discolored teeth: *"Betsy, front teeth change color over time like a white shirt or paint on a wall."*

The Illustration Dialogue is not designed to provide informed consent. The intention of the Illustration Dialogue is to give patients a memorable idea of what's going on in their mouths. Metaphors, comparisons, and photographs are great ways to make your explanations memorable. Avoid getting into a detailed show-and-tell about their conditions at this point. This part of your conversation is for discovering their awareness and attitudes about their dental health. It's not designed as a patient education experience.

Once you've delivered Discovery Guide Dialogues A and B (Curiosity and Illustration), the conditions in quadrant four are now in quadrant three—the patient is aware of them and has a simple understanding of them.

Figures 12-12 and **12-13** show how Curiosity and Illustration Dialogues A and B look on the Discovery Guide™. Assume your patient has fractured amalgams on teeth #29 and #30 and is unaware of them. First, take an intraoral photograph so your patient can see the cracks while you're delivering the dialogues.

FIGURE 12-12

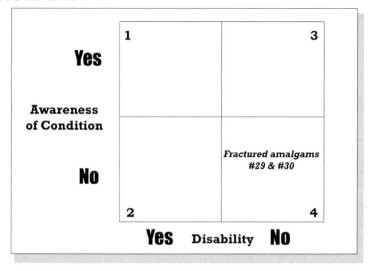

FIGURE 12-13

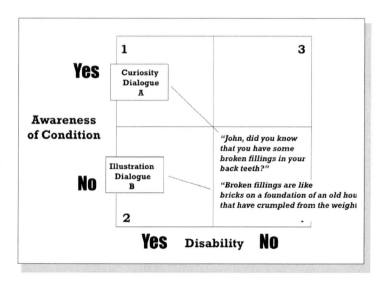

Once the Discovery Guide Dialogues A and B are delivered, the fractured amalgams (conditions) are now in quadrant three—the patient is aware of them (**Figure 12-14**).

FIGURE 12-14

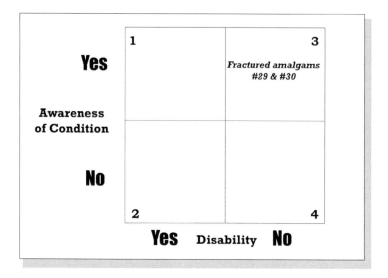

Discovery Guide™ Dialogue C: Consequences. Compares the patient's conditions to other patients with similar conditions and foreshadows the most likely associated disability if the condition remains untreated.

The Consequences Dialogue explains the most likely future disability arising from the condition identified in quadrant two. The intention here is to state the consequences of this condition if left untreated. It's important here to note that this dialogue is *not a threat* and should not be delivered with a threatening point of view or tone of voice. This is accomplished best by using an example of the consequences other patients with this condition have experienced. The patient will make the link between what's happened to others and what can happen to him or her. The intention of the Consequences Dialogue is to provide social proof that the patient's condition will likely worsen and result in a disability.

Here are some examples of the Consequences Dialogue C for typical quadrant two conditions:

Periodontal disease: *"Michelle, typically my patients who have untreated gum infections end up losing some teeth and are disappointed with their poor chewing* *and embarrassed about their appearance and speech."*

Fractured amalgam restoration: *"John, broken fillings in many of my patients result in decayed and broken teeth. Once teeth break, they can be painful or may be lost."*

Traumatic occlusion: *"Adam, my patients who have severe bite problems like yours often wear their teeth down or end up embarrassed by losing a lot of teeth. Tooth loss leads to problems with chewing, appearance, and speech."*

Keep in mind that the consequence of not treating a quadrant two condition should be stated as a disability, not a condition of increased complexity. For example, the consequence of untreated gum disease should *not* be stated as bone loss (another condition). The consequence of gum disease in Dialogue C is a disability (embarrassment about their appearance and speech).

Discovery Guide Dialogue D: Concern. Determines the level of concern the patient has for the most likely future disability and the patient's readiness to avoid it.

The Concern Dialogue's intent is to understand (discover) the patient's concern for avoiding the most likely future disability explained in Consequences Dialogue C (**Figure 12-15**). This question is asked immediately after you have the sense that the patient understands the consequences of her condition. This dialogue, like all dialogues, can take many forms. Here are some examples:

Periodontal disease: *"Michelle, does the thought of losing teeth and wearing dentures concern you?"*

Fractured amalgam restoration: *"John, does the idea of broken teeth or toothaches concern you?"*

Traumatic occlusion: *"Adam, is the idea of wearing dentures something you'd like to avoid?"*

FIGURE 12-15

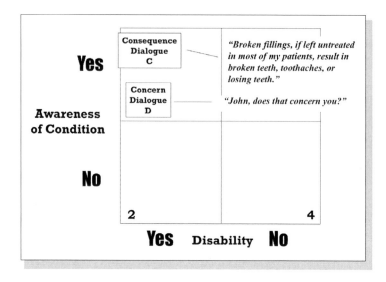

If the patient is concerned about the most likely consequences of their condition, then the condition now is in quadrant four because concern is a disability (**Figure 12-16**).

FIGURE 12-16

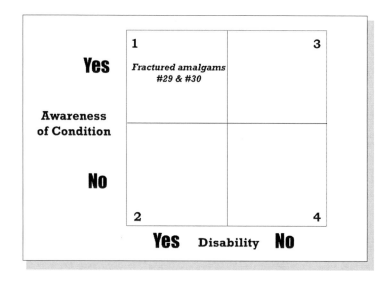

As you can see, the intent of the four Discovery Guide Dialogues is to move all conditions to quadrant four. In the real world of dentistry, however, not all conditions can be moved to quadrant one. <u>Later in this book we'll discuss how to handle conditions about which the patient expresses no concern.</u>

When in quadrant one, all conditions have associated disabilities. Those disabilities are either from the existing conditions or from the worry about avoiding disabilities in the future. Whether the treatment recommendations *fit* into the patient's life at this time is outside the scope of the Discovery Guide Dialogues. <u>We'll illustrate how to deal with quadrant one conditions a little later in this book.</u>

The Discovery Guide Dialogues in Action

Let's put the Discovery Guide™ Dialogues into action for Michelle. Here is a review of Michelle's conditions:

- Discolored mesial and distal composites in #6–11 with minor incisal edge wear and uneven incisal edge positions.
- Teeth #28 and #29 have large fractured amalgam restorations.
- Teeth #3 and #14 are missing, with slight adjacent tooth drift into the edentulous areas. No significant supraeruption has occurred in the opposing arch.
- Moderate subgingival calculus, bleeding in most posterior areas, 4- and 5-mm soft tissue pocketing, and minimal tooth mobility.

Figure 12-17 shows how it should look:

FIGURE 12-17

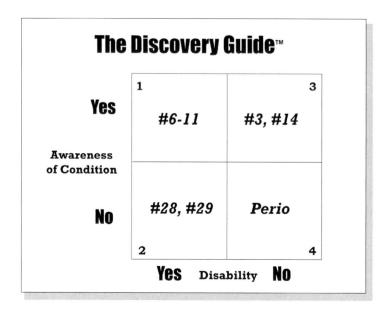

Imagine that you have completed this Discovery Guide™ and have it adjacent to your clinical examination charting. You now have the best of both worlds: the clinical charting important in your world, and a charting of the patient's concerns important in her world.

The Sequence of Discussion

The Discovery Guide™ directs the sequence of your discussion with Michelle. **Figure 12-18** illustrates the step-by-step process of your post-examination conversation. Remember, this conversation is not designed to offer solutions. Rather, its purpose is to create patient awareness of conditions and dentist/team awareness of disability and concerns. Also, this sequence is not the *treatment sequence*; it's the *discussion sequence* most likely to hold her attention and lead her to making good healthcare decisions.

FIGURE 12-18

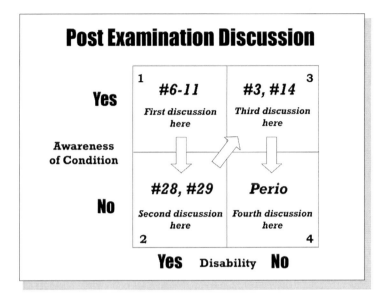

Use all four Discovery Guide Dialogues in all quadrants (**Figure 12-19**).

FIGURE 12-19

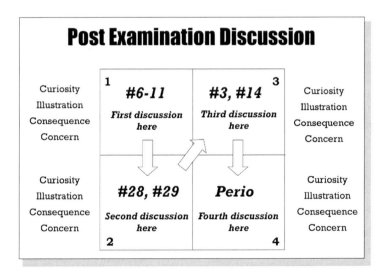

An important point to remember here is that the patient, if compelled or apathetic (quadrants one and three), is already aware of the conditions. Consequently, the Curiosity Dialogue is modified from a question ("*Michelle, did you know that you have missing teeth?*") to a statement that acknowledges her condition ("*Michelle, as you know you have a few missing teeth...*").

Similarly, with compelling and aggravating conditions (quadrants one and two), when we already know the patient has a disability and is concerned about it, the Concern Dialogue is modified from a question ("*Michelle, does the discomfort in your back teeth concern you?*") to a statement that acknowledges her disability ("*Michelle, I know you're concerned about your uncomfortable back teeth...*").

Here are sample post-examination dialogues using the sequence created by the Discovery Guide™, along with the four Discovery Guide™ Dialogues.

Quadrant One

Curiosity: "*Michelle, let's start by discussing your upper front teeth. I know you're embarrassed by their appearance and they're creating a lack of confidence when you're talking with customers. You have several large dark fillings in these teeth along with some chipped edges.*"

Illustration: "*Teeth can be like white shirts – over time they can yellow and lose their shape.*" (Showing patients' their own photos/x-rays of conditions help demonstrate conditions.)

Consequence: "*I see a lot of patients who are embarrassed by the appearance of their teeth. Over time, most of my patients find that the color and shape of their teeth worsens.*"

Concern: "*I know this concerns you and is the main reason you're here.*"

Quadrant Two

Curiosity: "*Michelle, you also mentioned that you're aggravated by the pain you have to hot and cold on your lower right side. Did you know that you have two broken fillings on that side?*"

Illustration: *"Fillings are like sidewalks–they can crack over time because of age and too much pressure on them. Here's a photograph of the cracked fillings."* (Showing patients' their own photos/x-rays of conditions help demonstrate conditions.)

Consequence: *"In many patients, cracked fillings can lead to decayed and cracked teeth and continued discomfort very similar to what you're experiencing."*

Concern: *"I assume this is something you want to take care of?"*

Quadrant Three

Curiosity: *"Michelle, I know you're aware that you have some missing molars on your upper left and right sides."*

Illustration: *"When teeth are missing, the teeth next to them can tip into the space like books on a book shelf."* (Showing patients' their own photos/x-rays of conditions help demonstrate conditions.)

Consequence: *"Often, patients with missing back teeth lose more teeth and end up chewing on their front teeth. This can cause problems with their health and appearance."*

Concern: *"I suspect this is something you want to avoid?"*

Quadrant Four

Curiosity: *"Michelle, the last area that I'm concerned about is your gum health. Are you aware that you have some gum infection?"*

Illustration: *"Gum infection can be like high blood pressure–you can have it and not know it. The infection in the gums is like the infection you get when you have a sliver in your hand–the gums get swollen, red, can bleed easily, and at times be uncomfortable. Here's a picture of an infected area in your mouth."* (Showing patients' their own photos/x-rays of conditions help demonstrate conditions)

Consequence: *"Many patients with gum infections experience bad breath and can lose teeth as the infections get worse. The leading cause of tooth loss is gum disease."*

Concern: *"Michelle, is tooth loss something you want to avoid?"*

In this example, I did not include Michelle's responses to my Curiosity or Concern questions. My goal here is to illustrate the flow of the Discovery Guide™ Dialogues used in the post-examination discussion.

Based on the patient's responses to the Concern Dialogue, the Discovery Guide™ now has a different distribution of conditions. Those conditions she's concerned about are now in quadrant one (compelling).

Don't pressure patients until all their conditions cross the disability line into quadrant four. Be patient and learn to take no for an answer to the Concern Dialogue. Our goal during the post-examination discussion is to organize the conditions onto the Discovery Guide™ for further conversation at the case presentation.

For example, let's assume that Michelle is concerned about the upper front teeth, the broken fillings and pain on her lower right, and the gum disease. At this time, she is not concerned about the missing upper molars. The Discovery Guide™ for this is shown in **Figure 12-20**.

FIGURE 12-20

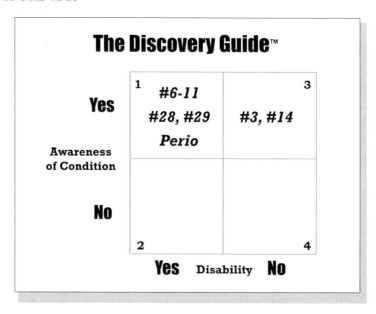

You've made her aware of all her conditions and told her the conse-quences of all of them. She's more concerned about some conditions than others. This post-examination discussion mapping of the Discovery Guide™ sets us up for the next appointment, where we'll recommend treatment.

As a preview of "coming attractions" in the next chapters, when we rec-ommend treatment to Michelle, conditions in quadrant one are discussed first and conditions in quadrant three are discussed last. We will recom-mend care for all conditions regardless of their quadrants. The difference is in our approach to the recommendation. Recommendations for treat-ment for conditions in quadrant one are offered in a slightly different way than for conditions in quadrant three. That difference, although slight, is huge in its impact. Treatment recommendations are discussed in Chapter Fourteen in the Warm-up Dialogue.

The goals for using the Discovery Guide™ as a post-examination tool are to:
- Create patient awareness of conditions in a way that makes it easy for them to listen and understand.
- Make it easy for us to understand patients' concerns and readiness to treat those concerns.
- Set the stage for treatment recommendations—understand patient's level of concern prior to making our treatment recommendations.

When patients are aware and concerned about a condition is when they are most open to a treatment recommendation. However, like Igor in *Young Frankenstein*, if they're not aware and not concerned about a condi-tion, their response to your treatment recommendation is predictable: *"What hump?"*

In a Nutshell
Chapter Twelve—The Discovery Guide™

- The Discovery Guide™ is a leadership communication tool. It helps your patients understand their conditions and helps you and your team understand the patients' disabilities. It also guides us in our discussions with patients when we present care.

- Confronting patients with a list of all the things wrong with their mouths, followed by a detailed description of how to fix them *without first understanding what's important to them* is a great way to confuse patients, overwhelm them with too much information, and motivate them to leave your practice.

- A *condition* is a clinical finding that is outside of normal/ healthy limits (what bothers the dentist and/or team member). A *disability* is what the patient is experiencing in his or her life as a result of a dental condition (what bothers the patient).

- The sequence of the post-examination discussion using the Discovery Guide™ is often not the sequence of treatment.

- Create patient awareness about their conditions by asking specific questions and offering illustrations and information (the Curiosity and Illustration Dialogues).

- To discover patients' concerns and their readiness to treat those concerns—means asking questions about their concerns. This is done by offering examples of the consequences of these untreated conditions from patients with similar conditions, then asking the patient whether the consequences of not treating these conditions are a concern (the Consequences and Concern Dialogues).

- The goals of the Discovery Guide™ are to: create patient awareness of their conditions in a way that makes it easy for them to listen and understand; make it easy for us to understand patients' disabilities and their readiness to treat them; and set the stage for treatment recommendations—understand patients' level of concern prior to making our treatment recommendations.

Chapter Thirteen
Practice Before You Preach:
Treatment Planning

A few years ago I returned to my hometown, Elmhurst, Illinois, to play in our annual Thanksgiving "Turkey Bowl" football game. The first Turkey Bowl was played in 1964. One team consisted of my brother Guy (the ultimate jock, who ended up playing for the Cleveland Browns) along with his Neanderthal friends (tough guys who'd kick you when you were down). The other team consisted of me, a violinist in the school orchestra, along with my friends, who got too drunk the night before to play decent football the next day. That rivalry has lasted to this day... and my friends and I have never won a single game.

For this particular game, Guy had recruited the daughters of his tough friends to play on his team. *"Girls!"* I thought, *"we're gonna get beat by girls!"* These weren't just any girls either—they were college soccer jockettes, wearing well-worn soccer cleats that would turn on a dime. Trying to catch them was like chasing rabbits. We were not prepared for them and they left us winded and whipped.

Have you ever been left winded and whipped following a case presentation because you didn't prepare well? When you don't prepare well, everyone loses—your patient, team, and you. This chapter shows you how to prepare for the patent consultation and to prevent case presentation from being an exhausting and frustrating experience.

Preparing for the Consultation Appointment

To prepare for the consultation appointment, you'll need to spend some time away from the patient, thinking about how to best approach her care. During this process, you will:

- Establish the clinical diagnosis and treatment plan.
- Determine essential versus elective conditions relative to her chief condition/disability.
- Organize and rehearse the Warm-up Dialogue on the Warm-up Dialogue Organizer.
- Prepare the Financial Options form.

Establish the Clinical Diagnosis and Treatment Plan

Develop Michelle's treatment plan to the best level of care you and your treatment team (including specialists) can offer. During this aspect of planning, don't worry about fees or other fit and readiness issues. Remember, she is already aware of her ballpark fees, financial arrangements, and time in treatment (this was accomplished through the use of the Advocacy Dialogue at the previous appointment). If there had been significant concerns, they would already have surfaced. You'll determine, along with the patient, the appropriateness of her treatment plan relative to her budget and other lifestyle issues at her consultation appointment. Your job during this phase is to establish a plan for a lifetime strategy for dental health.

Essential and Elective Treatment Recommendations

An important part of the diagnosis and treatment plan is determining which conditions, and their treatment recommendations, are essential or elective relative to the chief benefit the patient is seeking. For example, the chief benefit Michelle is seeking is more confidence in her appearance, which means her front teeth need to be restored. The issue of essential and elective conditions is this: What other conditions does Michelle have and how do they influence the outcome of restoring her front teeth?

Essential treatment recommendations are those that are crucial to a favorable long-term result of restoring her front teeth. Michelle's periodontal condition is an excellent example of an essential condition. *Elective* treatment recommendations, although desirable from an ideal treatment point of view, are not crucial in the short term to restoring her front teeth. A good example of an elective condition relative to restoring Michelle's front teeth is her missing maxillary posterior teeth.

Knowing which treatment recommendations are essential or elective is often an important way of helping patients fit treatment into their lives—some things have to be treated now (essential) and others can wait (elective).

Here is what you must consider when deciding whether treatment of a condition is essential or elective:

- Treating the condition is mandatory for medical/legal standards.
- Treating the condition is mandatory for your personal quality/ ethical standards.

Typically, essential treatment recommendations include periodontal care, endodontic procedures, equilibrations, orthodontics, nightguards, etc. Often, essential conditions have no disabilities—Discovery Guide™ quadrants three or four. These procedures are not "sexy." They don't bring dramatic visual change to the patient but nonetheless are essential to the longevity and functionality of the "sexy" procedures—veneers, crowns, etc.

In Michelle's case, the post-examination discussion Discovery Guide™ looks like this (**Figure 13-1**):

FIGURE 13-1

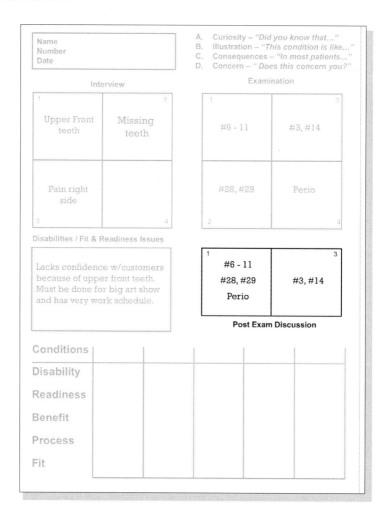

In this example, we know that her chief concern is the appearance of (and subsequent embarrassment about) #6–11 and the discomfort of #28 and #29. Additionally, through the use of the Discovery Guide™ Dialogues, we learn that her periodontal disease is also a concern. The missing teeth (#3 and #14) are not a concern for her (no disability), hence they remain in quadrant three for now. The periodontal treatment is an essential treatment recommendation relative to obtaining the best possible result for treating #6–11 and #28 and #29. You'll notice that it's in quadrant one (compelling). This makes Michelle more open to periodontal care because she is aware and concerned about it.

Essential treatment is either prerequisite (done before) or companion (done during/after) when treating quadrant one conditions. (In the next chapter on the Warm-up Dialogue you'll learn how to make it clear that treating essential conditions is mandatory for sustaining the benefit of the quadrant one procedures the patient wants.) In this example, the benefit of the periodontal care is to protect the confidence Michelle will have in the appearance of her front teeth. In the language of the Warm-up Dialogue, bundle/combine treating essential conditions with treating the chief condition as if the essential conditions and the chief condition are one condition. For example, when discussing periodontal treatment (essential treatment) with a patient planning to have cosmetic dentistry (chief condition), say, "*Part of enhancing the appearance of your front teeth is eliminating the gum infection through a series of very thorough cleanings and the use of some medications.*"

In this example it's convenient that her essential treatment is one she is aware of and concerned about—quadrant four. What gets more difficult is when an essential treatment recommendation is based on a condition that the patient is apathetic about—quadrant three. As before, we'll bundle/combine elective treatment recommendations with chief condition recommendations as if the elective conditions and the chief condition is one all-inclusive condition.

In Michelle's case, replacing teeth #3 and #14 is an example of elective treatment recommendations. Her maxillary anterior teeth and #28 and #29 can be treated well without the prerequisite or companion replacement of the missing teeth. Depending on fit and readiness issues, her tooth replacements can be completed later. (Don't interpret this paragraph as an indication that the patient is encouraged to postpone elective treatment recommendations; you'll see in the following chapter that essential as well as elective treatment recommendations are presented at the consultation appointment.)

The elective/essential distinction in conditions and their treatment recommendations is important because:

- It identifies which conditions need treatment now and which conditions can wait.
- It allows you to segment treatment plans, when necessary, to better fit into your patient's life.

After you've made the elective/essential distinctions, you may want to check the essential conditions on the post-examination Discovery Guide™ to remind you of your decisions. Once you've treatment planned the patient and identified which conditions are essential or elective relative to treating the chief condition, you are now ready to put together the Warm-up Dialogue Organizer.

The Warm-up Dialogue Organizer

At the bottom of the page on side two of the Discovery Guide™, you'll see the Warm-up Dialogue Organizer. It's where you'll organize your treatment recommendations and create a rehearsal tool for the Warm-up Dialogue, CD-4.

FIGURE 13-2

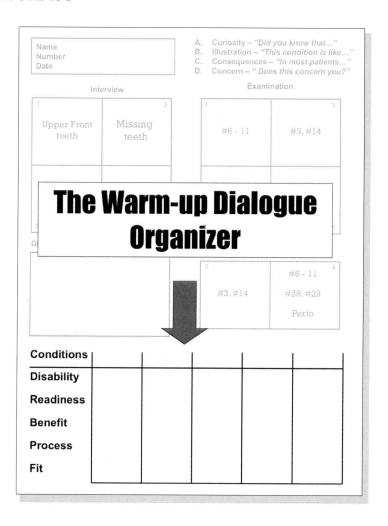

In this example (**Figure 13-2**), the top portion of the guide is already filled out. The Discovery Guide™ sections labeled Interview, Examination, and Post Exam Discussion have been filled in during the initial appointment and examination process. The bottom portion is completed when the patient isn't present, during your treatment planning process. Think of this portion of the process as "conversation planning." We spend a lot of time treatment planning—why not spend some time planning conversation? If you can't get through the treatment conversation, you'll never get to the teeth. Here are two steps for conversation planning: completing the fit and readiness summary and the Warm-up Dialogue Organizer.

If you can't get through the treatment conversation,
you'll never get to the teeth.

Fit and Readiness Summary

In the rectangle labeled Disabilities/Fit and Readiness issues, transfer a summary of the information from side one of the Discovery Guide™. Use short phrases summarizing those personal fit issues and specific disabilities important to the patient. A team member may be useful in making sure you have the current and relevant information recorded.

In Michelle's case, we've learned that her chief disability is her embarrassment around customers and her fit issues revolve around her art gallery and schedule. Here's how her summary box looks (**Figure 13-3**):

FIGURE 13-3

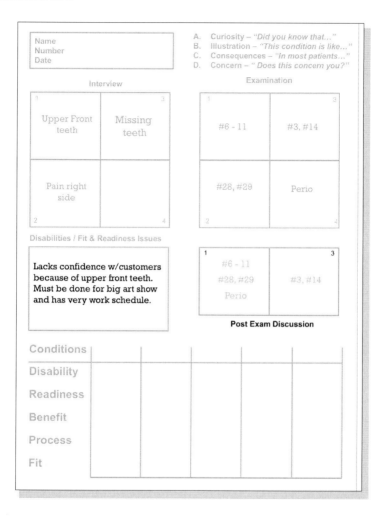

Post Exam Discussion

Warm-up Dialogue Organizer

Figure 13-4 shows the Warm-up Dialogue Organizer completed for Michelle. It's used to organize the sequence of the presentation of treatment recommendations (not treatment sequence), and to structure and rehearse the Warm-up Dialogue so it is easy for the patient to understand and for the dentist or team member to deliver. You'll complete the organizer during your treatment planning process.

FIGURE 13-4

Conditions	#6-11	#28, 29	Perio	#3,#14
Disability	Embarrassed w/ customers	Pain	Tooth loss	I'm concerned..
Readiness	3 month D/L	w/#6-11	w/#6-11	When it fits...
Benefit	Confidence w/ customers	Comfort	Maintain confidence	Maintain confidence
Process	New enamel	Restore	Special cleanings	Brush in mouth
Fit	Work schedule	Work schedule	Work schedule	Work schedule

Column Headings

The column headings (**Figure 13-5**) label the conditions to be treated. The sequence of presentation is from left to right. You'll notice that the sequence is taken from the post-examination Discovery Guide™, presenting treatment recommendations for conditions in quadrant one first, then quadrant three. Always list the chief condition first.

FIGURE 13-5

Presentation sequence				
Conditions	#6-11	#28, #29	Perio	#3, #14
Disability	Embarrassed w/ customers	Pain	Tooth loss	I'm concerned..
Readiness	3 month D/L	w/#6-11	w/#6-11	When it fits...
Benefit	Confidence w/ customers	Comfort	Maintain confidence	Maintain confidence
Process	New enamel	Restore	Special cleanings	Brush in mouth
Fit	Work schedule	Work schedule	Work schedule	Work schedule

The conditions in the column furthest to the right (#3, #14) are ones for which patients have no disability; they're apathetic to these conditions (quadrant three). It's useful to darken the line separating the columns between quadrant one (compelling) and quadrant three (apathetic) conditions to remind you to discuss conditions on either side of this line differently **(Figure 13-6)**. We'll get into the details of this in the next chapter.

FIGURE 13-6

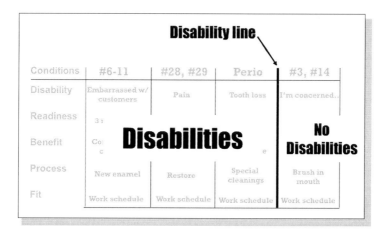

Row Headings

The row headings create the structure of the Warm-up Dialogue **(Figure 13-7)**. The sequence of the delivery of the structure is from the top row (Disability) to the bottom row (Fit).

FIGURE 13-7

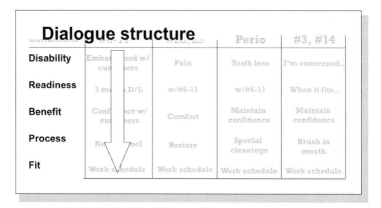

Each row heading has already been defined in previous chapters. Here's a quick review:

Disability: How the condition is affecting the patient's life (what's bothering the patient).

Readiness: The appropriate timing of the treatment.

Benefit: How the treatment will relieve the disability (essentially, it's the opposite of the disability).

Process: A simple one- or two-sentence description of how the treatment is done.

Fit: How the treatment must fit into the patient's life.

Let's look at the structure of the Warm-up Dialogue and how to use the Warm-up Dialogue Organizer one condition at a time. **Figure 13-8** shows the Warm-up Dialogue Organizer for condition #6–11, the chief condition.

FIGURE 13-8

Conditions	#6-11	#28, #29	Perio	#3, #14
Disability	Embarrassed w/ customers	Pain	Tooth loss	I'm concerned...
Readiness	3 month D/L	w/#6-11	w/#6-11	When it fits...
Benefit	Confidence w/ customers	Comfort	Maintain confidence	Maintain confidence
Process	New enamel	Restore	Special cleanings	Brush in mouth
Fit	Work schedule	Work schedule	Work schedule	Work schedule

Disability: It's abundantly clear that Michelle's chief disability is her embarrassment about the appearance of her front teeth. This is especially true for her at work. The importance of knowing the right-side patient's chief disability can't be overstated. You'll see how true this is in the context of the Warm-up Dialogue. Enter a few words in the Warm-up Dialogue Organizer that remind you of her chief disability—"embarrassed when with customers."

The importance of knowing the right-side patient's chief disability can't be overstated.

Readiness: In Michelle's case, she has an important black-tie event at her gallery in three months. The appropriate timing of her treatment is for her to be finished (disability relieved) before her event. Be sure to tell her you're aware of her timing issues—deadline (D/L) in three months.

Benefit: The benefit of care is the opposite of the disability. For Michelle, it means confidence in her appearance, especially when she's with customers. Again, jot a few words in the Warm-up Dialogue Organizer to remind you—"confidence with customers."

Process: State one or two sentences about how her treatment will be done. This is really difficult for most dentists, most of whom go into far too much detail. Remember, the dialogue we are organizing and rehears-

ing for (Warm-up Dialogue) is not informed consent. That comes later.
Here we want just a simple illustration or description. In Michelle's case,
a simple description of all-porcelain crowns on teeth #6–11 is:

> "Michelle, the way we'll improve the appearance of your front teeth is by
> removing the dark and chipped enamel and old fillings and replacing them
> with a new enamel-like material. This takes us about two appointments."

On the Warm-up Dialogue Organizer, write a few words to remind you
of this simple description—"new enamel."

Here are some other simple descriptions for some of the common dental
procedures:

Crowns, onlays, inlays, veneers, composites, and all other tooth-colored restorations: New enamel

Porcelain-fused-to-metal crowns: Restore teeth to their natural
shape and color

Periodontal treatment (nonsurgical): Special cleanings with an
occasional use of antibiotics

Periodontal treatment (surgical): Minor surgery

Equilibration: Adjust the bite by slight reshaping of the teeth's
biting surfaces

Implants: Artificial tooth roots

Bridgework and single-tooth implant replacements: Non-remov
able teeth that you brush right in your mouth

Endodontics: Pulp therapy

Fit: Offer a simple acknowledgment about those issues in the patient's
life that you know weigh on her decision about her dental care. In
Michelle's case, her work schedule and getting her gallery ready for her
event in three months are controlling her life right now. Let her know
that you're aware of her circumstances and offer to find the best way to
fit her dental care into her life. For example, *"... Michelle, I know you
have your hands full right now with your work schedule and the remodeling
you're doing at your gallery. I want to make sure these treatment
recommendations fit into what's going on in your life right now."*

On the Warm-up Dialogue Organizer, write a few words that remind you of this acknowledgment—"work schedule."

Before we review the rest of the Warm-up Dialogue Organizer, let's take a close look at four key entries on the organizer.

Four Key Entries

The entries for condition, disability, benefit, and fit in the first column (**Figure 13-9**) are the four most significant issues that impact the patient's decision to accept care.

FIGURE 13-9

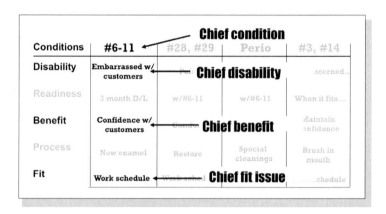

Remember: It's the conditions and issues of the first column that the patient is most aware of and concerned about (compelled)—chief condition. *When possible (and appropriate), relate the benefit of treating other conditions to first-column issues.* In Michelle's case, her desire to have confidence while with her customers and her work issues drive her decisions. Link the benefits of her gum treatment and tooth replacements to her desire to have more confidence when she's with her customers. More on this topic later.

Let's look at Warm-up Dialogue Organizer entries for teeth #28 and #29 (**Figure 13-10**).

FIGURE 13-10

Conditions	#6-11	#28, #29	Perio	#3, #14
Disability	Embarrassed w/ customers	**Pain**	Tooth loss	I'm concerned..
Readiness	3 month D/L	**w/#6-11**	w/#6-11	When it fits...
Benefit	Confidence w/ customers	**Comfort**	Maintain confidence	Maintain confidence
Process	New enamel	**Restore**	Special cleanings	Brush in mouth
Fit	Work schedule	**Work schedule**	Work schedule	Work schedule

Disability: Michelle's disability relative to #28 and #29 is pain. Usually you don't need to get any more detailed than stating you're aware a patient is in pain to let the patient know you're aware of the disability. In some cases, you might relate how her pain is affecting another area of her life (e.g., inability to concentrate or difficulty sleeping at night).

Readiness: The appropriate time to treat #28 and #29 would coincide with treatment of #6-11. It would save Michelle time and work well for you, too. Make a simple entry to remind you of this—"w/#6-11."

Benefit: Again, the benefit of care is the opposite of the disability. For Michelle, it means comfort. Enter a word in the Warm-up Dialogue Organizer to remind you—"comfort."

Process: The technical treatment plan for #28 and #29 is porcelain-fused-to-metal crowns. A simple way to explain this to the patient is, *"Michelle, we'll restore your lower right back teeth back to their normal shape and color."* A simple entry will remind you of this phrase—"restore."

Fit: The work- and schedule-related fit issues for Michelle are the same regardless of her condition—work schedule.

Figure 13-11 shows the Warm-up Dialogue Organizer entries for Michelle's periodontal care:

FIGURE 13-11

Conditions	#6-11	#28, #29	**Perio**	#3, #14
Disability	Embarrassed w/ customers	Pain	**Tooth loss**	I'm concerned...
Readiness	3 month D/L	w/#6-11	**w/#6-11**	When it fits...
Benefit	Confidence w/ customers	Comfort	**Maintain confidence**	Maintain confidence
Process	New enamel	Restore	**Special cleanings**	Brush in mouth
Fit	Work schedule	Work schedule	**Work schedule**	Work schedule

Disability: Michelle's disability relative to periodontal conditions is concern about tooth loss. Although she was unaware of her condition before her initial appointment, after her examination and Discovery Guide™ Dialogues she expressed concern about the probable disabilities associated with untreated periodontal disease: tooth loss, bad breath, poor appearance. Enter in the Warm-up Dialogue Organizer a simple reminder phrase—"tooth loss."

Readiness: The appropriate timing to treat the periodontal disease would coincide with treatment of #6–11. (Yes, I realize periodontal care would precede final restorations, but for the sake of this conversation, explanation of precise treatment sequencing is not our goal.) Make a simple entry to remind you of this—"w/#6–11."

Benefit: When relating the benefits of treatment for conditions about which patients were initially either clueless (quadrant one) or apathetic (quadrant two), link their benefits to the chief benefit they were seeking when they came to your office. In Michelle's case, that means linking the benefits of periodontal care (initially, she was clueless about her condition) to the benefit she wants the most—confidence when she's with customers **(Figure 13-12)**. Hence, the benefit of treating Michelle's gum disease is to keep the gum disease from destroying the stability of her front teeth, and preserving the confidence she'll have in her appearance. For example, say, *"Michelle, the last time we talked I mentioned the infection in your* *gums and you expressed a concern about it. While we're in the process of fixing your front teeth, we'll treat your gum infection to preserve your confidence in the appearance of your front teeth."*

FIGURE 13-12

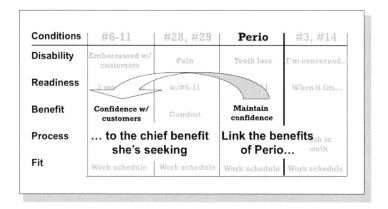

There are many ways to state the benefits of essential conditions and relate them to protecting the strongest benefit. Use words like safeguard, maintain, sustain, prolong, preserve, ensure, stabilize, shield, protect, care for, guard, and keep healthy. *"Michelle, to safeguard your appearance..."* *"Michelle, to maintain the confidence you'll have..."* *"Michelle, to preserve the appearance and health..."*

Use words like safeguard, maintain, sustain, prolong, preserve, ensure, stabilize, shield, protect, care for, guard, and keep healthy.

Process: The process of treating Michelle's gum disease is a nonsurgical approach. A few words is all you need to describe it—"special cleanings."

Fit: As before, the work- and schedule-related fit issues for Michelle are the same regardless of her condition—work schedule. **Figure 13-13** and **Figure 13-14** show the Warm-up Dialogue Organizer entries for Michelle's final conditions, missing teeth #3 and #14:

FIGURE 13-13

Conditions	#6-11	#28, #29	Perio	#3, #14
Disability	Embarrassed w/ customers	Pain	Tooth loss	I'm concerned..
Readiness	3 month D/L	w/#6-11	w/#6-11	When it fits...
Benefit	Confidence w/ customers	Comfort	Maintain confidence	**Maintain confidence**
Process	New enamel	Restore	Special cleanings	**Brush in mouth**
Fit	Work schedule	Work schedule	Work schedule	**Work schedule**

Disability: Look back at the post-examination Discovery Guide™ and you'll be reminded that her missing teeth #3 and #14 are not a concern for her; they have no negative impact on her life. She is apathetic to this condition (quadrant three). In other words, there is no disability associated with her missing teeth. Consequently, in the Warm-up Dialogue Organizer's first row calling for disability, we cannot state any disability from the patient's point of view, because her missing teeth don't bother her. Chances are excellent, though, that her missing teeth bother you. As professional healthcare providers, we have earned the right to express our opinion about what constitutes the best possible lifetime strategy for dental health. So state the disability in row one from *your* point of view. For example, *"Michelle I'm concerned about your missing teeth."* A simple entry in the Warm-up Dialogue Organizer should remind you—"I'm concerned."

Readiness: Michelle's missing teeth are not a concern for her and are an elective condition. Consequently the appropriate timing for care is up to her—"when she's ready," State this in the Warm-up Dialogue Organizer.

Benefit: Review how we handled stating the benefit of her periodontal treatment. We linked it to the strongest benefit she is seeking—confidence when she's with customers. Thus, the stated benefit of replacing Michelle's missing teeth is to prolong the health of her front teeth. Insert this phrase into the Warm-up Dialogue Organizer—"protect front teeth."

FIGURE 13-14

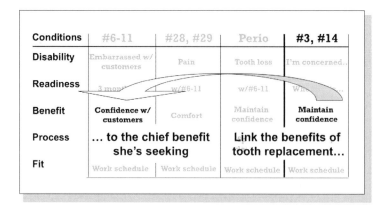

Process: The process of replacing Michelle's missing teeth can be simply stated as replacing her teeth so they don't come out and she can brush them in her mouth. Make the Discovery Guide™ Organizer entry— "brush in mouth."

Fit: As before, the work- and schedule-related fit issues for Michelle are the same regardless of her condition—"work schedule." The Warm-up Dialogue Organizer is now complete. Keep in mind that it's taken longer for you to read how to complete it than it does to actually do it—a few minutes at most. The goal is to help organize your presentation in a way that makes it easy for the patient to understand and easy for you to deliver.

Rehearsal

The Warm-up Dialogue Organizer is a rehearsal tool for you and your team. The word *rehearsal* is typically not in the glossary of terms that dentists use. How many of us rehearse (out loud) our treatment presentations? Not many. We spend more time vacuuming the trunk of our car than we spend on rehearsing one of the most important conversations we have with our patients.

What we've lacked in dentistry are good rehearsal tools and methods. Nobody likes to role-play, yet it is the one thing that can take us from good to great in our presentation impact. I recommend that you use the Warm-up Dialogue Organizer as a rehearsal tool for the Warm-up Dialogue. The organizer has one- and two-word descriptors of the key issues that need to be covered. Practice with a team member who's familiar with the patient. Talk through the rows and columns of the Warm-up Dialogue Organizer several times until you become accustomed to the words and sequence. You'll find that, with rehearsal, you won't have to think too much about the content of the presentation. Instead, you'll be able to connect better with your patient through eye contact and tone of voice. You'll be able to create everything that right-side patients want: you'll sound better, you'll create more of a personal feel to your conversation, and patients will experience a greater sense of relationship with you.

Preparing the Financial Options form

The last step in preparing for the consultation appointment is to complete the Financial Options form **(Figure 13-15)**.

FIGURE 13-15

Financial Options Form

Patient Name: Date:

Estimated fee for your treatment is: $_____
Est. Specialist: $_____
Total Combined: $_____
Less estimated insurance: $_____
Estimated Patient Responsibility: $_____
Payment Options:

1. **Lowest Monthly Payment**
    • No initial payment
    • Payments ranging from 18 to 60 months with payments as affordable as
      $_____ per month which includes a low fixed rate of interest
      Prepayments can be made anytime without penalty
    • Fast, confidential approval by phone 1-888-XXX-XXX or online at their
      secure website www.XXXX.com. Good credit standing required.

2. **3, 6 and 12 Months Interest Free Plan**
    • 12 monthly payments of _____, interest free. ($1,500 minimum)
    • 6 monthly payments of _____, interest free. ($1,000 minimum)
    • 3 monthly payments of _____, interest free. ($300 minimum)

3. **Pay fee as treatment is provided.**
    One-third of the total treatment fee at the beginning of care, one third in the
    middle, and the remaining one-third when the final restorations are inserted

4. **Payment in full (cash or check)**
    • A bookkeeping courtesy of _____% or $_____ is given for direct payment
    in full at the start of treatment, resulting in a one-time payment of
      $_____ .

5. **Other Payment Options**
    • Visa and MasterCard are accepted for payment in full.

Financial Option forms can be customized with your practice letterhead. This form is completed by the financial coordinator and used during the financial discussion at the consultation appointment. We'll discuss the use of this form in the next chapter.

Now that you've treatment planned Michelle, identified essential and elective conditions, completed the Warm-up Dialogue Organizer, rehearsed your Warm-up Dialogue, and prepared the Financial Options form, you're ready for the consultation appointment.

In a Nutshell
Chapter Thirteen—Treatment Planning

- To prepare for the consultation appointment, you will establish the clinical diagnosis and treatment plan, determine essential versus elective conditions relative to her chief condition/disability, organize the Warm-up Dialogue Organizer and rehearse the Warm-up Dialogue, and prepare the Financial Options form.

- *Essential* treatment recommendations are those that are crucial to a favorable long-term result and must be done as soon as possible. *Elective* treatment recommendations, although desirable from an ideal treatment point of view, do not have to be done as soon as possible. Knowing which treatment recommendations are essential or elective is often an important way of helping patients fit treatment into their lives.

- The Warm-up Dialogue Organizer is used to organize the sequence of the *presentation* of treatment recommendations (not treatment sequence). It's also used to structure and rehearse the Warm-up Dialogue so it is easy for the patient to understand and for the dentist or team member to deliver.

- The structure of the Warm-up Dialogue Organizer is: **Disability, Readiness, Benefit, Process,** and **Fit.**

Chapter Fourteen
What If Dentists Worked At Nordstrom?:
The Warm-Up Dialogue

It's midmorning on a Saturday and your husband and kids are away camping. You find your way to your favorite mall and notice that Nordstrom has a sale on women's clothing. You stroll in, take a look around sportswear and end up in eveningwear, where you see an absolutely beautiful dress. You want this dress—now.

Out of the corner of your eye you see a salesman approaching, a former dentist who's going to use everything he learned in dentistry to sell you this dress.

You say, *"Hi, I'm interested in this evening gown. It's beautiful. Do you have it in a size eight?"*

He frowns, eyes your figure and says, *"Well before we talk about the dress, don't you think we should discuss your weight first?"*

You can't believe what you just heard. *"My weight! You want to talk about my weight?"*

"It's not just your weight. There are other things you need to know here," he says, eyeing his manicure.

"Other things? What other things?" you howl.

"Well, first off, we need to do something about your hygiene. Before I sell you any of my clothing, I want to make sure you know how to keep it clean."

"Well, you can just...." and before you can finish your suggestion, he

butts in and says, *"The first thing we'll have you do is watch this videotape on textile manufacturing. Then after the video you'll see our tailor, who'll chart your measurements and go over how to keep your clothes clean. Then I'll be in to tell you what you need."*

"I know what I need. I need this dress!" you shout, as your face turns fire-engine red.

"I'm sorry, but we don't let our customers diagnose themselves. If you're uncomfortable with this policy, then I'll be glad to refer you to a store which will do what you want."

"You don't have to. I'm outta here!" you roar, as you shoulder him into a display of pantyhose.

What if dentists worked at Nordstrom? Many would make it difficult for people to buy things they want by complicating the process. Do you? This chapter shows you how to make it easy for your patients to understand what they need and get what they want.

The Consultation Appointment

Think of the consultation appointment as having three parts: the Warm-up Dialogue, CD-4; the Financial Options Dialogue, CD-5; and the technical case presentation (informed consent) (**Figure 14-1**).

FIGURE 14-1

Consultation Appointment

Warm-up Dialogue CD-4:
offers hope and opens fit/readiness conversation

Financial Options Dialogue CD-5:
total fee, total time, affordable options,
negotiation

Technical Case Presentation:
informed consent

The consultation appointment begins with the Warm-up Dialogue, which usually takes just a few minutes to deliver. Typically, after the patient has heard the Warm-up Dialogue, she asks questions related to fit issues: cost, time, insurance, etc. These questions are answered in the context of the Financial Options Dialogue. Finally, after your patient, your financial coordinator, and you have decided on the scope of care and its financial arrangements and administrative issues, the technical case presentation is done, fulfilling the medical/legal consent aspect of the consultation appointment.

The Warm-up Dialogue (CD-4)

The intention of the Warm-up Dialogue is three-fold:
- Provide a simple layman's description of treatment recommendations
- Give the patient hope that the disability can be relieved.
- Reopen the conversation about how the recommended treatment fits into the patient's life.

At this point in the relationship with Michelle, we've planned her clinical care, identified essential and elective conditions, completed the Warm-up Dialogue Organizer, rehearsed the Warm-up Dialogue, and completed the Financial Options form. We're now ready for the consultation appointment.

Michelle is a typical patient in that she has conditions with and without disabilities. She's aware of her conditions because we used the Discovery Guide™ Dialogues. However, we're not certain how our treatment recommendations will fit into her life, or her readiness to treat all her conditions. We started the conversation about fit issues at the previous appointment using the Advocacy Dialogue. As a result of that dialogue we had a discussion about ballpark fees, financial arrangements, and time in treatment. We know going into the consultation appointment that she has a good idea of the circumstances and requirements of complete dental treatment. What we don't know is what she is really ready to do. The Warm-up Dialogue is designed to satisfy this uncertainty.

The Warm-up Dialogue is designed to be short (less than three or four minutes) and sweet (not dwelling on technical details). Its intention is to "warm up" the relationship, give the patient hope, and build a positive and optimistic conversational tone.

The Warm-up Dialogue is not intended to meet the test for informed consent. It is not designed to explain the technical aspects of care. Attempts to get into the technical aspects cause this dialogue to lose focus and dilute its intention. Do not educate the patient in this dialogue.

Do not educate the patient in this dialogue.

We want the patient to be in an optimistic, positive frame of mind for many reasons, the chief one being that at the end of the Warm-up Dialogue the patient will ask, *"How much does this cost?"* Conversations about fit issues always are easier for everyone when buoyant moods prevail. (Think back to Chapter Four on the Spectrum of Appeal™ and remember why it's important to create broad appeal before asking for action.)

Find a quiet, peaceful place. To start the Warm-up Dialogue, find a quiet and peaceful place. I like using a private consultation area or an operatory that has a door on it to keep out the sounds and interruptions. Like the initial appointment for the right-side patient, the consultation appointment is best scheduled as a first appointment in the morning or right after lunch.

Start with a question. After the patient is seated in your consulta-tion area, begin the dialogue with a question similar to, "*Michelle, since we last talked about your care, have any questions or concerns come up for you?*" We want to start the conversation with things that are important to the patient. It's good leadership to first address those issues important to the patient, then present your recommendations. If a patient has a significant unaddressed concern, she will be a far better listener if you can satisfy her curiosity/concerns upfront. Chances are good that most of the patient's concerns at the beginning of the consultation appointment relate to fit issues. If so, reassure her that you'll get to those issues immediately.

> *It's good leadership to first address those issues important to the patient, then present your recommendations.*

The Warm-up Dialogue is structured to make it easy to deliver and easy for the patient to understand. In the previous chapter, we completed the Warm-up Dialogue organizer and rehearsed the Warm-up Dialogue. **Figure 14-2** shows the Warm-up Dialogue organizer completed for Michelle.

FIGURE 14-2

Conditions	#6-11	#28, 29	Perio	#3,#14
Disability	Embarrassed w/ customers	Pain	Tooth loss	I'm concerned..
Readiness	3 month D/L	w/#6-11	w/#6-11	When it fits...
Benefit	Confidence w/ customers	Comfort	Maintain confidence	Maintain confidence
Process	New enamel	Restore	Special cleanings	Brush in mouth
Fit	Work schedule	Work schedule	Work schedule	Work schedule

Remember, we discuss her conditions in the columns from left to right. We present the structure of the Warm-up Dialogue in the rows from top to bottom (**Figures 14-3** and **14-4**).

FIGURE 14-3

Presentation sequence				
Conditions	**#6-11**	**#28, 29**	**Perio**	**#3,#14**
Disability	Embarrassed w/ customers	Pain	Tooth loss	I'm concerned...
Readiness	3 month D/L	w/#6-11	w/#6-11	When it fits...
Benefit	Confidence w/ customers	Comfort	Maintain confidence	Maintain confidence
Process	New enamel	Restore	Special cleanings	Brush in mouth
Fit	Work schedule	Work schedule	Work schedule	Work schedule

FIGURE 14-4

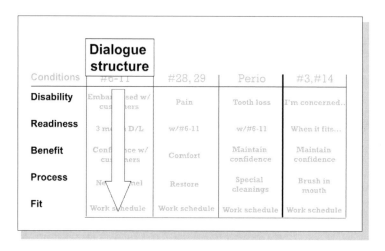

Dialogue structure				
Conditions	#6-11	#28, 29	Perio	#3,#14
Disability	Embarrassed w/ customers	Pain	Tooth loss	I'm concerned...
Readiness	3 month D/L	w/#6-11	w/#6-11	When it fits...
Benefit	Confidence w/ customers	Comfort	Maintain confidence	Maintain confidence
Process	New enamel	Restore	Special cleanings	Brush in mouth
Fit	Work schedule	Work schedule	Work schedule	Work schedule

Here's the entire Warm-up Dialogue for Michelle. The cued key phrases prompted by the Discovery Guide organizer are in bold type. Also notice in this dialogue that the fit issues for #28, #29, and perio are not repeated. When multiple conditions exist, do not repeat fit issues following every process. You want to avoid sounding overly repetitive.

"Michelle, I know you're **embarrassed** by the appearance of your upper front teeth when **talking with customers**. I know that you have an important **black-tie event coming up in three months** and you'd like to be finished with your care by then. After reviewing your photographs and models, I know we can make you feel very **confident in the appearance** of your teeth by removing the dark and yellowed enamel and chipped edges and replacing them with a **new enamel-like material**. This usually takes three appointments. I know this is **your busy season** at the art gallery, so let's find a time when this makes the most sense for your **work schedule**."

"At the examination appointment, you mentioned you're **aggravated by the discomfort** on your lower right back teeth. **While we're working with your upper front teeth**, I recommend we get these teeth **comfortable** for chewing and changes in temperature. We do this by **restoring** these teeth to their natural shape and color."

"The last time we talked, I mentioned the **infection in your gums** and you expressed a **concern** about it. I recommend that while we're in the **process of fixing your front teeth** we eliminate the gum infection to **maintain the confidence you'll have in the appearance** of your front teeth. We do this through a series of **very thorough cleanings** and the use of some medications."

"Michelle, the last thing I'd like to mention is an area that I know you're not concerned about—your missing upper molars. Although you're not concerned I want you to know that **I am concerned**, and **when you're ready** my recommendation is to replace the missing back teeth. The reason I say this is that back teeth protect the **front teeth** from heavy chewing. I want to protect the health and **appearance of** your **front teeth** as long as possible. The way we'd replace the back teeth is with teeth that **you would brush right in your mouth**. They would look and feel exactly like natural teeth."

"I know I've made a lot of recommendations to you. Of course, let's make sure we do this dentistry for you in a way that fits into your work schedule and budget. What questions do you have for me?"

When you ask, "What questions do you have for me?" most of the time the patient will ask questions related to fit—fee, time in treatment, financial arrangements. These questions are answered in the next chapter, on the Financial Options Dialogue, CD-5.

Warm-up Dialogue Debriefing

Keep it short and conversational. The Warm-up Dialogue example above takes about two-and-a-half minutes to deliver. You can use the Warm-up Dialogue organizer as well as the patient record as a memory jogger during the dialogue. This dialogue doesn't have to be memorized; in fact, it's better if it isn't—it's important that you stay connected to your patient during this dialogue. That means sustaining normal friendly eye contact, smiling, and speaking in a conversational (not clinical) tone. Use of visual aids, radiographs, and other props are not part of this process (save them for the technical case presentation coming up later in this appointment). Part of the goal of the Warm-up Dialogue is to move past the clinical aspect and into the financial options aspect. Let's determine what dentistry fits into the patient's life before we spend a lot of time and energy explaining clinical issues.

The Discovery Guide

Figure 14-5 shows how the Warm-up Dialogue looks when put on the Spectrum of Appeal.

FIGURE 14-5

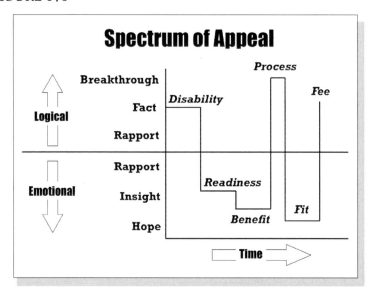

You'll notice in **Figure 14-5** how the great majority of the appeal of the Warm-up Dialogue is in the emotional spectrum (10% logic, 90% emotion). The structural elements of readiness, benefit, and fit all are emotionally appealing. **Figure 14-6** represents Michele's Warm-up Dialogue with the key words on the Spectrum of Appeal.

FIGURE 14-6

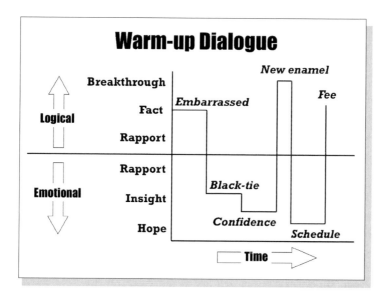

You begin the Warm-up Dialogue in the blue spectrum by stating what you know about the patient's **disability**—how her dental problems are affecting her life—*"Michelle, I know that you're embarrassed about the appearance of your front teeth."*

Then you shift into the red spectrum with a **readiness** statement—the appropriateness of the timing of her care—*"I know you have an important black tie affair in three months..."*

Now you deepen the emotional appeal by stating a specific, strong **benefit**—*"After studying your case, I feel really good that we can completely restore the confidence you have in your appearance."*

Shift back to the blue spectrum and give the patient an easy-to-understand idea of the **process** of fixing her teeth—*"We'll replace the dark and chipped enamel from your front teeth with a new enamel-like material."*

Here's where you'll need to discipline yourself and not get deep into technical details. If you do, the Warm-up Dialogue loses its focus of providing hope.

Return to a deep level of emotional appeal by stating your willingness to *fit* the cost and time factors of restoring her teeth into the realities of her life circumstance—*"Let's make sure we can fit this into your work and travel schedule."* Fit issues are very red spectrum for the patient and give the patient hope and demonstrate that you're her advocate. This is a very powerful, positive moment for the patient and it's presented immediately prior to quoting the blue spectrum fee. **When presenting fees, the best emotional state for the patient to be in is one of feeling hope.**

This case presentation model is *not* designed to provide informed consent. Rather, it's designed to create an appealing process for presenting care that inspires hope and opens the conversation about how to fit the dentistry the patient needs into the circumstances of her life.

Outcomes Versus Inputs

You'll discover that when you present care from your advocacy role that your consultations with the patient take on more leader-like qualities. Advocates talk in terms of outcomes—*comfort, confidence, peace of mind,* etc. Providers talk in terms of inputs—*crowns, bridges, implants.* For right-side dentistry, presenting care from the perspective of preferred outcomes far outperforms presenting care from the perspective of inputs. Outcomes are far easier for the patient to understand and help them to see the light at the end of their tunnel. Talking in terms of outcomes provides a positive resonant energy patients need to endure the rigors of right-side dentistry.

Essential and Elective Conditions

In the previous chapter we discussed essential and elective conditions. Periodontal treatment is an essential condition relative to treating Michelle's chief condition, #6-11. Replacing missing teeth #3 and #14 are elective at this time, relative to treating #6-11.

How elective and essential conditions are handled during the Warm-up Dialogue depend on where they exist relative to the post-examination Discovery Guide. **Figure 14-7** shows the post-examination Discovery Guide for Michelle.

FIGURE 14-7

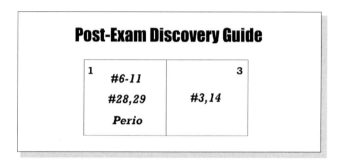

We know that Michelle is concerned about #6–11, #28, #29, and her periodontal conditions; therefore, they're in quadrant one. Because she is not concerned (no disability) about missing teeth #3 and #14, this condition is in quadrant three.

Figure 14-8 is a table relating essential and elective conditions to quadrant three conditions (no disability) and quadrant one conditions (disability).

FIGURE 14-8

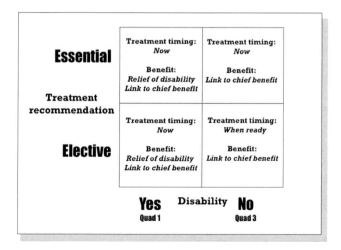

Essential and Elective Conditions With Disability

In the Warm-up Dialogue for essential and elective conditions with disabilities, the recommendation for the timing of their treatment is *now*—disability is present and patients usually are anxious for relief. When stating the benefit of the treatment, link it to the chief benefit as well as to relieving the disability. In Michelle's case, periodontal care is an essential condition with disability. As we've seen in the previous chapter, its benefit is linked to maintaining the confidence she'll have in the appearance of her teeth—chief benefit—as well as removing her concern about tooth loss from gum disease (**Figure 14-9**).

FIGURE 14-9

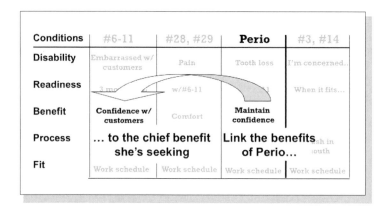

Conditions	#6-11	#28, #29	**Perio**	#3, #14
Disability	Embarrassed w/ customers	Pain	Tooth loss	I'm concerned..
Readiness	3 mo	w/#6-11		When it fits...
Benefit	Confidence w/ customers	Comfort	Maintain confidence	
Process	... to the chief benefit she's seeking		Link the benefits of Perio...	sh in outh
Fit	Work schedule	Work schedule	Work schedule	Work schedule

Essential Conditions With No Disability

There are many right-side patients who have essential conditions with no disability, and they are *not* interested in treatment. Examples of this are patients wanting crown and bridgework but who aren't interested in having the periodontal disease treated; patients with severe attrition with end-to-end occlusions who want their anterior teeth restored but don't want their posterior teeth restored; or patients who want cosmetic dentistry but aren't interested in treating the periapical abscesses. In the Warm-up Dialogue for cases where quadrant two *essential* conditions exist:

- The disability is stated from the dentist's point of view (i.e., *"I'm concerned..."*)
- The readiness (timing) of care is linked to the timing of the chief condition (i.e., *"While we're treating your front teeth..."*).

- The benefit is tied to supporting the chief benefit (i.e., *"Treating the abscesses protects the health of the front teeth and the confidence you'll have in your appearance"*).

When patients are adamantly against treating essential conditions, and further explanation and patient education do not change their decision, then treating the chief condition is not within the standard of care and should not be provided. Patients in this category are not ready for care. (Refer to the dialogue "Taking No for an Answer" in the next chapter.)

In the Warm-up Dialogue for cases where quadrant three *elective* conditions exist:
- The disability is stated from the dentist's point of view (i.e., *"I'm concerned..."*).
- The readiness (timing) of care is at the patient's discretion (i.e., *"When you're ready..."*).
- The benefit is tied to supporting the chief benefit (i.e., *"Replacing your missing back teeth will ensure the longevity of your front teeth and the confidence you'll have in your appearance"*) (**Figure 14-10**).

FIGURE 14-10

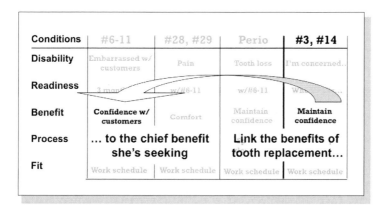

When a condition is quadrant three and elective, its presentation during the Warm-up Dialogue is prefaced with the acknowledgment of the patient's lack of concern: *"Michelle, the last thing I'd like to mention is*

an area that I know you're not concerned about–your missing upper molars." Additionally, we let her know that the timing to replace her missing teeth is her decision, *"...when you're ready."*

When discussing elective conditions, your language in the Warm-up Dialogue is less assertive. Offer patients more choices relative to elective conditions–remember that all elective conditions are more subject to a patient's fit and readiness issues. If there is only so much dentistry that can fit into the patient's life at this time, make sure it's the essential conditions. If the elective conditions fit too, great. If not, you can treat elective conditions when the patient is ready.

By acknowledging her lack of concern and giving her control over the timing of treatment, we are:
- Making a clear distinction between what care needs to be done now, and what care can wait.
- Honoring her point of view.
- Demonstrating we're listening to her concerns.
- Helping her find ways to fit her dentistry into her life.
- Creating opportunities for future treatment.

Points of Emphasis
Let's revisit the Warm-up Dialogue organizer and look at where the points of emphasis are (**Figure 14-11**).

FIGURE 14-11

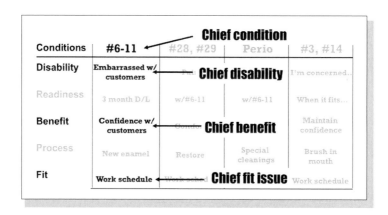

The bulk of the emphasis during the Warm-up Dialogue is on the disability, benefit, and fit issues. Almost no emphasis is given to the process. Be crystal-clear with right-side patients that you're aware of their chief conditions, chief disability, chief benefit, and chief fit issues. Treatment of all other conditions and their benefits call back to supporting the chief benefit and must be subordinate to chief fit issues.

Be crystal-clear with right-side patients that you're aware of their chief conditions, chief disability, chief benefit, and chief fit issues.

Contrast this with the traditional case presentation approach. How much emphasis is given to process? Almost all of it. In fact, during the traditional case presentation process, the disability, benefit, and fit issues are rarely mentioned. For right-side patients you must know and emphasize disability, benefit, and fit issues. Without that emphasis you'll focus on process and technical issues that do not support the objectives of the Warm-up Dialogue—providing hope and reopening the issues of fit and readiness.

Dr. Mark V. Davis, of Clearwater, Florida, is a Board Certified Diplomate examiner and past president of the American Board of Oral Implantology, thinks that getting into too much technical details with patients is almost always a problem. He says;

"It took me a while to understand how to best lead patients into accepting complex care treatment plans. In the early years of my practice I did a lot operative and quadrant dentistry. As long as I was not dealing with significant dental disease, I had a very high level of predictability.

Now it's clear as the complexity of care increases that patients vary widely relative to their treatment tolerance, healing capacity, homecare, and recall faithfulness. Consequently, the exact course and outcome of treatment is not always totally certain. If I present a treatment plan carved in stone, and I encountered variables that require me to modify my treatment plan, this is an opportunity for the patient to lose confidence in me and may cause a failure in the relationship.

Over the years I've developed a way to give a patient confidence in my ability to get them to the best place they can be with their given circumstances, within the limitation of dental materials, and do it through a complex series of events that are not completely predictable. In other words I do not sell on the basis of the technical details of the case, I sell myself.

I focus on making sure the patient understands their problem, understands the things we could possibly could do for them, and have them come to the belief that whatever their condition is, that I have the skills, understanding, and knowledge that I am able to bring them to the best possible level of dental health that they can achieve given the limitations of their circumstances. I point out to the patient that it is impossible to know the precise pathway we're going to follow in order to get them to the best possible place. We'll discover along the way what we need to do to get them to the best place possible.

When I begin a complex treatment plan, by the third or fourth appointment I know more about what would work best for this patient than I know from even following a very thorough examination. Change is good when it benefits the patient and is based on a deeper understanding of the case. Once you begin treatment, the pathway of treatment evolves.

So the answer to your inquiry on how I sell complex dentistry is this: I don't sell based on treatment details, I sell myself."

The next chapter, the Financial Options Dialogue, CD-5, addresses how to talk about money. When you've prepared your patient and yourself well through the use of the Warm-up Dialogue, you've made it easy to be successful at the Financial Options Dialogue.

In a Nutshell
Chapter Fourteen—The Warm-up Dialogue

- Think of the consultation appointment as having three parts—the Warm-up Dialogue, the Financial Options Dialogue, and the technical case presentation (informed consent).

- The intentions of the Warm-up Dialogue are to: provide a simple description of treatment recommendations, give the patient hope that the disability can be relieved, and reopen the conversation about how the recommended treatment fits into the patient's life.

- The Warm-up Dialogue is not intended to meet the test for informed consent or to explain the technical aspects of care.

- The dialogue does not have to be memorized; in fact, it's better if it isn't.

- The bulk of the emphasis during the Warm-up Dialogue is on the disability, benefit, and fit issues. Almost no emphasis is given to the process.

Chapter Fifteen

The Discovery Guide™:

New and Improved Version

E verything you're read about the Discover Guide™ was written in 2005 with some slight adjustments along the way. In this revised edition of my book you're reading now (2017) I'm going to introduce the most current version of the Discovery Guide™ and its associated processes. Keep in mind the foundational concepts of the original version are still 100% valid. In fact, learning the foundational concepts in the previous chapters is a huge advantage to you as you're introduced to the new Discovery Guide™.

To facilitate understanding the new Discovery Guide™ let's look at a new case study – Christine. Here is a summary of Christine's clinical and personal history.

Case Study

Name: Christine
Age: 49
Profession: Public Relations

Telephone and In-office Interview

Christine is 49 years old and is a public relations (PR) professional. Her employer, Providence Hospital, has her traveling to all major hospitals in the western US where she collaborates with other PR professionals. She's married, has three grown daughters, and her husband is a contractor who works for Myerson Homes.

She's concerned about a sharp edge on a broken tooth on her lower right side. When asked about how it gets in her way, she explained that it interferes with her speech. It's a big problem for her at work.

When asked about other concerns, she mentioned an on-and-off ache in the back of her mouth on the left and right side. She thought it might be her wisdom teeth and the cause of her mouth odor and a bad taste in her mouth.

From further inquiry into her concerns, she mentioned that her previous dentist had told her that she had minor tooth decay. She doesn't remember which teeth. She has no other concerns.

Christine is remodeling her kitchen, has a daughter getting married in 5 months, another daughter in college, and one in high school getting ready for college.

The Discovery Guide™

A companion to the Four Chiefs™ is the Discovery Guide™. It's a two-sided form and one of its functions (side one) is to document the Four Chiefs™ conversation. Side one can also be used as a guide to providers during the Four Chiefs™ conversation. Either during the Four Chiefs™ conversation or immediately after providers or team members document what was discovered about patients on side one. Keep in mind additional patient discovery can occur during the entire new patient process. Stay mindful of Four Chiefs™ discoveries and document them as they occur.

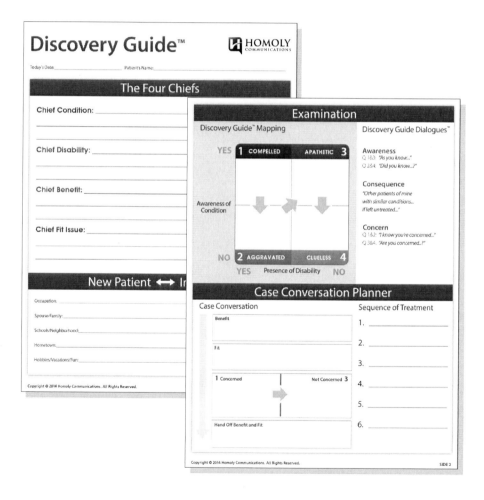

Christine's Discovery Guide™ - Side One

Here's side one of the Discovery Guide™ completed for our case study Christine. Once completed it can be scanned and put into providers' practice management software. It's a good idea to update side one at each recall visit for the same reasons providers update periodontal charting and medical histories; things change in patients' lives.

You'll see later in this program how the information on side one is used to connect with and influence Christine to make good dental health care decisions and accept provider treatment recommendations.

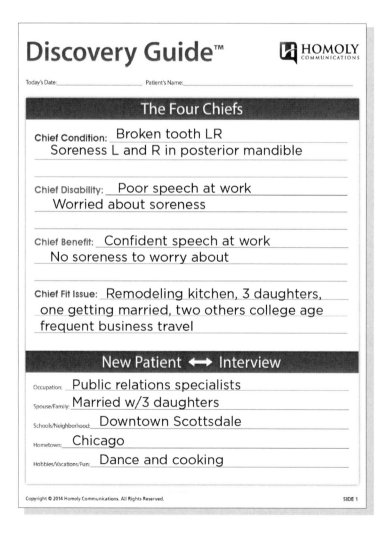

Discovery Guide™   HOMOLY COMMUNICATIONS

Today's Date:_____   Patient's Name:_____

The Four Chiefs

Chief Condition: Broken tooth LR
Soreness L and R in posterior mandible

Chief Disability: Poor speech at work
Worried about soreness

Chief Benefit: Confident speech at work
No soreness to worry about

Chief Fit Issue: Remodeling kitchen, 3 daughters,
one getting married, two others college age
frequent business travel

New Patient ⟷ Interview

Occupation: Public relations specialists
Spouse/Family: Married w/3 daughters
Schools/Neighborhood: Downtown Scottsdale
Hometown: Chicago
Hobbies/Vacations/Fun: Dance and cooking

Sequence of Treatment Rarely is the Sequence of Influence

Most providers start the patient education process immediately after the initial examination in the form of the post examination discussion. Most often it's done chairside. Providers reveal conditions to patients and often offer treatment recommendations during this discussion. The sequence of this discussion is usually determined by the sequence of treatment starting with soft tissue and periodontal considerations, then onto endodontic, restorative, and prosthetic treatment recommendations. All of this is done with the belief that educating patients is influencing them.

There is a more influential way to structure the post examination discussion. It's called the Sequence of Influence and it is assembled using side two of the Discovery Guide™.

The Sequence of Influence

The Sequence of Influence is developed using side two of the Discovery Guide™. The top half is used during the examination and charting process and the bottom half for assembly and delivery of the case conversation.

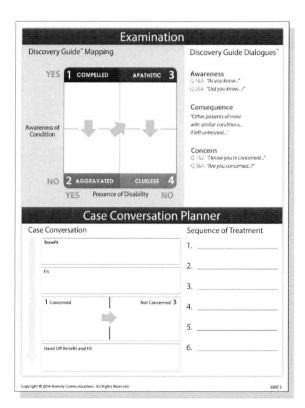

Here's the top half of the Discovery Guide™. It is divided into four quadrants. Each quadrant describes the conditions within it. Quadrant one are conditions which patients have awareness and disability. Quadrant two are conditions which patients are unaware but are experiencing disability. Quadrant three are conditions which patients are aware but are not experiencing disability. Quadrant four are conditions which patients are unaware and are not experiencing disability.

For Christine, our case study, her conditions are documented in their appropriate Discovery Guide™ quadrants. This documentation process is called Mapping. In contrast to charting which is documenting conditions in patients' clinical record, Mapping is documenting the same conditions on the Discovery Guide™. Charting and Mapping are done during the examination process.

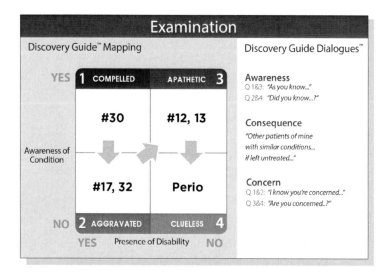

Mapping

Tooth #30 is Mapped in quadrant #1 because Christine is aware of her cracked tooth and it bothers her (disability).

Teeth #'s 17 and 32 are Mapped in quadrant #2 because Christine is not aware of the clinical problem in the area but it is bothering her (disability).

Teeth #'s 12 and 13 are Mapped in quadrant #3 because Christine is aware of the presence of tooth decay but has no symptoms (disability).

Periodontal disease is Mapped in quadrant #4 because Christine is not aware of her soft tissue issues nor does she have any symptoms/problems (disability).

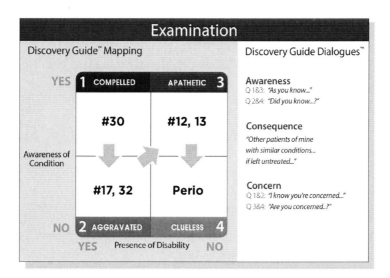

The Sequence of Influence is the order in which providers discuss patients' conditions during the post examination discussion, i.e., which conditions do providers discuss first, second, third, etc. **This sequence is rarely the sequence of treatment**.

The Sequence of Influence is based on human nature; patients are most interested and influenced by discussion of conditions that are bothersome. They are far less interested in discussion of conditions that are not. For patients to be influenced, they first must be interested enough to listen. A big mistake many providers make during post examination discussions is to begin this discussion with conditions in quadrants #'s 3 and 4. Instead have post examination discussions in the sequence of quadrants #'s 1, 2 ,3, then 4. This is the sequence patients will listen to and be most influenced by. It is The Sequence of Influence. It is rarely the sequence of treatment. The sequence of treatment is part of informed consent and patient education which come later in the new patient appointment.

.

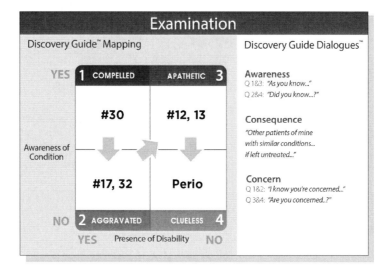

During the post examination discussion done in the Sequence of Influence patients will be made aware of all their conditions. Providers will discover which conditions patients are concerned about and those they are not. This is done by addressing each condition's consequences if left untreated and whether patients are concerned about those consequences.

In Christine's case study let's assume she is concerned about #'s 30, 17 and 32, and her gum condition. She is not concerned about the early decay in teeth #'s 12 and 13.

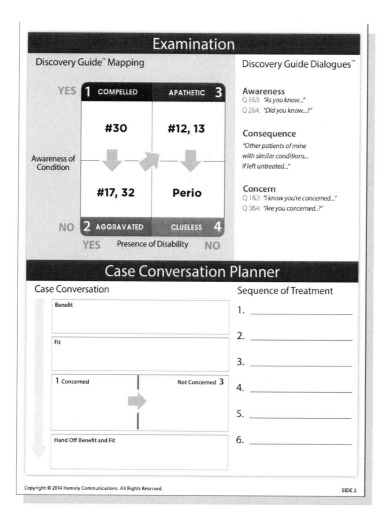

After providers have discovered which conditions patients are concerned and not concerned about, they are documented in the Case Conversation area in the bottom half of the Discovery Guide™. The distinction, concerned vs. not concerned, is an important one. During Case Conversation, treatment recommendations for concerned conditions are presented differently than non concerned conditions. You'll learn more about this distinction later in this program.

The remaining portion of the bottom half of the Discovery Guide™ is completed while providers prepare to present treatment recommendation during the Case Conversation. Usually Case Conversation occurs during the initial appointment for left-side patients and during the second appointment for right-side patients.

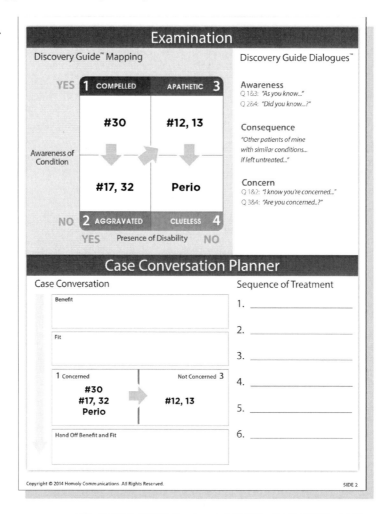

SIDE 2

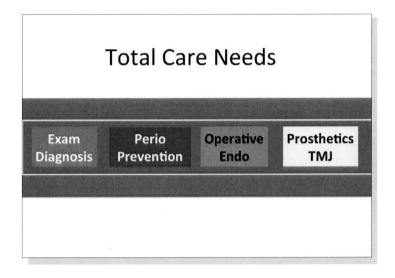

Providers Have the Responsibility of Offering Total Care Needs

Patients' Total Care Needs is the clinical care to restore optimal structure, function, comfort, esthetics, and phonetics. In many practices Total Care Needs include breathing conditions and facial cosmetics. Most providers acknowledge they have the responsibility of informing patients of all conditions along with treatment recommendations including the benefits, risks, and treatment alternatives. In fact informing patients of their Total Care Needs along with treatment recommendations is an ethical and legal requirement. Unfortunately many providers cite the leading stressor in their practice is offering Total Care Needs to patients who are not concerned about some/all of their conditions.

The source of the stress comes from the fear of patients abandoning their practice due to the "sticker shock" brought on by the fees associated with Total Care Needs. The repeated stressful experience of patients rejecting Total Care Needs make providers shy away from presenting Total Care Needs. Instead treatment plans presented by many providers offer far less care than Total Care Needs and center on treatment for chief complaints. This is not good for patients, providers, or the profession. Side two of the Discovery Guide™ eliminates the stress for providers and patients when offering Total Care Needs.

Here's how.

Presenting Total Care Needs

Here's the bottom half of side two of the Discovery Guide™ for Christine. During the post examination discussion it's determined she is interested in treating #30, #'s 17 and 32, and her periodontal condition. She is currently not interested in treating #'s 12 and 13.

The technique required to recommend Total Care Needs to Christine without stressing her or providers is to preface all treatment recommendations acknowledging Christine's concern or lack of for each condition.

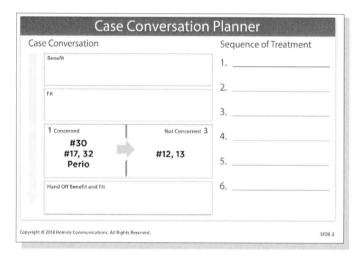

By acknowledging Christine's concern or lack of for each condition removes perceived sales pressure from provider recommendations. It gives providers complete confidence in recommending care for conditions patients are not concerned about with no fear of patient rejection or practice abandonment.

Here's an example dialogue for our case study Christine.

"Christine, I know you're concerned about the cracked molar on your lower right side. I recommend we...(offer treatment). Additionally you expressed interest in relieving the discomfort in the back of you mouth. I recommend we...(offer treatment). As for your gum health you're concerned about I recommend we... (offer treatment). The last thing I want to talk about is something I know you're not concerned about. That is the early tooth decay on your upper left side. Even though you're not concerned, I am, and when you're ready I recommend we...(offer treatment)."

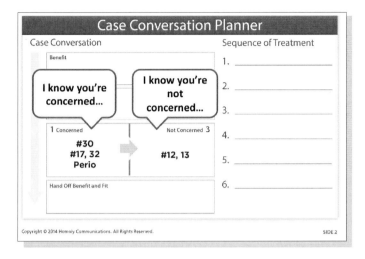

The phrase *"...and when you're ready..."* in this dialogue keeps treatment options open for Christine in the future with no sales pressure on her or stress on providers.

By acknowledging concern or lack of concern for conditions and adopting a *"when you're ready"* attitude for conditions patients are not yet ready, allows providers to offer Total Care Needs with complete confidence.

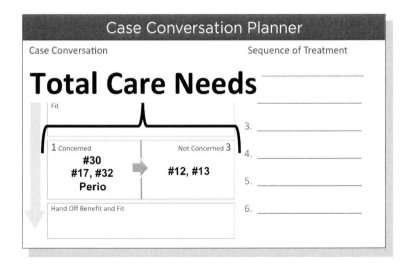

Influence Requires Rehearsal

The Case Conversation Planner is the rehearsal tool for Presenting Total Care Needs care to patients. You've already populated it with concerned and not concerned conditions. Following the examination and post examination discussion and before the Case Conversation, providers will complete the Case Conversation Planner. For left-side patients this will occur during the initial appointment. For right-side patients it may be better to reappoint patients to give providers time to treatment plan and rehearse.

The first step to completing the Case Conversation Planner you've already done; documenting concerned and not concerned conditions.

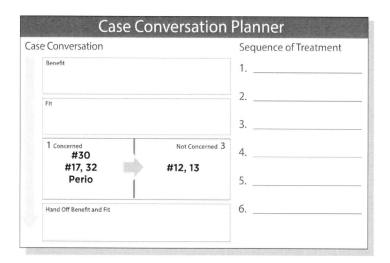

The Case Conversation Planner

The second step in completing the Case Conversation Planner is to enter patients' benefits. In Christine's case it's confidence with speech at work. Providers learn Chief Benefit(s) during The Four Chiefs™.

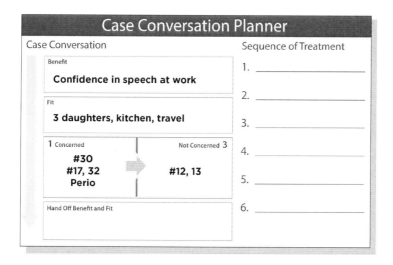

The third step is to enter patients' fit issues. For Christine it's her three daughters, kitchen remodeling, and travel.

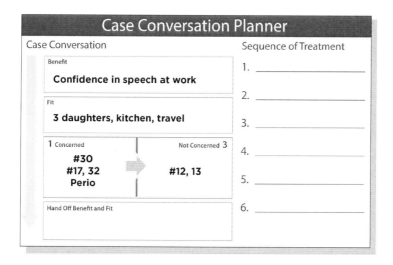

The last step is to enter a summary of benefit and fit issues. This may seem redundant but it's important that patients and treatment coordinators/financial arrangement team members hear and understand the benefits and fit issues related to dental care.

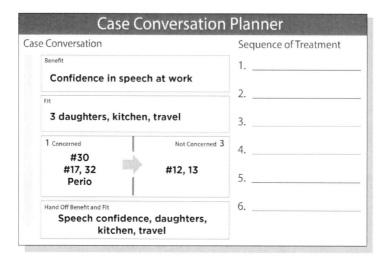

Here's a review of assembling the Case Conversation Planner.

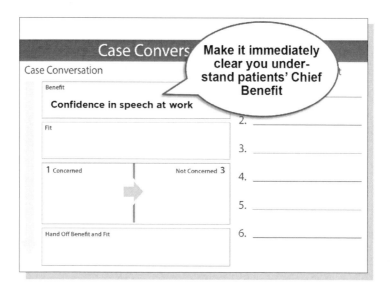

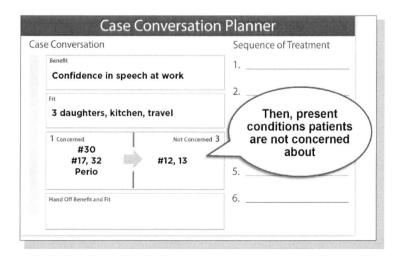

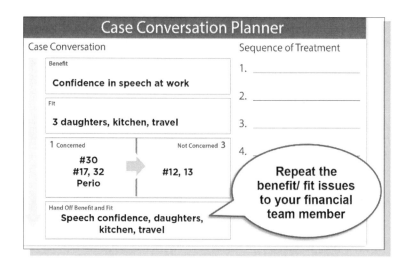

With this Case Conversation Planner completed and adequately rehearsed, providers have the privilege and responsibility of presenting Total Care Needs with total confidence.

Here's the Case Conversation with Christine.

"Christine I know you're main concern is getting comfortable and confident with your speech, especially at work. I know we can do that for you. I also know you have your hands full with your 3 daughters, remodeling your kitchen, and all your travel. I bring this up because we need to decide how soon you want to proceed with care. In a minute let's talk about how you need to best fit all this into your life. I know your main concern is the broken tooth on your lower right side. We can rebuild this tooth by removing all the broken enamel and replacing it with a new enamel like material. For the discomfort in back of your jaws I recommend you have these wisdom teeth removed. I'll refer you to Dr. Sullivan. She's an oral surgeon we have a lot of confidence in. You'll be safe and comfortable during the procedure. You mentioned concern about the gum infection. I'll introduce you to our hygienist Rita. She's terrific and she'll help you eliminate the existing infection and show you how to prevent it from returning. The last thing I found during your exam was the early tooth decay on your upper left side. I know you're not concerned about it and I understand. Even though you're not concerned, I am, and when you're ready I'd recommend we remove the early decay and replace it with tooth colored fillings."

Addressing the treatment coordinator/financial arrangements team member, "Joy, *as you heard Christine is interested in being more comfortable with her speech especially at work. She also has a busy schedule and family life. Spend time with her and help her figure out how to best fit all this into her budget and schedule.*"

Case Conversation Planner

Case Conversation	Sequence of Treatment
Benefit **Confidence in speech at work**	1. _____
	2. _____
Fit **3 daughters, kitchen, travel**	3. _____
1 Concerned Not Concerned 3 **#30** **#17, 32** **#12, 13** **Perio**	4. _____
	5. _____
Hand Off Benefit and Fit **Speech confidence, daughters,** **kitchen, travel**	6. _____

At this point I'll let Christine and Joy talk about fees, insurance, payments, and appointments. Following their conversation, assuming Christine has accepted total care or a portion of it and financial arrangements/insurance issues are settled, providers return to the conversation with Christine and present informed consent, including benefits, risks, and alternative to care along with the sequence of treatment.

In a Nutshell
Chapter Fifteen—The Discovery Guide™ - New and Improved Version

- Learning the fundamentals of the original version will make it easier learning the newer version.

- Side one of the Discovery Guide™ is used to document the Four Chiefs™ and record patients' personal details.

- The Case Conversation Planner on side two of the Discovery Guide™ provides a template for an efficient Case Conversation.

- Patients' Total Care Needs is the clinical care to restore optimal structure, function, comfort, esthetics, and phonetics. In many practices Total Care Needs include breathing conditions and facial cosmetics.

- The Case Conversation Planner is designed to present Patients' Total Care Needs.

Chapter Sixteen
Money Talks:
The Financial Options Dialogue

Early in my practice I would rather take a fork in the eye than discuss money with patients. In fact I had a subtle way of slipping out of the consult room just before the patient was about to ask me about fees. I'd say, *"Mrs. Bamber, why don't I get my office manager, Joy, in here and she can go over financial arrangements with you,"* and I'd high-tail it back into an operatory to drill a tooth.

Over time, however, I learned that financial discussions don't have to be tough... and so can you. Money is one of the most emotional topics in dentistry. Talking about it intelligently without creating stress and contests demonstrates an extremely high level of empathy and common sense that patients love. To avoid financial conversations with patients is to avoid great opportunities to build strong relationships that endure. This chapter is about making it easy to talk about money in a way that makes *everyone* comfortable.

The Financial Options Dialogue

The Financial Options Dialogue, CD-5, is the second step in the consultation appointment. It immediately follows the Warm-up Dialogue **(Figure 15-1)**.

FIGURE 16-1

Consultation Appointment

Warm-up Dialogue CD-4:
offers hope and opens fit/readiness conversation

Financial Options Dialogue CD-5:
total fee, total time, affordable options,
negotiation

Technical Case Presentation:
informed consent

The intentions of the Financial Options Dialogue are to:
- Quote the total treatment fee (including estimated specialists' fees).
- State the total time in treatment.
- Discuss the financial arrangement options.
- Agree on the scope of dental treatment and when to begin care.

During the Warm-up Dialogue, the Financial Options Dialogue, and subsequent negotiations, it can be helpful to have your treatment coordinator/financial coordinator present. In fact, if you have a strong team member in this role, she can have these dialogues with the patient. The only part of the consultation appointment you can't delegate to her is the technical case presentation/informed consent.

Immediately following the Warm-up Dialogue, you'll say something like, *"Michelle, I know we've talked about lot of things. What questions or comments do you have for me?"* That usually triggers the "fit" questions: *"How much does it cost?" "How long will it take?" "How much will my insurance pay?"* Remember, the patient already knows the ballpark estimates of costs, time, and financial arrangements as a result of the Advocacy Dialogue at the initial appointment. There should be no great "sticker shock" experiences during the Financial Options Dialogue. If there are, then you didn't do the job during the initial appointment and the Advocacy Dialogue.

When the patient asks fit questions, immediately go into the Financial Options Dialogue. There are three parts: total fee, total time in care, and financial arrangements.   Here's an example of the Financial Options Dialogue for Michelle:

"Michelle, the total fee for your treatment is $17,000. It will take us about three months from start to finish. We have some affordable options for you. Most patients enjoy beginning care with no initial payment, and then making monthly payments. We've estimated your monthly payments to be $xxx."

"We also have a twelve-month, no-interest payment option of $xxx a month."

"Another financial option for you is to make an initial payment of one-third when we begin care, one-third in the middle, and the final third as we finish your treatment."

"Or if you'd like to take care of the fee when you begin your treatment, we offer a bookkeeping courtesy of xxx percent. That means you'll save xxx dollars, for a total treatment fee of xxx."

"Michelle, which one of these plans is best for you?"

Notice that the dialogue has three distinct elements: total fee, total time in care, and financial options. Don't dilute the dialogue with fillers like *"...that's a good question,"* or apologies, *"...I know this sounds expensive."*

It's best to accompany your Financial Options Dialogue with a financial options form **(Figure 15-2)**. This **makes it easy** for the patient to follow along with your options and gives the person a record of your conversation to take home.

This form is completed prior to the consultation appointment. If decisions are made during the Financial Options Dialogue that are not reflected on the financial options form, make those corrections on a new form.

FIGURE 16-2

Financial Options Form

Patient Name: Date:

Estimated fee for your treatment is: $_____
Est. Specialist: $_____
Total Combined: $_____
Less estimated insurance: $_____
Estimated Patient Responsibility: $_____
Payment Options:

1. **Lowest Monthly Payment**
    • No initial payment
    • Payments ranging from 18 to 60 months with payments as affordable as
    $_____ per month which includes a low fixed rate of interest
    Prepayments can be made anytime without penalty
    • Fast, confidential approval by phone 1-888-XXX-XXX or online at their
    secure website www.XXXX.com. Good credit standing required.

2. **3, 6 and 12 Months Interest Free Plan**
    • 12 monthly payments of _____, interest free. ($1,500 minimum)
    • 6 monthly payments of _____, interest free. ($1,000 minimum)
    • 3 monthly payments of _____, interest free. ($300 minimum)

3. **Pay fee as treatment is provided.**
    One-third of the total treatment fee at the beginning of care, one third in the
    middle, and the remaining one-third when the final restorations are inserted

4. **Payment in full (cash or check)**
    • A bookkeeping courtesy of _____% or $_____ is given for direct payment
    in full at the start of treatment, resulting in a one-time payment of
    $_____.

5. **Other Payment Options**
    • Visa and MasterCard are accepted for payment in full.

Four Keys to a Successful Fee Presentation

Barb Hertzog, a Dayton, Ohio, orthodontic office manager for twenty years and also a dental consultant, emphasizes four keys to a successful fee presentation:

1. Use a written presentation form

Reasons

- Simplifies the presentation for both you and the patient.
- Patients retain more when they can see and hear their options.
- Gives all patients the same choices.
- Ensures presentation consistency among team members.

Results

- Patients listen to all options.
- Patients understand their options.
- Patients' payment information is in one place so any team member can help with future questions.

2. Present patient financing to all patients

Reasons

- Presents options in an unbiased manner.
- Can't judge a book by its cover.
- Gives everyone the same opportunity for treatment.

Results

- Simplified presentation for you and your patients.
- Patients will tell their family and friends about your affordable payment options.
- Increased case acceptance.

3. Present the monthly payment plan first

Reasons

- Lowers your stress.
- Removes financial barriers to treatment.
- Patients know they can start treatment with no initial payment, if desired.
- People often make purchase decisions based on their monthly budgets.

Results

- You and team members are at ease.
- Patients are at ease.
- Patients listen attentively to their options.
- Patients shift their focus from *"Can I afford this?"* to *"When can I begin?"*

- The total treatment fee becomes less important in the decision-making process.

4. Let the patient choose

Reason
- Allows your patients to choose the option that works best for them.

Results
- Patient satisfaction.
- Patient referrals.

Negotiation

The negotiation following the Financial Options Dialogue should be relatively stress-free for several reasons.

First, the patient chose to purse a lifetime strategy for care instead of treating a single chief condition (Choice Dialogue). This choice signaled readiness for complete care and gave an indication that the patient's life circumstances (fit issues) had room for the budget required for complete care. If the patient didn't have some level of budget, he or she would have opted out of complete care and treated only the chief condition.

Second, the Advocacy Dialogue clearly states, *"Let's find a way that we can fit your dentistry into what's going on in your life..."* This dialogue foreshadows the Financial Options Dialogue. Because we initiated the discussion about fit issues (ballpark fees and time estimates), when and if fit issues come up during the Financial Options Dialogue, we can go back to the Advocacy Dialogue to find a suitable way to fit the dentistry into the person's life—either now or later.

Concerns

Here are the most common concerns patients have relative to the Financial Options Dialogue and how to address them in a way that maintains an advocacy relationship with the patient.

If the patient refuses monthly payments, *"I don't like to pay interest..."* or, *"I don't believe in going into debt for things like this..."* then offer the other two options: payment in full or payments over the course of treatment. A good response to a patient refusing monthly payments is, *"I understand.*

Which one of the other two options works better for you?"

If these options don't fit for the patient, offer to do the dentistry (when possible) over time. Recommend specific dollar amounts over a certain period and give the patient an idea of how long it will take to complete her care by working within a budget. For example, I might say:

"Michelle, another way we can help you get the dentistry you need and fit it into what's going on in your life is to do it over time. If you're comfortable with a budget of xxx dollars a year, we'll have you finished in two years. Does that work better for you?"

Notice I immediately reminded Michelle that she think about staying within her budget and fit issues. Almost always, the best response to fee objections and other fit issues is to remind your patient of the promise you make during the Advocacy Dialogue: *"... let's find a way to fit your dentistry into what's going on in your life."* So when you and Michelle are talking about fees, remind her that it's your goal to help her fit it in her life. This attitude will keep the conversation on track and eliminate uneasiness for everyone. This response reminds the patient that you want to work within his or her budget and fit issues. It also keeps you from having to defend your fees, treatment plan, and ethics. If you have not suggested that she think about her budget and fit issues in the Advocacy Dialogue, then it's less credible to suggest a budget for her care now.

I've discussed using the Advocacy Dialogue at the end of the complete examination. However, this dialogue, which is intended to reassure the patient that we'll work within her fit issues, can come at any point in the relationship with the patient. Here are some situations where fee concerns can occur and how you and your team can take an advocacy attitude toward them:

- Receptionist on telephone: *"I understand your concern about costs. Dr. Jarvis is excellent about staying within patients' budgets."*
- Chair-side assistant taking radiographs: *"I guarantee you Dr. Allen will work with you to find a way to fit your dentistry into your work schedule."*
- Hygienist at initial appointment: *"You'll appreciate how Ginger, our financial coordinator, will help you find ways to afford the best dentistry."*

Crossover Zone

The Crossover Zone is the general fee level at which you or your team members get anxious about quoting the fee. For some, this zone is in the range of a few hundred dollars; for others, it may be over $30,000.

Another situation that establishes the Crossover Zone is the fear a dentist feels—especially if the fee is high—about the patient becoming embarrassed or angered, and responding, *"Hell no!"* I'm convinced it's not the fee that makes us uptight—it's not knowing what to say when patients say "No." Prove it to yourself. Would you have any fear of quoting very large fees, way beyond your Crossover Zone, if you knew your patient would say "Yes"? Probably not. The anxiety over fees comes from the fear of confrontation, not from the fee itself. Logically, if we can use a process that makes it nearly impossible to create confrontational events with patients over fees and fit issues, then it would follow that our fear of quoting large fees would diminish. Indeed, that is precisely what the Making It Easy approach does.

Spectrum of Appeal

Let's use the Spectrum of Appeal™ to look at fees and budgets (**Figure 16-3**). The fee/dollar amount of the case is blue spectrum (fact). However, budget is a personal (emotional) relationship with money, which makes it red spectrum.

FIGURE 16-3

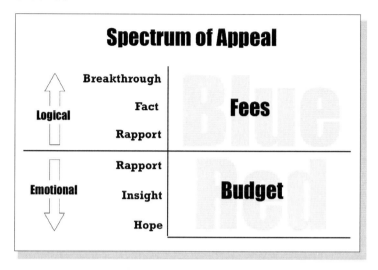

If you think of fees only in terms of dollar amounts, you're missing an essential opportunity to create appeal. By showing that you're aware of and sensitive to budgets, you can create red spectrum (emotional) appeal to the patient. The Choice, Advocacy, and Warm-up Dialogues are great opportunities to do this. It's been my experience that our ability to be emotionally intelligent about discussing money offers the patient a huge helping of empathy. It distinguishes us and our leadership from the long line of dentists most right-side patients have encountered.

Our ability to be emotionally intelligent about discussing money...
distinguishes us and our leadership from the long line of dentists
most right-side patients have encountered.

Fee levels for left-side patients usually range up to $5,000 (in 2005 dollars). For most dentists and team members, this level of fee is in the blue spectrum—they don't get emotional when quoting it. However, fees for right-side patients typically can start at the $5,000 level. The fee level that makes you anxious is your Crossover Zone. In the example in Figure 15-4, you're comfortable quoting fees up to $5,000. Fee discussions about money above your Crossover Zone are emotional (stressful) for you.

FIGURE 16-4

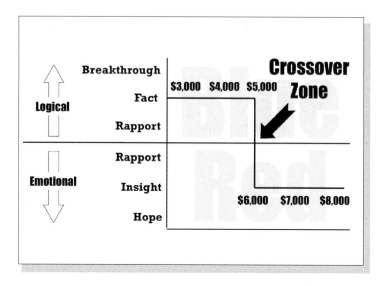

Assessing Your Crossover Zone

Let's determine your Crossover Zone. Write down the fee level at which you begin to get nervous about quoting. I know it depends on a lot of things, but write down a fee that is difficult for you to say.

Next, write down a typical fee for an average total treatment plan you offer. Another way of asking the same thing is, what fee range do you quote a lot? Again, it depends, but give it a try.

Now, look at the two numbers. The first one is your Crossover Zone; the second one is your typical treatment fee. Which one is higher? If you're like the hundreds of dentists and team members I've done this exercise with, *your average treatment fee is less than your Crossover Zone.* In other words, many dentists are treatment planning within their financial comfort zone.

If you're treatment planning within your comfort zone, what will taking an advanced CE course on occlusion do to increase your Crossover Zone? Probably nothing. Having a Crossover Zone that works with left-side patients holds you back with right-side patients. Many dentists complain that lack of dental insurance holds patients back from accepting complete care. I'd bet dental insurance limitations are a minor deterrent to complete care compared to low Crossover Zones.

> *Having a Crossover Zone that works with left-side patients holds you back with right-side patients.*

Assessing Your Team's Crossover Zone

At your next team meeting, have everyone write down the minimum patient fee dollar amount at which they get nervous about quoting. Have them work independently, no collaborating. Encourage them to be honest about the number. Once they're done, collect their answers and write their Crossover Zone amounts on an easel or white board, then average them. Here are some questions to think about:

- Is the average of your team greater or less than your fee for a target right-side patient?
- Can you guess which individual Crossover Zone goes with which team member?
- What are the dangers of having clinical team members with low Crossover Zones?
- What are the dangers of having administrative team members and treatment coordinators with low Crossover Zones?
- How close is your team's average Crossover Zone to yours?
- What would your practice be like if the team average Crossover Zone was doubled?
- What would your practice be like if your Crossover Zone was doubled?

Your Crossover Zone Creates Your Ceiling

Your Crossover Zone and that of your team are a big part of what sets the limits on your ability to grow your practice qualitatively (percentage of right-side patients) and quantitatively (net income). If your Crossover Zone is $5,500, you're not going to treat many full-mouth restorative/cosmetic patients, regardless of your clinical training or specialty degrees. If this is the case for you, then it makes perfect sense for you to work on increasing your Crossover Zone as a companion to your clinical skills.

Increasing Your Crossover Zone

I've never experienced a dentist making a huge leap—greater than $10,000—all at once. I have, however, seen many dentists and team member steadily nudge up their Crossover Zones over time. Here's how to do it (**Figure 16-5**).

FIGURE 16-5

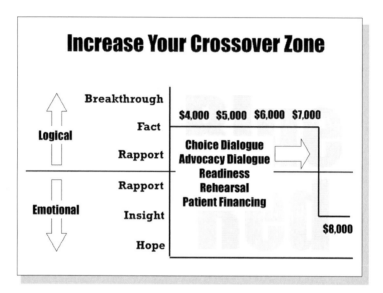

Choice Dialogue: Start increasing your Crossover Zone by offering the Choice Dialogue. This dialogue really is the start of your awareness of what is financially comfortable for the patient. In the context of the Choice Dialogue, if patients have financial limitations, they will opt for treating their chief condition only and not pursue comprehensive (expensive) dentistry. Likewise, if they choose a lifetime strategy for dental health, their decision begins to qualify them as having some level of budget to work with. This knowledge should strengthen your confidence in fee discussions.

Advocacy Dialogue: Your Crossover Zone is affected by patients' Crossover Zones—the fee ranges at which they get uncomfortable. The Advocacy Dialogue continues the financial qualification process started by the Choice Dialogue. You'll recall the objective of the Advocacy

Dialogue is to reassure patients that we'll find the best way to fit their dentistry into their lives. This dialogue leads to a fit issue discussion that should give the patient a ballpark estimate of fees, time in treatment, and financial arrangements. If the patient is all right with your estimates, your Crossover Zone should increase at least to the level of the ballpark estimate, and maybe higher. If you know your patient is comfortable with your ballpark fee estimate quoted at the initial appointment, you should be comfortable during the Financial Options Dialogue.

Readiness: As you know, a big part of the Making It Easy approach is the concept of readiness. Readiness is tested at many points in the process. Additionally, the phrase *"when you're ready..."* is used both at the start and end of treatment recommendations: *"Hunter, when you're ready, we can replace your missing front teeth you lost in your soccer game."* Alerting patients to your sensitivity to their readiness issues and knowing what patients are ready for will increase your Crossover Zone.

Don't use the fee to discover readiness. Too often, we find out what patients are ready for too late—after we've quoted the big fee. When you quote big fees without being aware of patient readiness, you risk embarrassing or angering the patient, and causing a confrontation.

Rehearsal: Rehearsal helps raise your Crossover Zone. I've coached many dentists on quoting fees far beyond their Crossover Zones. The way I've done it is to have them quote the fee below their zones and the total time in treatment, and ask me (the "patient") how this fits into my life. Then I have them repeat the drill many times and each time I have them increase the fee by $2,000 until they're way over their zones. My response each time they do the drill is overwhelmingly positive. In fact, the higher the fee, the more enthusiastic I become. In coaching situations, it's amazing how comfortable dentists become quoting fees ten times above their Crossover Zones. Then when they have to do it for real, they've already said the fee many times and their confidence is evident in the tone of their voice and eye contact.

Patient Financing: The single fastest way I've seen to increase dentists' and team members' Crossover Zones is to use patient financing from outside service providers. What's less stressful for you to say and for patients to hear: *"Your fee is $10,000. How would you like to pay for it?"* or *"Your fee is $10,000, and most patients like to start their care with no initial payment and make monthly payments in the range of $xxx."*

It's hard to imagine what the automobile and real estate industries would be like if purchasers didn't have the ability to pay over time through consumer financing. There's no question that modern dentistry is now in the same league as other high-end consumer purchases such as cars, homes, and luxury vacations. Dental fees at the ten-, twenty-, and thirty-thousand-dollar levels (and higher) are common. How many people do you know who can pay cash at these levels? Not many. If you're not using patient financing from a financial services provider, you need to start.

Don't Try to Overcome Fee Objections

The topic of overcoming fee objections for right-side patients always irritates me, for several reasons.

The strategies for overcoming objections come directly from the sales industry. In fact, there are seminars in our industry led by salespeople who have never sold ten cents worth of dentistry in their lives, but who are telling us how to use sales ploys that work in the "real world." I've heard and read many times what these "experts" say we should tell our patients. Too often the advice is manipulative and demeans the dentist/patient relationship. Here are a few of my "favorite" examples:

After you quote a fee for a crown, a patient says to you, "Wow, that's expensive." The "expert" response is, *"Don't think about the crown as being expensive, think of it as an......"* Can you complete the sentence? Of course you can, and so can every businessperson who sits in your chair.

Or, you learn that your patient wants better-looking teeth but is reluctant to shell out $10,000. The "expert" advice is to say something like: *"Vicky, now you've told me you're interested in having a beautiful smile. If you mean what you say, other than money, is there any other reason why you shouldn't go ahead and make a commitment now?"* If anyone said that to me I'd say, *"If you mean what you say, then, other than money, is there any reason why I shouldn't walk right out of here now?"*

Or, how about this "expert" advice: *"After you quote a fee, say nothing, because whoever speaks first loses."* I tried that—once—and felt like hell. So will you.

A big problem with using sales techniques is that most patients already know these techniques. One of my best friends is Kevin Humbert. Kevin lives in Chicago and sells high-end financial software to the big boys like Charles Schwab, Fidelity, and the Chicago Mercantile Exchange. He's been in the high-pressure corporate sales environment for thirty years and he's heard it all. If you laid one of the lame sales techniques on him, *"Don't think of it as expensive, Kevin, think of it as an investment,"* he'd laugh in your face and you'd lose every shred of credibility. You're not going to outsell your patients. They know the sales process better than we do and they use it every day. Dental team members will mutiny if you pressure them to pressure your patients. It's hard enough to get teams to role-play asking patients for referrals, let alone expecting them to learn sales scripts, only to go toe-to-toe with the Kevin Humberts of the world.

Another reason I'm against the mind-set of overcoming objections is that many of the objections we hear are not the real problem. A patient's objections to cost may have deeper issues, like the fact that he is paying his in-laws' nursing home bills. Or fee objections may be due to a child starting college. How do you overcome these objections—tell him to boot his wife's parents out of the nursing home or suggest community college for his kid? Revisit the discussion of the Personal Fit issue (Chapter Nine). Often the objections we hear are symptoms of deeper issues, and attempts to overcome them are inappropriate and destroy relationships.

Acknowledge Objections

Instead of overcoming patients' objections, think about *acknowledging* them and then offering them hope. Here's how it works. For example, when a patient states an objection:

1. Acknowledge it. *"Kristen I understand that you're concerned about... the cost of care,"* or *"...the lack of insurance benefit."* Acknowledging it does not

mean you agree with it. Just repeat how you think she feels so she knows you're listening.

2. Offer social proof. *"A lot of patients are surprised about... the costs of dental care,"* or *"... the poor benefits of dental insurance."* The truth is, many patients are surprised about the costs of care. Let her know that her concern is common and you're not afraid or defensive about discussing it.

3. Give her hope and act as her advocate. *"Kristen, we've helped a lot of our patients find ways to get the care they need. What can I do to help make this fit for you?"* If you can find a way to help fit the treatment into her life by treatment sequencing or financing, great. If not, then keep the door open for future care. The key here is being open to the fact that complete care may not be in the cards for her now.

Acknowledging objections and giving patients hope will cut your case-presentation stress to nil. Remember, being an advocate means not making treatment acceptance a condition of having a good relationship with your patient. I can't emphasize enough that the heart of the Making It Easy approach is creating an environment where right-side patients who *aren't* ready feel welcome. Then, when they become ready, they choose you to do their care.

Learn To Take "No" For An Answer

Occasionally, you'll have a patient who won't accept any of your treatment recommendations offered during the Warm-up Dialogue, nor the various financial arrangement and treatment sequencing options offered during the Financial Options Dialogue. Even though this person favored complete care and chose a lifetime strategy during the Choice Dialogue, and was comfortable with your ballpark fee estimates during the Advocacy Dialogue, the patient is still not ready. Remember, people's lives change and so do their levels of readiness. Many times I've heard of amazing things that happen to patients between their initial appointment and the consultation appointment, which change their level of readiness:

- *"My husband left me ... lost his job ... has been diagnosed with cancer."*
- *"I'm sick ... my cat's sick ...my boyfriend's sick."*
- *"I had to buy a new car... a new TV... a new house."*

When it's obvious patients are not ready, take "No" for an answer—gracefully—and remind yourself that time and life circumstances will help re-ignite their readiness and they'll be back. Here's an example of taking "No" for an answer:

"Mr. Crawford, sounds like this is not a good time for you to get your teeth fixed. I understand that this is a big step for you. Let's keep you on our recall program and when you're ready, we'll be here."

Patients' budgets, fit issues, and life circumstances change. Don't think that restating the clinical reasons for care will change their life circumstances. Patient education efforts in the face of an obvious lack of readiness feels like sales pressure to patients. Don't make them wrong or pressure them. Don't make a contest out of case acceptance. If your patients aren't ready, give them a way to feel good about staying in your practice, and when they're ready, they'll say so. If you pressure them and make them wrong, when they become ready, they'll go somewhere else.

> **Patient education efforts in the face of an**
> **obvious lack of readiness feels like sales pressure to patients.**

Assuming the patient is ready and has made a mutually agreeable financial arrangement with your office, you're now ready to do the technical case presentation and informed consent.

In a Nutshell
Chapter Sixteen—The Financial Options Dialogue

- The intentions of the Financial Options Dialogue are to quote the total treatment fee (including estimated specialists' fees), state the total time in treatment, discuss the financial arrangement options, and agree on the scope of dental treatment and when to begin care.

- It's best to accompany your Financial Options Dialogue with a financial options form. This makes it easy for the patient to follow along with your options and gives the person a record of your conversation to take home.

- The Crossover Zone is the general fee level at which you or your team members get anxious (self-conscious) about quoting the fee.

- Things that increase your Crossover Zone (make you more comfortable discussing fees) are using the Choice Dialogue and Advocacy Dialogue, understanding the patient's fit and readiness issues, rehearsal, and patient financing.

- Instead of overcoming patients' objections, think about *acknowledging* them and then offering them hope.

- When it's obvious patients are not ready, take "no" for an answer—gracefully.

- Patients' budgets, fit issues, and life circumstances change. If your patients aren't ready, give them a way to feel good about staying in your practice, and when they're ready, they'll say so. If you pressure them and make them wrong, when they become ready, they'll go somewhere else.

Chapter Seventeen
Famous Last Words:
The Technical Case Presentation

The following is one of my favorite quotations of famous last words:

> *"They couldn't hit an elephant at this dist... "*
> —General John Sedgwick, Union Army Commander,
> killed by a sniper's bullet during the Civil War

Can you imagine the blinking expressions and bitter surprise of the general's nearby officers as his horse galloped away, leaving their general face first in the dust?

If we're not careful, our words can be like sniper's bullets to relationships. This chapter on the technical case presentation explains how to shape our language with patients, so that the potentially difficult to understand and intimidating technical case presentation won't become our famous last words.

Technical Case Presentation

Technical case presentation is the third part of the consultation appointment **(Figure 17-1)**.

FIGURE 17-1

Consultation Appointment

Warm-up Dialogue CD-4:
offers hope and opens fit/readiness conversation

Financial Options Dialogue CD-5:
total fee, total time, affordable options,
negotiation

Technical Case Presentation:
informed consent

Its objective is to inform the patient of the benefits, risks, and alternatives to care; and to obtain informed consent for your intended procedures. The structure and scope of the consent conversation is defined by the standard of care in your area. In this chapter, I won't get into the structure of your technical case presentation. In my first book, *Dentists: An Endangered Species*, I provide a complete description of the structure and content of the consent procedures I use along with a computer disk containing all the forms and letters (you can order this book online at www.paulhomoly.com). The ADA also has information on proper consent structure and content. The consent aspect of the consultation appointment is not a task you can delegate; it must be done by the dentist.

The Traditional Case Presentation

Typically, under the traditional approach, a case like Michelle's may take thirty to forty-five minutes to discuss. Remember, the traditional approach presents the technical aspect of care first, then fee information and financial arrangements. Woven into all of that is the traditional case presentation's focus on influencing the patient.

Think about it. With the traditional approach, we attempt to have a conversation that mixes scientific/biological/clinical information with financial options (many of which may be surprising/unacceptable to the patient) with legal consent issues, while trying to sound appealing, all within thirty to forty-five minutes—on a patient who may not be ready for any of it. This can be too much for patients to take. It's no wonder so many patients have to "go home and think about it."

Spectrum of Appeal

The traditional process for the case presentation appointment on the Spectrum of Appeal™ is shown in **Figure 17-2**.

FIGURE 17-2

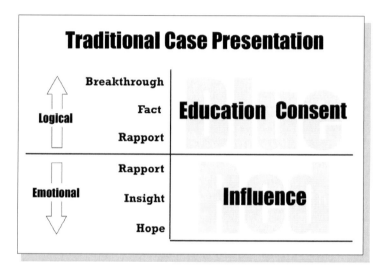

As you can see, there is a strong presence of logical appeal in the form of patient education and consent issues. As we are educating and informing the patient, we are simultaneously hoping to influence the patient, which is an emotional spectrum domain. And that's the core of the problem with the traditional approach of case presentation: we're trying to influence (emotional spectrum) a patient to say "Yes" by using overwhelming logic. If you want to influence someone, you need to include emotional appeal. The traditional case presentation is *not* designed to be emotionally appealing.

Learning Domains

Experts in adult learning and instructional designers cite four domains of learning:

- Cognitive: thinking, like reading and mathematics
- Psychomotor: moving, like dancing and golf
- Interpersonal: relating to others
- Affective: feelings and preferences

When instructional designers are designing programs for adults, they avoid mixing learning domains in a single lesson. Mixing domains makes learning any one of them more difficult than if you taught each domain individually. If an instructional designer were to look at the consultation appointment as if it were a classroom situation, in which the student (patient) had to learn something (the treatment plan, the financial requirements and arrangements, and consent issues), the designer would separate the domains into individual lessons, allowing the student to learn one domain at a time.

This is exactly the *opposite* of how the traditional case presentation appointment is structured—all domains are mixed into one conversation (lesson). Consequently, the student (patient) learns little and feels overwhelmed.

- Cognitive: dental conditions, solutions, treatment modalities and options, consequences, fees, etc.
- Psychomotor: patient education and home care instructions
- Interpersonal: rapport, empathy, listening, relating, understanding
- Affective: personal appeal, decision making

The "Making It Easy" Approach Technical Case Presentation

Under the circumstances we've created for the Making It Easy approach, we *already* have a patient who understands and has accepted the general concepts of the treatment (Warm-up Dialogue) and has agreed to the financial requirements (Financial Options Dialogue). Now when we present the technical aspects of care with the intention of obtaining informed consent, it is a much simpler and less stressful conversation for the patient and the dentist because:

- The patient is a much better listener, because fit issues (costs, time, schedule) have been resolved.

- The case is already "sold," allowing the dentist to do a better job of communicating because he/she can focus on one topic—consent.

The Making It Easy approach has separated the four domains of learning into individual lessons, making each one easy to learn.

The Making It Easy approach has separated the four domains of learning into individual lessons, making each one easy to learn.
- Cognitive: technical case presentation (Financial Options Dialogue)
- Psychomotor: this lesson (home care instructions) to be taught during the treatment process
- Interpersonal: (Warm-up Dialogue)
- Affective: (Warm-up Dialogue)

Figure 17-3 shows how it looks on the Spectrum of Appeal.

FIGURE 17-3

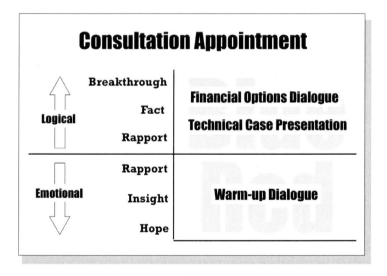

What If...

Because the technical case presentation follows the Financial Options Dialogue, I'm often asked, *"What if the patient learns something about their intended treatment during the technical case presentation that they don't like and won't agree to? Does that undo all that you've done?"*

Yes, it does, but this rarely happens. Depending on the objection, part of the entire treatment plan may need to be reengineered. However, using the traditional approach doesn't make you immune to patients' objections. If a patient doesn't want surgery or root canals or orthodontics, etc., then it's not going to happen, regardless of how you present care.

Save Time

You'll find that your technical case presentation will take less time than under the traditional approach. Dentists tell me they were spending up to an hour discussing complex restorative treatment plans, and now with the Making It Easy approach, they spend up to two-thirds less time. A big part of the reason you'll spend less time is that you'll feel less compelled to get into a lot of technical details. It's been my experience that dentists dwell on details, in part, to help justify the fee (the more you tell them what you're going to do, the more your fee should make sense). You'll discover that patients will accept your care regardless of them knowing all the details.

> *You'll find that your technical case presentation*
> *will take less time than under the traditional approach.*

"Review of Findings" Letter

After the consultation appointment and the scope of care and financial considerations have been agreed upon, the patient is scheduled for the next appointment. It's a really good idea to mail the patient a review of findings letter. This letter is structured almost identically to the Warm-up Dialogue. I suggest it be mailed ASAP following the consult. Put it in a large envelope so the letter is unfolded and include brochures on intended procedures. This letter is a nice touch, serves as a reminder of your discussions, and combats post-purchase dissonance. Here's an example for Michelle.

Michelle Flame
815 Poplar Avenue
Oakbrook, Illinois 60126

Dear Michelle,

Here's a summary of your treatment recommendations. These recommendations are based on our conversations and from my clinical examination and analysis of your dental health. This treatment plan is designed to provide for you a lifetime strategy for dental health. This plan is offered with the understanding that it must be financially comfortable for you and fit into your lifestyle.

I understand that you're embarrassed by the appearance of your upper front teeth when talking with customers. We can help you feel confident in the appearance of your teeth by removing the dark and yellowed enamel and chipped edges and replacing them with a new enamel-like material. This usually takes three appointments. I know this is your busy season at the art gallery, so let's find a time when this makes the most sense for you to do it.

You mentioned you're aggravated by the discomfort on your lower right back teeth. While we're working with your upper front teeth, I recommend we get these teeth comfortable for chewing and changes in temperature. We do this by rebuilding the teeth and when we're done they'll look and feel completely normal.

The last time we talked, I mentioned the infection in your gums and you expressed a concern about it. I recommend that while we're in the process of restoring your front teeth, we eliminate the gum infection, helping preserve the appearance of your front teeth and protecting you from tooth loss. We do this through a series of very thorough cleanings and the use of some medications.

I know you're not concerned that you have some missing molars on your upper left and right side. We talked about how when teeth are missing, the teeth next to them can drift into poor positions. I'm concerned that eventually you may lose more teeth and have more problems with the appearance of your front teeth. When you're ready, either while we've fixing your front teeth or soon afterward, we can replace these missing teeth. You'll be able to brush these replacement teeth right in your mouth. That will safeguard the foundation of your bite, protecting the appearance of the front teeth.

Follow-up care—We know that you want to keep your teeth for a lifetime. It's important that you keep regular checkup visits with us every six months. Your total fee includes all anticipated treatment along with follow-up visits for one year and all the supplies (special toothbrushes, mouth rinses, etc.) you need to keep your teeth and gums healthy.

Michelle, your total care will take about two months from start to finish. We look forward to providing you with the very best care.

Yours for better dental health,

Dr. Paul Homoly

The technical case presentation ends the consultation appointment. When preceded by well-structured and delivered Warm-up and Financial Options Dialogues, the technical case presentation should be one of the most stress-free and enjoyable conversations you have with your right-side patient.

The next chapter is about managing right-side patients who haven't completed care who are in your recall system. You have more untreated right-side patients in your recall system than you'll see as new patients in many months. Read on.

In a Nutshell
Chapter Seventeen—Technical Case Presentation

- The objective of the technical case presentation is to inform the patient of the benefits, risks, and alternatives to care, and to obtain informed consent for your intended procedures. The structure and scope of this consent conversation is defined by the standard of care in your area.

- Experts in adult learning cite four learning domains: cognitive, psychomotor, interpersonal, and affective.

- When we present the technical aspects of care with the intention of obtaining informed consent, it is a much simpler and less stressful conversation for the patient and the dentist because: 1) the patient is a much better listener, because fit issues (costs, time, schedule) have been resolved; 2) the case is already "sold," allowing the dentist to do a better job of communicating because he/she can focus on one topic—consent.

Chapter Eighteen
Whatever Happened To What's-Her-Name?:
Hygiene Dialogues

It's 2:30 in the morning—you're wide awake and you have this dim memory of a patient you examined months ago, a nice woman in her mid-forties; owns an art gallery, you think. You can see her face, but you can't remember her name. You know she needs a lot of work, but you have no clue what happened to her. You spend the rest of the night in a fitful half-sleep, and when you walk into your office the next day, you storm the front desk, demanding to know, *"Whatever happened to that lady we saw a few months ago who owns the art gallery who needed some anterior crowns? Did she ever schedule?"*

Your administrative team runs for cover and you think you hear someone call out, *"I'll check into it."*

It's 2:30 the next morning— you're wide awake and you have this dim memory of a patient you examined months ago and you can see her face... Does this happen to you? You're not alone. We all have flashbacks at night wondering, *"Whatever happened to what's-her-name?"*

This chapter should help you sleep better. It's about how your hygiene team and recall system can help get your right-side patients, who aren't ready for treatment, out of your nightmares and into your schedule.

Choice, Readiness, Advocacy, and the Dental Hygienist
Of all the team members in your practice, the dental hygienist is in the best position to help your practice and your right-side patients maintain an excellent relationship. Hygienists spend more time with patients, have more frequent contact, and, if they're paying attention, know more about patient fit and readiness issues than anyone in the office. Consequently,

it makes perfect sense that the dental hygienist be a superstar in the concepts of choice, readiness, and advocacy.

Think of all the right-side patients who enter your practice and how most of them aren't ready. I'd bet that you have more untreated right-side patients in your recall system right now than new right-side patients that you'll see over many months. Some of your greatest opportunities for starting right-side cases are already on your recall schedule. Also, as you mature into the Making It Easy approach, you'll be encouraging many right-side patients, who aren't ready, to remain in your recall system. Remember the phrase, *"When you're ready, we'll be here. I'll wait with you"*? It's the hygiene recall system that reminds the patient, *"We're still here!"*

> *Some of your greatest opportunities for starting right-side cases are already on your recall schedule.*

Managing the Right-Side Patient Who's Not Ready

There are three steps in managing the right-side patient who isn't ready, in the hygiene recall system. You and your team complete these steps at you daily *"huddle"*:

1. Identify all right-side patients in the hygiene schedule who need additional care.
2. Evaluate where they are in their treatment plan and decide what their next step is.
3. Agree on how these patients will be managed today if they elect to take the next step in their treatment plan.

Identify the right-side patient. Generally speaking, there are two types of untreated right-side patients in your recall system: those who've had a complete examination and been presented with a complete-care treatment plan, but have followed through with part or none of the dentistry; and those who have not had a complete examination or treatment plan. Both types of right-side patients should be identified either the day prior to their appointment or at the morning huddle. Everyone on the team should be aware of which recall patients are right-side patients and where they are in the treatment process.

Evaluate the treatment plan. With input from other team members, decide what the patient's next step is if the patient decides to proceed with complete care. This next step varies widely. It might be to make financial arrangements, study models and photographs, a complete examination, or talk with the dentist. It's been my experience that most dental hygienists need support in determining the next step in the treatment process. Don't make the mistake of inappropriately delegating this step to your team members; they may not be comfortable or may not have enough information or confidence to make this decision.

Agree on how to manage the right-side patient. This step varies widely depending on the day's clinical schedule. The thing to keep in mind here is the word agree. If you agree on what will happen when this patient is ready to move forward with complete care, then it makes the process much less stressful for everyone. For example, you notice that Wanda is due for her recall appointment tomorrow and have identified she is a right-side patient who has a complete treatment plan but has only completed part of it. Her next step is to restore her maxillary molars and she needs to make financial arrangements before you start. You agree that, if she is ready to proceed with care, the hygienist will save some time at the end of the hygiene appointment for Wanda to talk to Ginger, your treatment coordinator. If Wanda wants to talk to you, your schedule is light enough for you to see her at the beginning of the hygiene appointment. This type of conversation puts everyone on the same page and makes Wanda feel like you've got your act together.

Hygiene Choice Dialogue

After you've identified the untreated right-side patient, determined the next step, and agreed on how the patient will be managed today if she elects to go ahead with care, you've really set the stage for a smooth appointment. After the patient is seated in the hygiene chair, review with her the changes in her health and dental history. Then, before you start the clinical aspects of care, offer the Hygiene Choice Dialogue. The Hygiene Choice Dialogue is similar to the Choice Dialogue (CD-2) the dentist uses in the new patient experience. In this dialogue the dentist asks, *"Are you interested in addressing your (disability) or, in addition to that, are you interested in us developing a lifetime strategy for dental health. What's best for you now?"* The intention of the Hygiene Choice Dialogue is to reveal your patient's level of readiness for complete care by giving your patient a choice relative to today's care.

The structure of the Hygiene Choice Dialogue is: *"Guy, I'm glad to clean your teeth today, but tell me, in addition to that, is this a good time for us to talk about the recommendations that Dr. Homoly made the last time you were in? What's best for you today?"* The Hygiene Dialogue is designed to reintroduce the choice of taking care of today's concerns (adult prophy) or, in addition to that, revisiting the idea of developing a lifetime strategy for dental health.

If the patient is interested in proceeding with complete care (ready), or has questions about it, use the strategy that you and the team discussed at the morning huddle to best manage this patient. If your team has prepared well, there should be minimal confusion, stress, and wasted time moving this patient toward the goal of lifetime care.

If the patient is not ready for complete care, complete the clinical aspects of hygiene care. At the end of the appointment, let the patient know that you'll offer the choice each time he's in—not to bug him, but to keep in touch with his level of readiness. For example, Clark is not interested in revisiting complete care recommendations at his hygiene visit. Your hygienist performed her clinical care and either during her treatment or at the end she said to Clark, *"Clark, each time you visit us I'm going to ask if this is a good time for you to discuss Dr. Kaiser's recommendations. If it is, all you have to do is say so."*

Offer the Choice Early

It's important that you offer the Hygiene Choice Dialogue early in the appointment. Here are two good reasons. First, if the patient says "Yes" to your offer of revisiting complete care, then you have the remaining appointment time to "maneuver" and meet the objectives you set for yourself at the huddle on how to best manage the patient taking the next step. Second, if the patient says "No" to your option of revisiting complete care, you have the balance of the appointment to discover the fit/readiness issues behind your patient's decision, using indirect "fit-chat" or direct inquiries.

Find a Way To Make It Happen

It's been my experience that significant differences exist among hygienists with respect to their ability/willingness to deliver the Hygiene Choice Dialogue. This dialogue could be as simple as, *"Daniel, I know that you and Dr. Homoly at one time discussed some ideas for helping you achieve a more beautiful and comfortable smile. Does today seem like a good time to explore that further?"*

Yet the simplicity of this invitation may still be out of the comfort zone of some hygienists and/or dentists. My recommendation is that you and your team find a way to make it happen. The Hygiene Choice Dialogue represents one of the best and most frequent opportunities for untreated right-side patients to begin complete care.

> *The Hygiene Choice Dialogue represents one*
> *of the best and most frequent opportunities for*
> *untreated right-side patients to begin complete care.*

How Not To Do It

A big mistake at the hygiene visit for right-side patients who aren't ready is to overeducate them about their conditions. Too much education feels like nagging. For example, Marlene comes in for your recall visit and your hygienist asks, *"Are you ready for your bridge yet?"* and Marlene says *"No."* Six months later your hygienist asks, *"Are you ready for your bridge yet?"* and Marlene says *"No."* Six months after that your hygienist asks, *"Are you ready for your bridge yet?"* and Marlene says *"No."* Six months later Marlene sits in the hygiene chair and screams, *"Don't talk to me about the bridge!"* You know you're overeducating/nagging patients when they say, *"You aren't going to find anything wrong today, are you?"* I guarantee your hygienist has heard that; they all have.

Hygiene Crossover Zone

Hygienists have a crossover zone of comfort related to restorative treatment discussion similar to that of the crossover point related to quoting fees. The crossover zone of comfort for hygienists is the point at which having treatment discussions becomes uncomfortable for them. The crossover zone is the point at which the hygienist switches from the safety of logic (knowing what she is talking about) to the discomfort of emotion (not being confident or knowledgeable about what she is talking about). It's critical that the dentist and hygienist know each other's expectations. If the dentist expects the hygienist to discuss complex care that has been previously treatment planned but the hygienist doesn't know this, or lacks confidence to do it, then there will be unnecessary stress.

Figure 18-1 shows a continuum of care from periodontal care to advanced restorative dentistry. Somewhere along this continuum, the hygienist can lose confidence and avoid specific conversations about care. Remember, it's human nature to avoid situations that make us uncomfortable.

FIGURE 18-1

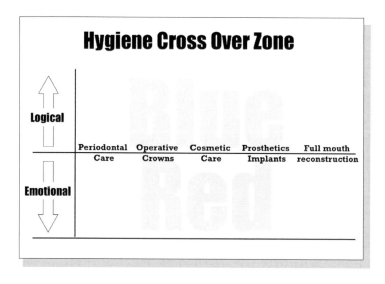

FIGURE 18-2

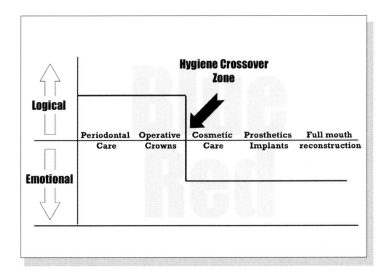

In the example shown in **Figure 18-2**, the hygienist is comfortable with treatment conversations about periodontal care and operative and single crowns. She gets uncomfortable when the complexity of care increases past the single-crown level into cosmetic dentistry and beyond. It's helpful to have your hygienists rate their crossover zones. Then assess your crossover zone relative to how comfortable you feel about your hygienists discussing care. Some dentists are very confident in their hygiene staff's ability to initiate treatment discussions at the highest comprehensive clinical level. Other dentists are far less confident in their hygiene team's ability to discuss complex care.

FIGURE 18-3

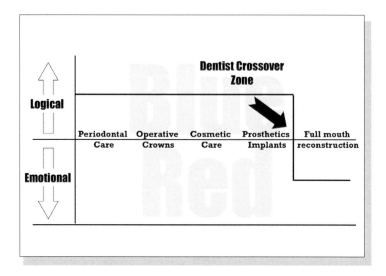

As shown in **Figure 18-3**, the dentist is confident in his or her hygienists discussing care up to full-mouth reconstruction. It's important to assess, then reconcile, the comfort zones and expectations of hygienists and dentists relative to right-side treatment discussions.

FIGURE 18-4

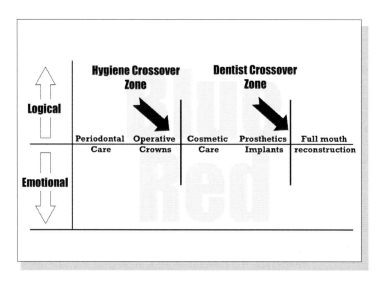

As **Figure 18-4** indicates, where there is a gap between the hygienist's and dentist's crossover zones, developmental work needs to be done. **Figure 18-5** depicts the four situations of crossover zone comparisons—the hygienist's comfort in discussing right-side care and the dentist's comfort in the hygienist discussing right-side care.

FIGURE 18-5

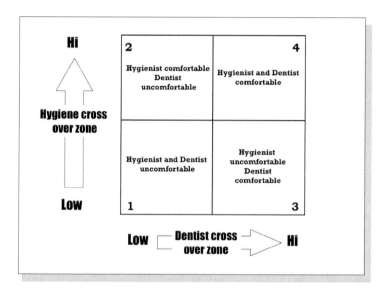

Quadrant 1: Neither hygienist or dentist is comfortable with the hygienist discussing recommendations for complex treatment.

Quadrant 2: Hygienist is comfortable, but dentist is uncomfortable with hygienist discussing recommendations for complex treatment.

Quadrant 3: Hygienist is uncomfortable, but dentist is comfortable with the hygienist discussing recommendations for complex treatment.

Quadrant 4: Both hygienist and dentist are comfortable with the hygienist discussing recommendations for complex treatment.

If your team is in quadrants 1, 2, or 3, then your ability to upgrade untreated right-side patients in the recall system is limited. Additionally, being in quadrants 1, 2, or 3 is a predictable source of stress, disharmony, and limited career satisfaction. Being in quadrants 1, 2, or 3 strongly suggests there are developmental needs to bring about harmony among the members of the dental team. And above all, being in quadrants 1, 2, or 3 handicaps your patient's opportunities for complete dental health.

Hygiene Handoff

The "Hygiene Handoff" is a conversation the hygienist initiates with the dentist as he or she enters the hygiene room to check the hygiene patient. The Hygiene Handoff is structured such that the hygienist, in a few short sentences, summarizes her findings to the dentist in a way that's easy to understand and respond to. The handoff goes a long way in showcasing to the patient that the hygienist has heard and understood her patient's concerns. The handoff also honors the time and talent the hygienist has invested in her patient.

The Hygiene Handoff is important because one of the more stressful situations in the dental office is the scene involving the hygiene check—the dentist leaving his/her patient to go into the hygiene room to examine a recall patient. A big part of the stress comes from the dentist having to shift gears from what he was doing to what he thinks is important to the hygiene patient and, at the same time, make small talk. Compounding this is when a right-side untreated hygiene patient is involved. The huddle work involving identifying the right-side patient, establishing the next step, and agreeing on how to manage the patient today if he or she elects to move ahead with complete care, goes far in reducing confusion and stress, and in making the right-side patient feel like you've got your act together. The Hygiene Handoff brings together all the work you've done to properly manage that patient.

> **The Hygiene Handoff brings together all the work you've done to properly manage that patient.**

Here's how the Hygiene Handoff is designed to work. The hygienist finishes her clinical care and the dentist enters the room. The dentist greets the patient and then asks the hygienist how the appointment went. The hygienist then describes the aspects of the hygiene appointment in a specific sequence so it's easy for the dentist to understand and easy for the hygienist to deliver. The Hygiene Handoff should be delivered before the dentist begins any clinical discussion.

Here's a good structure for the hygienist to follow:
- Positive framing—*"Michelle has done a good job of..."*
- Disability—*"She's concerned about..."*
- Conditions—*"I've also noticed..."*
- Next step—*"Michelle's next step is..."*
- Fit/readiness—*"Michelle is ready/not ready because..."*

Positive Framing: Your hygienist starts the conversation with you by saying something complimentary about the patient's teeth, attitude, current events, or life. For example, *"Dr. Homoly, Kevin is here today for his six-month recare appointment. He's really done a great job of taking care of the new crowns you made for him."*

Disability: Put the patient's concerns (disability) first in your conversation. This lets the patient know he's been heard and his concerns are your concerns. *"Dr. Homoly, Kevin is concerned about some discomfort when he chews on his right side."*

Conditions: Conditions are those areas in the patient's mouth that your hygienist is concerned about that she's discovered during her exam. *"Dr. Homoly, I've noticed that some of the silver fillings on Kevin's right side are showing signs of breakage. I've shown these areas to Kevin and he understands how these may be a problem in the future."*

Next Step: The next step is what needs to happen to advance the treatment plan or relieve the disability or condition. *"Dr. Homoly, I told Kevin that I thought your recommendation would be to restore the broken molar on his right side. I've explained the details to him."*

Fit/Readiness: Fit/readiness relates to the readiness of the patient to take the next step. If your patient is not ready, get an idea of why. *"Dr.*

Homoly, Kevin is ready to take care of the broken molar on his right side as soon as possible. He's not sure, though, when he'll be able to take action on the tooth whitening I recommended—he's got two sons starting college this fall and he's concerned about costs."

The Hygiene Handoff gives the patient the sense of being heard, gives your hygienist the satisfaction of getting her thoughts out, and honors the time she's invested in the patient. You'll love it because it gives you the right information and eliminates the need to "ad-lib" conversations with patients. Everyone wins!

Case Study: Michelle

In this case study we'll assume that Michelle never followed through with treatment. Even though she was excited about having a gorgeous smile for her black-tie event, too many things were on her plate. Consequently, she called your office and canceled her appointment to begin care. Your receptionist put her in your recall system and scheduled Michelle for a hygiene appointment in four months.

It's now four months later and at your morning huddle you notice Michelle is on your hygiene schedule. You and your team go through the three steps in managing her.

1. You identify her as an untreated right-side patient.
2. You establish that her next step in pursuing complete care is an adult cleaning and a short consultation with you.
3. You agree that if Michelle is interested in moving forward with complete care today that her cleaning will be done first, saving ten minutes at the end of the appointment to bring you in to discuss her decision.

Michelle comes in for her appointment and is seated in the hygiene chair. Her medical history is updated and she's in good spirits. Here's a sample dialogue between your hygienist and Michelle:

Hygienist: *"Hi, Michelle, it's nice to have you back again. I'm curious, how did your black-tie event at your gallery go?"*

Michelle: *"It was great. I did a lot of business and things worked out fine."*

Hygienist: *"Wonderful! Today, you're scheduled to have your teeth* cleaned. Dr. Homoly and I reviewed your record this morning and we decided to offer you a choice. I can go ahead and clean your teeth as planned, or in addition to that, we can revisit the recommendations for restoring your front teeth and some of the other things you discussed a few months ago. What's better for you today?"

Michelle: "I'd like to do both. I know my front teeth are getting worse and the ache on the right side is still there."

Hygienist: "OK, let's go ahead and clean your teeth now and I'll save a few minutes at the end of this appointment and get Dr. Homoly in here so you two can talk."

Your hygienist completes her clinical care and alerts you that Michelle is ready to be checked in the hygiene room. You enter and your hygienist uses the Hygiene Handoff.

"Michelle is in good spirits today and did really well during her visit with me. She had a terrific black-tie open house last month." (Positive framing)

"She's concerned about the appearance of her front teeth and occasional pain on her lower right side." (Disability)

"I've noticed that #28 and #29 are more broken down now than a few months ago and that #10 has a loose composite filling in it." (Conditions)

"I suggested to Michelle that her next step is to visit with you and discuss her concerns." (Next step)

"Michelle is ready now for you to talk to her about her continuing care." (Fit/readiness)

At this point, follow Michelle's lead—let the conversation go in the direction she takes it. Avoid dominating it with a technical discussion about periodontics or restorative dentistry.

In the event that Michelle might *not* be ready for complete care, the readiness aspect of the Hygiene Handoff sounds like this:

"Michelle told me that it isn't a good time for her to think about restoring her

*teeth. I mentioned our payment options to her; she's interested but with the
new computers she's getting for her gallery, now just isn't a good time for
her. I'm keeping her on six-month recall and we agreed to talk about things
then."*

Because the Hygiene Handoff has a specific structure, you can anticipate
talking about one or all aspects of the structure.

- Positive framing—*"Michelle, I'm glad to hear that your black-tie event
  went well."*
- Disability—*"Tell me more about your front teeth."*
- Conditions—*"Let's take a look at that loose filling in front."*
- Next step—*"Where would you like to get started first?"*
- Fit/readiness—*"If now is not a good time for you, let's revisit it again
  in six months. By then you may have your computer situation all
  figured out."*

The Hygiene Choice Dialogue and the Hygiene Handoff are two huge
components of Making it Easy approach. Over time, if you accumulate a
few hundred right-side patients who aren't ready but who've had complete
examinations and treatment plans, with the correct implementation of
the Hygiene Choice Dialogue and the Hygiene Handoff you can expect
one to two right-side patients a month to begin complete care.

In a Nutshell
Chapter Eighteen—Hygiene Dialogues

- Of all the team members in your practice, the dental hygienist is in the best position to help your practice and your right-side patients maintain an excellent relationship. Consequently, it makes perfect sense that the dental hygienist be a superstar in the concepts of choice, readiness, and advocacy.

- There are three steps in managing the right-side patient who isn't ready, in the hygiene recall system. You and your team complete these steps at your daily "huddle:" 1) Identify all right-side patients in the hygiene schedule who need additional care; 2) Evaluate where they are in their treatment plan and decide what their next step is; 3) Agree on how these patients will be managed today if they elect to take the next step in their treatment plan.

- The structure of the Hygiene Choice Dialogue is as follows: *"(Patient name) I'm glad to clean your teeth today, and in addition to that, this a good time for (discussing treatment recommendations). What's best for you today?"*

- The Hygiene Handoff is a conversation the hygienist initiates with the dentist as he enters the hygiene room to check the hygiene patient. The Hygiene Handoff is structured so that the hygienist, in a few short sentences, summarizes her findings to the dentist in a way that's easy to understand and respond to.

- The structure of the Hygiene Handoff is:
    - Positive framing—*"Michelle has done a good job of..."*
    - Disability—*"She's concerned about..."*
    - Conditions—*"I've also noticed..."*
    - Next step—*"Michelle's next step is..."*
    - Fit/readiness—*"Michelle is ready/not ready because..."*

Chapter Nineteen
What's Good For The Right Is Good For The Left:
Case Acceptance for Left-Side Patients

I remember years ago, after I first started offering case acceptance workshops for complex-care dentistry, I called one of the attendees a few weeks after he attended the workshop and asked how he was doing. He said, *"We haven't had any new right-side patients come in since I've taken the workshop, but I've been using what we learned for left-side patients and it seems to work really well!"*

I've heard that response many times over the years and the serendipity is that even though I never set out to teach left-side patient management, the right-side patient process described in this book is a superb match for case acceptance for the left-side patient. This chapter is about taking the lessons from the Making It Easy approach and applying them to the left-side patient. This creates continuity in your approach to patients and, at the same time, allows you to make adjustments for individual patients. It's good leadership to let the lessons of the Making It Easy approach influence the left-side practice.

> **It's good leadership to let the lessons of the**
> **Making It Easy approach influence the left-side practice.**

The Right-Side Dentist

A major theme throughout this book is that to experience case acceptance for right-side patients, you need to become a stronger leader. In other words, to consistently treat right-side patients, you need to evolve into a right-side dentist. Dr. Betsy Bakeman makes this point:

"The left- and right-side distinction is really more about the dentist than the patient. To have patients with severe conditions accept our treatment recommendations, right-side dentists need better communication and leadership

skills. But once the dentist learns those skills, they'll lead all patients that way. In my practice, with only minor differences, we lead left- and right-side patients the same."

Evolving into a right-side dentist has significant impact on the relationships you have with your team. The concepts of the Making It Easy approach—choice, advocacy, readiness, fit, etc.—impact the team/dentist relationship in a powerful way.

To be a right-side dentist means you become conscious of and use the foundational principles and dialogues required for complex-care patients. Once in place, these principles shape the culture of your entire practice and impact all patients, left- and right-side.

Foundational Principles and Dialogues

The foundational principles and dialogues of the Making It Easy approach are:

The Identity Dialogue—the dialogue that identifies and schedules left- and right-side patients

Disability—the impact of the dental disease on the patient's life

Condition—the intraoral finding outside of normal limits

The New Patient Interview—the conversation that begins the process of you and your patient learning about each other

The Choice Dialogue—the dialogue that helps discover the patient's level of readiness for care

Readiness—the willingness of the patient to undergo treatment immediately

The Advocacy Dialogue—the dialogue reassuring patients that you and your team will work to find the best way to fit their dental care into their life circumstances

Fit—how your treatment recommendations suit patients' life circumstances

The Warm-up Dialogue—the dialogue communicating hope to the patient and reopening the conversation about fit issues

The Financial Options Dialogue—the dialogue stating the fee, time in treatment, and payment options

Technical Treatment Plan—this provides informed consent

Hygiene Choice Dialogue—the dialogue that helps discover the level of readiness of recall patients who need dentistry

Hygiene Handoff—the dialogue summarizing the hygienist's findings to the dentist in a way that's easy to understand and respond to.

Let's look at these principles and dialogues and describe the adjustments necessary, if any, for left-side patients.

The Left-Side Dentist

The Initial Telephone Call

The initial telephone call is managed using the Identity Dialogue. When the caller is identified as a right-side patient, she is scheduled either first thing in the morning or afternoon, with no other patients scheduled during that time. For left-side patients, it's not as important to isolate their appointment from other treatment activities. Left-side patients typically have fewer issues to deal with and can fit more easily into your schedule.

I'd recommend that practices with experienced administrative team members with strong telephone skills offer the Choice Dialogue during the initial telephone call. This is especially useful after determining that the caller is a left-side patient. In this case the Choice Dialogue helps you schedule patients for what they're ready for—emergency care, a cleaning, or examination.

Initial Interview

I believe that regardless of whether a patient is left- or right-side, it's always good to have the dentist (along with a team member, if appropriate, to document the interview in the record) conduct the new patient interview. It signals to patients that they are important. The interview for the left-side patient usually is less complex than for a right-side patient because of less-complicated clinical conditions and related disabilities. However, connecting well with left-side patients can positively influence their referral behavior.

> *Connecting well with left-side patients can positively influence their referral behavior.*

My next order of preference is to have the new left-side patient interview conducted by a team member who reports her findings to the dentist. This can be very effective and efficient if handled by a properly trained team member.

I know many practices initiate patient care (both left- and right-side patients) not with an interview but with an appointment with the hygienist, where the hygienist conducts a cursory interview before she cleans the patient's teeth. This approach is the least of my preferences.

It's always good leadership to have some level of interview/conversation with a new patient before starting clinical procedures. If you want to be in a relationship style of practice, then start the relationship with an interview, whether left- or right-side.

Disability and Conditions

The greatest distinction between left-and right-side patients is the complexity of their conditions and the level of related disability. Because left-side patients have fewer and less-complex conditions, the disabilities related to those conditions can be much less severe (other than acute emergencies). This lack of disability is at the heart of why many left-side patients are apathetic about care, resistant to patient education efforts, and have the *"I'll do it if my insurance pays for it"* mentality. It is what causes the frustration most dentists experience with left-side patients.

An important tool to discover and manage the concerns and lack of concerns in the left-side patient is the Discovery Guide™ and the related Discovery Guide Dialogues. The Discovery Guide provides a process for you to discover the patient's disabilities (if any), optimizes the impact of your post-examination discussion, and acts as a template for the Warm-up Dialogue. The Discovery Guide makes it easy for patients to listen to and understand your clinical findings and treatment recommendations. It is a versatile tool that serves both left- and right-side patients well.

Choice and Readiness

The intention of the Choice Dialogue, CD-2, with right-side patients is to discover their level of readiness for complex care. Although the fees and complexity of care are much less for left-side patients, knowing their level of readiness for care and acknowledging it is just as important as it is for the right-side patient.

A good example of where readiness is an issue for left-side patients is periodontal care. Your patient, Bob, is being seen by your hygienist and he's requested a cleaning, but his clinical conditions indicate that he needs full-mouth root planing, which he may or may not be ready for.

You say, *"I see, Bob, that you've got bleeding gums and you've asked us to clean your teeth. Are you aware that this bleeding indicates a disease state that a simple teeth cleaning isn't really going to help very much at all?"*

Bob says, *"No, I didn't know that."*

You reply, *"Well, your choice here is that we can keep it simple and clean your teeth, but not really affect the disease that's going on in your mouth. Or we can offer you some treatment that has some reasonable chance of being successful in making your gums healthy. Which is best for you today?"*

The hard part about offering choices when discovering readiness is accepting the answer. You may argue that it's up to us to convince that patient to have root planing. But, how many times have patients been driven out of offices by too much education and treatment lectures? Plenty. If patients are driven out of the office or driven out of dentistry, what good does that do anyone? How does their health improve under that scenario? In the event that the left-side patient is not ready for care, then as with right-side patients who aren't ready, acknowledge their lack of readiness, treat what they are ready for, and let left-side patients know that when they're ready, you'll be there for them.

Dr. Phil Potter has used the concept of readiness for many years. He says:
"When my team and I learned to manage left- and right-side patients in a way where we stopped feeling the need to exceed the patient's readiness, it was liberating for everybody. Patient education is important, but it's only important in the context of continuing to maintain a level of relationship

where you can continue to influence them. As you know, we can drive
people out of the office with education. What we need to be sensitive to is
that we're trying to heighten their sense of awareness to a clinical problem
and trying not to drive them into it. That's what dentists do; we drive
education into patients and make them mad. We're famous for it!"

Assertiveness

A distinction between left- and right-side patients relative to choice and readiness is that at times with left-side patients, you need to be assertive in your treatment recommendations and de-emphasize the *"when you're ready"* point of view. In fact, emphasizing a legitimate sense of urgency with left-side patients helps them make good decisions about preventing their left-side conditions from becoming right-side conditions.

> ***Emphasizing a legitimate sense of urgency with left-side***
> ***patients helps them make good decisions about preventing their***
> ***left-side conditions from becoming right-side conditions.***

It's important to know when to be assertive. There are times when patients resist treatment recommendations that you know they need immediately. Good leadership means communicating assertiveness in a way that protects the relationship. For example, your patient, Barb, has a large, asymptomatic abscess and is apathetic about care. Being assertive and protecting the relationship may sound like this: *"Barb, in order to save this tooth and protect you from further infection it needs to be taken care of right now. I wish I could say you can wait on this."*

Be careful, however, when creating a sense of urgency. The issue of creating a sense of urgency relates to ethics. What really constitutes an urgent condition? If a patient has a simple chipped tooth, does this constitute a legitimate emergency? Telling patients they have a condition that requires urgent treatment when, in fact, they do not has a huge negative impact on the team and often patients can sense they're being oversold.

Patients need leadership when it comes to readiness. Creating too much urgency or not enough are both leadership mistakes. You must lead and give them a truthful and appropriate time frame. This is more difficult with right-side patients because their problems are often chronic. For example, if you believe that delaying treatment will significantly add costs, time, and risks to a treatment plan, saying so is good leadership. Dr. Carl Misch says:

> *"With implant patients with advanced bone loss, intervening immediately often keeps them from having more extensive bone grafting and assuming much more risk in their treatment. It's our responsibility to tell patients, especially people with severe time-sensitive conditions, that to delay care can mean greater treatment challenges."*

On the other hand, it's easy to get into trouble by creating urgency with patients who have chronic conditions that are not time-sensitive. Tooth wear is a good example. You say, *"Your teeth are wearing down and you'd better get something done here before it gets much worse."* Your patient answers, *"You know, Doc, Dr. O'Malley told me that twenty-five years ago and I still have my teeth!"*

The fact is that disease is episodic and tooth wear is cyclic and some of the contributing factors to the wear might be gone. If you tell the patient, *"You'd better do something soon"* and the patient knows it has been a problem for decades, you might be putting your foot in your mouth and lose credibility.

The irony here is that with left-side patients, with few conditions, we often need to create a legitimate sense of urgency and encourage treatment ASAP; with right-side patients with more severe (non-time sensitive) conditions, adopting a *"when you're ready"* attitude often is what they need to hear to start getting ready.

Fit and Advocacy

Fit issues are how your treatment recommendations suit patients' life circumstances—budget, work schedule, vacations, etc. Although the cost of left-side dentistry is less than right-side, the issue of fit is important for many left-side patients. Spending a hundred dollars is a big decision for many people. Remember, too, that fit is more than just money—it's also how your treatment recommendations fit their schedules and the current events of their lives.

Fit issues occur all the time with left-side patients. Patients say, *"I'm fly-ing to New York on Tuesday, I'll be back on Wednesday, and I'm going to Europe on Friday, and I need this crown done before I go!"*

Because fit issues are important, so is the Advocacy Dialogue, CD-3, the intention of which is to reassure patients that you and your team will work to find the best way to fit their dental care into their life circumstances. For example, Natalie is a recent college graduate who has just started her first job as a physician's assistant and is looking forward to moving into her new condo. She's self-conscious about a rotated lateral maxillary incisor and has a few fillings that need replacing. Here's an Advocacy Dialogue for Natalie:

> *"Natalie, I know you've just started a new job and are saving for your condo. I also realize that you're self-conscious about your front tooth and are concerned about your two broken fillings. Why don't you talk with Ginger, my financial coordinator, and she can help find the best way for you to fit this dentistry into your budget and your work schedule."*

The key to making the concept of fit work is letting patients know that you need input from them on how dentistry can fit into their lives. This works for everyone—left- and right-side patients. Dr. Susan Maples says:

> *"Pay attention to the fit issues of your patients. A phrase I like to use with patients when discussing fit issues is, 'Dentistry of this nature can be surprisingly expensive. We work hard to provide a lot of financial options for our patients. Let's see how we can make this work for your budget.' Don't assume what your patients can or cannot afford. We need to treat everyone the same when it comes to fit issues and offer financial options to everyone, regardless of what we think they can afford."*

Many patients think that if they can't do all of the recommended den-tistry, they can't do any of it. The combination of readiness (urgency) and advocacy encourages patients to begin their care even if means taking just one step.

> *"Matt, I know we've talked about a lot of dentistry for you. Don't be dis couraged if you can't do it all right now. Let's start with the most urgent situation, and when you're ready we'll do more. If you move quickly you can avoid further complications. I think you'll be glad you did."*

A problem many dentists have is deciding how much time to spend trying to build relationships and influencing left-side patients who don't have much dentistry to do. How much time are you or your team willing to spend influencing someone when there is minor benefit from an economic point to view? In a traditional model of case presentation, patient education techniques are used to raise dental IQs and designed to influence patients to accept care. This can be a time-consuming and frustrating experience, both for the clinician and patient. Understanding the principle of fit and using the Advocacy Dialogue is highly influential and takes little time. Then, after the patient has accepted care, you can feel confident that the time spent on patient education is a good investment for you and your patient.

The Consultation

Many left-side patients can be diagnosed and treatment planned well during the examination. Then, immediately following their examination is the consultation (a separate appointment for consultation for a left-side patient is usually not necessary). The structure of the consultation for the left-side patient is the same as for the right-side patient—Warm-up Dialogue, CD-4; Financial Options Dialogue, CD-5; and technical case presentation. This structure and the supporting communication skills function extremely well for the left-side patient.

Case Study for a Left-Side Patient: Adam

Adam is thirty-two years old, married, and he and his wife are expecting their first child in seven months. Adam works long hours as a construction supervisor for a large regional home builder. He and his wife are both working and saving to move to a larger home in a nicer neighborhood.

Adam has just been promoted and is working more with homeowners, and he's concerned about the appearance of his teeth. He recently quit smoking and his wife suggested a cleaning to remove the tobacco stains and improve his appearance. He also has noticed food packing between his teeth on his upper left. Adam learned about your office from the yellow pages and your office is close to where he works.

Figure 18-1 illustrates how Adam is managed using the principles and dialogues of the Making It Easy approach. This illustration shows all the dialogues and principles of the Making It Easy approach applied to a left-side patient at his initial appointment.

FIGURE 19-1

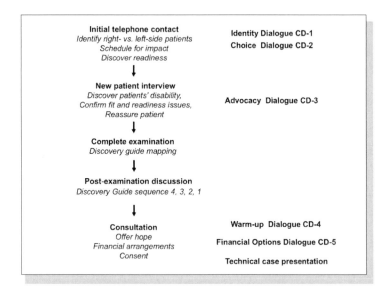

You notice that I'm introducing the Choice Dialogue at the initial telephone contact and the Advocacy Dialogue during the initial interview. In fact, in the example you'll read below, the Advocacy Dialogue is introduced on the telephone. The words and attitude related to choice and advocacy can and should be used throughout the new patient experience for left- and right-side patients by all members of the team.

Initial Telephone Call

Here's the Identity Dialogue, where being curious, listening for clues, and asking the right questions reveal Adam to be a left-side patient (the left-side clues and other key information that will help us best serve him are in bold type).

Ring-ring...

Ginger: *"Hello, this is Ginger at Dr. Homoly's office. How can I help you?"*

Adam: *"Hi, my name is Adam Taylor and I'd like to make an appointment to see Dr. Homoly."*

Ginger: *"Thanks for calling, Adam. How can we help you?"*

Adam: *"I want to get my teeth cleaned. I used to smoke and I'd love to get the stains off. Plus I've got an area on my upper teeth that always packs food and the gum gets sore occasionally."***(Chief condition)**

Ginger: *"How long has food packing between your teeth been a problem?"*

Adam: *"For awhile now. I've noticed that if I don't get the food out that my gums get sore."*

Ginger: *"You said you'd like to get your teeth cleaned. Sounds like the appearance of your teeth is important."*

Adam: *"Yes, it is. I'm a home builder and I work with homeowners and at times I worry about what kind of impression I'm making."*

(Chief disability)

Ginger: *"Adam, let me ask you, how urgent is this problem for you? Is this something that's important for you to get solved right away?"*

Adam: *"It's not an emergency or anything like that but the sooner the better."* **(Urgency)**

Ginger: *"So you're a home builder. Where do you work?"*

Adam: *"I work for Ryland Homes and we have projects all over the city."*

Ginger: *"Sounds like you've got your hands full. Do you live in the area?"*

Adam: *"Yes, my wife and I live near Lake Norman."*

Ginger: *"Is she in the home-building business, too?"*

Adam: *"No, she runs the catering department at Maggiano's Restaurant at SouthPark mall. We're expecting our first baby this October so we've got our hands full now getting everything ready."* **(Current events)**

Ginger: *"Adam, how did you find out about us? Who can we thank for referring you?"*

Adam: *"I saw your ad in the yellow pages."* **(Referral)**

Ginger: *"If you have a few more minutes, I'd like to ask you a few questions about your health history. Do you have any allergies?"*

Adam: *"No."*

Ginger: *"Are you taking medications or do you have any medical conditions that we need to be aware of?"*

Adam: *"No, I'm very healthy."* **(Medical history)**

Ginger: *"For your health history, could I have your date of birth?"*
Adam: *"December 2, 1972."* (**Date of birth**)
Ginger: *"Adam, do you have any missing teeth?"*
Adam: *"No, I have all my teeth."* (**Missing teeth**)
Ginger: *"How long has it been since you've been to the dentist?"*
Adam: *"It's been about five years."*
Ginger: *"What's kept you away so long?"*
Adam: *"I really haven't had any problems until now."*
Ginger: *"Is there anything else we need to know about you or your dental condition before we see you?"*
Adam: *"Not really. I just need to get this food-packing problem fixed, and a cleaning."*
Ginger: *"Adam, because you haven't been to a dentist in awhile, let me ask you this: When you come in do you want us to just look at the food-packing problem and clean your teeth or, in addition to that, would you be interested in Dr. Homoly doing a good examination for you and evaluating your overall dental health? What would be best for you at your appointment with us?"* (**Choice Dialogue**)
Adam: *"I can't spend a lot of time, so if I can get my teeth cleaned and the examination all at the next appointment, that's fine. Plus I need for him to look at the food-packing problem."*
Ginger: *"OK, I'll schedule an hour-and-a-half appointment for you so we can get all this done for you. I'll put in the mail your medical history questionnaire, a map to our office, and patient registration information so you can fill it out before you come in. That will save you time. You can visit our Web site, www.paulhomoly.com, and learn more about us and how we help lots of people like you."*
Adam: *"Do you have an idea of how much all this will cost?"*
Ginger: *"The fee for our complete examination is $125 and the cleaning is $90. As far as the food-packing problem, Dr. Homoly will need to take a look at it. If there's something he can do immediately, he will."*
Adam: *"I have dental insurance. Do you think my insurance will cover all of this?"*
Ginger: *"Most dental plans cover exams and cleanings. We'll be glad to look at that for you. As far as the food-packing problem, whatever needs to be done, Dr. Homoly is really good about finding a way to fit our patients' dental work into their budgets. We'll do the same for you."*

(Advocacy Dialogue)

Adam: *"That sounds good."*

Ginger: *"At your appointment, Dr. Homoly will sit down with you and have a short conversation about your concerns. I'll show him the notes I made today during our conversation. Then Dr. Homoly will do an examination, our hygienist will clean your teeth, and you and Dr. Homoly will figure out the best thing to do about the food-packing problem. How does next Monday at 2:30 fit your schedule?"* **(Left-side new patient appointment)**

Adam: *"I'll make it fit."*

Ginger: *"Adam, thanks for calling and we'll take good care of you."*

Discovery Guide

Figure 19-2 shows how side one of the Discovery Guide looks after the telephone conversation with Adam.

FIGURE 19-2

Use the information on side one of the Discovery Guide and the information on the telephone slip to the new patient interview with Adam.

New Patient Interview

The new patient interview with Adam did not reveal any new information about Adam's conditions or disabilities (references to the structure of the new patient interview as described in Chapter Six are shown in bold). When asked about his past dental experiences (**Adam's story**), he talked about having his wisdom teeth removed when he was in college and a few minor fillings he's had. When asked what he'd like for his dental health in the future, Adam said he'd like to keep his teeth and avoid emergency situations. Adam and talked about his first child being born in October and I used this information to segue into a short story about when my first child was born (**Dr. Homoly's story**).

I confirmed Adam's desire for a complete examination and to have his teeth cleaned (**Confirming Choice Dialogue, CD-2**). I used side two of the Discovery Guide to map out Adam's clinical concerns.

Near the end of the new patient interview, I offered the **Advocacy Dialogue, CD-3**, to reassure Adam that every effort will be made to fit treatment recommendations into his life.

"Adam, I understand that you have a busy work schedule and you and your wife are expecting your first child this fall. I also know that you have some concerns about the appearance and comfort of your teeth. After your cleaning today, you and I will sit down and we'll find the best way to fit fixing your teeth into what's going on with your job and home life."

Initial Examination

Adam's initial examination reveals moderate cigarette stains on all his teeth. Teeth #13 and #14 have large broken amalgam fillings, creating a food trap. Both teeth need full crowns. Adam has slight to moderate gingival inflammation around all his teeth. He has a diastema between #8 and #9.

Discovery Guide

Figure 19-3 shows how side two of the Discovery Guide looks following his examination.

FIGURE 19-3

Post-Examination Discussion

Here's the post-examination dialogue using the sequence created by the Discovery Guide along with the four Discovery Guide Dialogues. The Discovery Guide Dialogues are used to create awareness and determine concern.

Quadrant One

Curiosity: *"Adam, let's start by discussing the appearance of your teeth. I know you're embarrassed by the stains and they're creating a lack of confidence when you're talking with customers."*

Illustration: *"Teeth can be like the inside of a coffee cup—over time they can pick up stains."*

Consequence: *"I see a lot of patients who are embarrassed by the appearance of their teeth. Over time, most of my patients find that if they don't do something about the stains, they just get worse."*

Concern: *"I know this concerns you and is the main reason you're here."*

Quadrant Two

Curiosity: *"Adam, you also mentioned that you're concerned by food packing on your upper left side. Did you know that you have two broken fillings on that side?"*

Illustration: *"Fillings are like sidewalks—they can crack over time because of age and too much pressure on them. Here's a photograph of the cracked fillings."*

Consequence: *"In many patients, cracked fillings can lead to decayed and cracked teeth and food traps very similar to what you're experiencing."*

Concern: *"This is something we should put on our 'most urgent' list. Is that OK with you?"*

Quadrant Three

Curiosity: *"Adam, I know you're aware that you have a gap between your two front teeth. Has this gap always been there?"*

Illustration: *"Sometimes teeth erupt into positions that are less than ideal. Here's a close-up photo of your two front teeth."*

Consequence: *"At times, I find with some patients that these gaps can get worse."* Or, *"Many of my patients think their appearance would be better without the gap between their teeth."*

Concern: *"Is the gap between your front teeth a concern for you?"*

Quadrant Four

Curiosity: *"Adam, the last area that I'm concerned about is your gum health. Are you aware that you have some gum infection?"*

Illustration: *"Gum infection can be like high blood pressure—you can have it and not know it. The infection in the gums is like the infection you get when you have a sliver in your hand—the gums get swollen, red, can bleed easily, and at times be uncomfortable."*

Consequence: *"Many patients with gum infections experience bad breath and can lose teeth as the infections get worse."*

Concern: *"Adam, is this something that worries you?"*

In this example, I did not include Adam's responses to my Curiosity or Concern questions. My point here is to illustrate the flow of the Discovery Guide Dialogues used in the post-examination discussion.

Based on the patient's responses to the Concern Dialogue, the Discovery Guide now has a different distribution of conditions as depicted in the post-examination discussion Discovery Guide. As you can see in **Figure 19-4** , Adam is concerned about the appearance of his teeth, the broken fillings, and the gum disease (quadrant one), but not the anterior diastema (quadrant three).

FIGURE 19-4

Treatment Planning

Adam goes to the hygienist for his cleaning. While the cleaning is underway, you and your team prepare his treatment plan using the Discovery Guide™ Organizer. Adam's treatment plan includes two crowns on teeth #13, and #14, three quadrants of root planing, and veneers on #8 and #9. During the treatment planning session, you also prepared the financial options form. Figure 19-5 depicts how the Discovery Guide™ Organizer looks when completed.

FIGURE 19-5

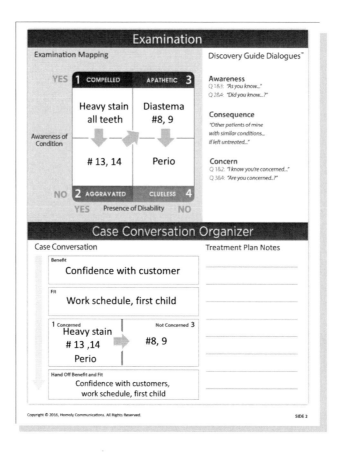

Consultation

Adam's consultation is immediately after his visit with the hygienist. The structure of the consultation is exactly the same as if he were a right-side patient: Warm-up Dialogue, CD-4; Financial Options Dialogue, CD-5; and technical case presentation. Here are examples of each dialogue.

Start Here

Warm-up Dialogue: Here's the entire Warm-up Dialogue for Adam. In bold type are the cued key phrases prompted by the Discovery Guide Organizer. Also notice in this dialogue that the fit issues for periodontal care *are not repeated*. When multiple conditions exist, do not repeat fit issues following every process. You want to avoid sounding overly repetitive.

When reading this Warm-up Dialogue, remember the patient just finished his appointment with the hygienist. His teeth are now stain-free and his chief disability related to the appearance of his teeth is relieved and is not included in the Warm-up Dialogue.

"Adam, I know you're concerned by the food packing on your upper left and the **gums are sore in that area**. *I recommend that we get that area* **comfortable for you as soon as possible**. *The way we do it is by removing the old fillings and broken enamel and* **replacing them with a new, enamel-like material**. *This usually takes two appointments. Now I know you're busy at work, so let's look at what we need to do* **to fit it into your schedule**.*"*

"I mentioned the **infection in your gums** *and you expressed a concern about it. I recommend that while we're in the* **process of fixing your upper left teeth** *we eliminate the gum infection to* **maintain the comfort and confidence** *you'll have in your teeth. We do this through a series of* **thorough cleanings** *and the use of some medications. We got a good start on that today with your cleaning."*

"Adam, the last thing I'd like to mention is an area that I know you're not concerned about—the space between your upper front teeth. If you **ever become concerned** *about it I can make your front teeth* **look completely natural** *and eliminate the space. The way I'd do it is by adding an* **enamel-like layer** *to the fronts and sides of the two front teeth."*

*"Adam, I know we've discussed a lot of things. Let's make sure we do this dentistry for you in a way that **fits into your work schedule and budget**. What questions do you have for me?"*

Typically the questions that immediately follow the Warm-up Dialogue relate to fees and financial arrangements. When asked these questions, go immediately into the Financial Options Dialogue, CD-5.

Financial Options Dialogue, CD-5: Here's an example of the Financial Options Dialogue for Adam. This dialogue is accompanied by the financial options form that Adam can refer to as the financial options are discussed. (The fee for correcting the anterior diastema is not included.)

"Adam, the total fee for your treatment is $2,400. It will take us about four appointments over one-and-a-half months from start to finish. We have some affordable options for you. Most patients enjoy beginning care with no initial payment and then making monthly payments. We've estimated your monthly payments to be $xxx. We also have a twelve-month, no-interest payment option of $xxx a month."

"Another option for you is to make an initial payment of one-third when we begin care, one-third in the middle, and the final third as we finish your treatment. Or if you'd like to take care of the fee when you begin your treatment, we offer a bookkeeping courtesy of X percent. That means you'll save xxx dollars for a total treatment fee of xxx."

"Adam, <u>which one</u> of these plans is best for you?"

Now you and/or your financial coordinator and Adam find the best fit for Adam's dentistry. At the end of the financial-arrangements conversation, I'd recommend you or your team revisit the offer to close the diastema and give Adam an idea of the fee and time required. Don't push it; just plant the seed. As Adam's appointment is ending, invite him to have his wife join the practice as a patient. Tell him that if she needs dental work it might be a good idea to get it done before she is too far along in her pregnancy. Depending on the financial services company you use, Adam and his wife may be able to combine their treatment plans and finance both over time.

Technical Case Presentation

The technical case presentation for Adam at this point is a simple matter of describing the processes for crowns and root planing, along with some brochures on the procedures. For left-side patients such as Adam, written informed consent is usually not necessary.

In a Nutshell
Chapter Nineteen—Left-Side Dentistry

- To be a right-side dentist means you become conscious of and use the foundational principles and dialogues required for complex-care right-side patients. Once in place, these principles shape the culture of your entire practice and impact all patients, left- and right-side.

- The initial telephone call is managed using the Identity Dialogue, CD-1. For left-side patients, it's not as important to isolate their appointment from other treatment activities.

- Whether a patient is left- or right-side, it's always good to have the dentist (along with a team member, if appropriate, to document the interview in the record) conduct the new patient interview. It signals to patients that they are important.

- Although the fees and complexity of care are much less for left-side patients, knowing their level of readiness for care and acknowledging it is just as important as it is for the right-side patient. The Choice Dialogue, CD-2, helps you to determine this.

- The Advocacy Dialogue, CD-3, is important for left-side patients. Spending a hundred dollars is a big decision for many people. Remember, too, that fit is more than just money—it's also how your treatment recommendations fit their schedules and the current events of their lives.

- Many left-side patients can be diagnosed and treatment planned well during the examination. Then, immediately following their examination is the consultation. A separate appointment for consultation for a left-side patient is usually not necessary.

Chapter Twenty
The Delicate Art of Referrals:
The Team Approach to Right-Side Patients

Mr. Chambers, a right-side patient, makes an appointment with a general dentist, Dr. Sally Hill. Mr. Chambers arrives at the office; Dr. Hill examines him and concludes that the best way to replace his missing posterior teeth is to use dental implants. She explains this to him and recommends that he see a surgical specialist for implant evaluation.

Mr. Chambers takes Dr. Hill's advice and seeks the opinion of the specialist. Following the examination, the specialist describes the use of dental implants, shows a few visual aids, and gives him a consent form to read at home. Just as the specialist is ready to escort the patient to the front desk, Mr. Chambers says, *"I'm not sure I can afford all this. How much does a new partial denture cost?"* The specialist winces. *"Didn't your general dentist explain any of this to you?"* *"No,"* Mr. Chambers says, *"the only thing she did was send me here to talk to you about 'transplants.'"* Then he asks the "knock-out" question: *"I can't do anything unless my insurance pays for this. How much will my insurance pay for this work?"*

Ouch! Have you ever felt "knocked out" by a question like that? When a patient refuses treatment within the team approach to care, it can raise lots of questions and concerns: *"Didn't the patient like the specialist or one of the team members?"* *"Were the specialist's fees too high?"* *"Why didn't the general dentist explain more to the patient?"* *"Who's in charge of this case?"*

The team approach to dental care is delicate from a relationship point of view. Compounding that is the growing complexity of technology. However, technology is rarely the culprit when the team approach to case acceptance fails. It fails most often because of communication problems during the case acceptance process.

*Technology is rarely the culprit when the
team approach to case acceptance fails.*

During the past thirty years, I have experienced the team approach for right-side dentistry from every point of view: as the dentist accepting the referral, as the dentist making the referral, as a patient experiencing the referral, and now as a coach teaching the referral process. From these multiple experiences I know this to be true: the referral process can harbor both the best and the worst patient experiences. Whether you're a general dentist making the referral or a specialist receiving the referral, I know you have been delighted by and disappointed in the referral process. This chapter takes the concepts of the Making It Easy approach and applies them to the team approach to case acceptance. The referral process is a critical one relative to right-side dentistry because often the conditions of the right-side patient require extraordinary care and teamwork in order to fulfill the requirements of a lifetime strategy for dental health.

The Traditional Referral Process

Figure 20-1 is an example of the traditional referral process that many of us follow.

FIGURE 20-1

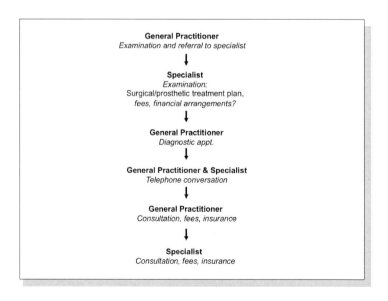

Let's go through this process with the assumption that the patient is a right-side patient who is a good candidate for implant dentistry.

It begins with the patient being examined by the general dentist. After discovering that this patient has edentulous areas suitable for implant dentistry, the general dentist refers the patient to the surgical specialist for implant evaluation.

The patient goes to the specialist's office, where an examination is done followed by a discussion of the surgical aspects of care. Often the prosthetic treatment plan is not clear at this time because the general dentist, before treatment planning using dental implants, needs to make sure that implants are a good option for this patient. Consequently, the specialist is not in a good position to discuss a definitive treatment plan, quote the total fees and financial arrangements, and discuss insurance issues. Following the examination, the specialist usually writes a review-of-finding letter to the general dentist.

If implant dentistry is a good option for the new right-side patient, the patient returns to the general dentist for diagnostic records and the development of the prosthetic treatment plan. At some point, the general dentist and specialist have a telephone conversation outlining care.

The patient returns to the general dentist's office for the prosthetic consultation and treatment plan, fees, consent, and financial arrangements. Following that, the patient goes to the specialist's office for the surgical treatment plan, fees, consent, and financial arrangements. Once everyone is on the same page, treatment begins.

The "Making It Easy" Referral Process
Figure 20-2 outlines how the Making It Easy process works within the team approach.

FIGURE 20-2

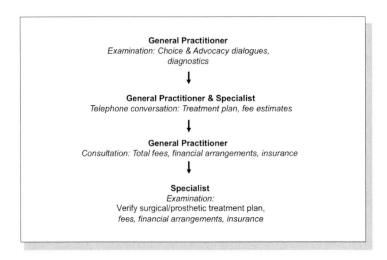

The Making It Easy referral process begins with the general dentist going through the examination and post-examination discussion as outlined earlier in this book, using the Choice and Advocacy Dialogues to discover the new patient's readiness and fit issues. If the patient is ready and the ballpark fee estimates are within the patient's budget, then diagnostic procedures (models, photographs, facebow, etc.) are completed.

The diagnostic materials are duplicated (or shared) and sent to the specialist, and together the generalist and specialist treatment plan the patient. This can be done over the telephone or in person. The assumption here is that both practitioners have sufficient clinical experience to look at well-done diagnostics (mounted study models, CT scans, radiographs, etc.) and treatment plan the case. If definitive treatment planning cannot be done because of the experience of the operators and/or the complexity of the case, then an estimate of the definitive treatment plan is done.

The patient returns to the generalist's office for the consultation appointment of the definitive or estimated treatment plan. During this appointment the Warm-up and Financial Options Dialogues are completed. The general dentist presents the entire treatment plan, including the specialty procedures, along with all fees and financial arrangements. If the treatment recommendations are agreeable to the patient, the general dentist does the technical case presentation for the prosthetic aspects of care.

The patient is referred to the specialist for an examination and verification of the treatment plan. The specialist has all the diagnostic materials from the general dentist along with the treatment plan. If the specialist discovers conditions that were not apparent from the original conversation with the general dentist, then the treatment plan is adjusted. Minor adjustments are discussed with the patient immediately. Major adjustments are discussed with the general dentist before they are explained to the patient. After the specialist verifies the treatment plan with the patient, the fees and financial arrangements are made. At this point the patient is already aware of the specialist's fees and financial arrangements from the previous consultation with the general dentist. Once the patient is comfortable with the specialist's recommendations, the specialist completes the technical case presentation and consent procedures. The patient is now ready for right-side dentistry.

The Traditional Versus the "Making It Easy" Team Approach

Let's compare the traditional and the Making It Easy method in the team approach to right-side care.

The traditional process, under the appropriate circumstances, works very well. It gives both the general dentist and specialist plenty of time to examine the patient and make their treatment decisions. If the patient is ready and has the budget for complex care, the traditional process for the team approach to care is predictable.

However, as described in many areas of this book, if the patient is not ready and/or does not have the budget for complex care, the traditional process to the team approach stalls.

If the patient is not ready and/or does not have the budget for complex care, the traditional process to the team approach stalls.

At times in the team approach to right-side care, there is a large knowledge gap between each office—one office is far more experienced and knowledgeable than the other. Using implant dentistry as an example, some specialists are more knowledgeable than general dentists. This often leads to the general dentist relying on the specialist to "sell" the case. The knowledge gap also can prompt some specialists to encourage general dentists to let specialists "sell" the case. Either way, when one office is in charge of the "sale" and the patient says "no," it can lead to fractured relationships between offices.

The advantage of the Making It Easy method to the team approach is to eliminate surprises and contests when the patient is seen by the specialist. Here's how:
- The patient has already built a strong relationship with the general dentist prior to the referral, making the recommendation for referral more significant from the patient's point of view.
- The general dentist presents the total treatment fees, financial arrangements, and insurance issues for the entire case (including specialty care), making the decision process for the patient easier than if the consultation process is split between offices (i.e., "Here's your fee for the teeth. You'll have to talk to the specialist to learn what your fee for the implants is.").
- When the patient is seen by the specialist, the patient already has a good idea of what the specialist is going to recommend, how much it will cost, how long it will take, how much insurance will pay, and a good idea of what financial arrangements will be. This takes all of the "sales" pressure off the specialist.
- If the patient is not ready for specialty care, this is discovered before the referral is made, eliminating the wasted time and aggravation for everyone. The referral is made *after* the patient becomes ready for specialty care. (Note: If the condition is essential and time-dependent [acute infection, neoplasm, etc.]—referral is not based on patient readiness. Referral is immediate.)

Common Mistakes in the Referral Process

Case acceptance of specialty procedures is predictable if all previous steps of the team approach to case acceptance have been followed. If the patient refuses specialty procedures, it's usually a direct result of poor patient preparation. Here are some typical reasons a patient rejects specialty care:

- The patient doesn't understand why the referral is important. Whether specialty procedures are essential or elective to the clinical outcome, the patient needs to know why she's being referred before she sees the specialist.

- Too often the team approach is based on the assumption (hope) that one dentist of the team (generalist or specialist) will "sell" the case. This often leads to a "lopsided" patient experience—one office is far more engaged than the other.

- One member of the treatment team (generalist or specialist) is not fully committed to the treatment plan. Patients can sense tacit disagreement between dentists.

- Wide knowledge gaps exist in the technical understanding/ experience about the dentistry planned by the respective teams. For example, in team treatment within implant dentistry, the general dentist may not understand the fundamentals of the surgical diagnosis, implant placement, and healing, and the specialist may not understand the reconstructive and occlusal requirements. Each team doctor should do what it takes to be able to competently diagnose the respective team member's dentistry.

- The patient gets confused within the team approach. Often, patients become confused because the teams are confused. This occurs when the patient arrives at the specialist's office after there has been little discussion of the patient's treatment plan. It's not the patient's responsibility to make the team offices communicate. It's insulting to patients when the treatment teams don't communicate and prepare well.

- The patient is surprised by the fees, financial arrangements, and insurance coverage of the team offices. These issues are nearly always avoidable if both teams communicate to each other their financial policies. Be sure to prepare patients for anticipated specialty fees whenever possible.

- The patient becomes discouraged because the dentists don't agree with or understand each other's treatment plan. If the dentists don't agree with a treatment plan, the patient should never be the messenger bringing that "news" to the other dentist.

A major mistake within the team approach to case acceptance is to refer without informing the patient of expected fees, financial arrangements, and insurance issues.

> *A major mistake within the team approach to case acceptance is to refer without informing the patient of expected fees, financial arrangements, and insurance issues.*

Great Referrals

Let's list the components of great referrals, many of which are a direct result of the Making It Easy approach. Most of these examples are based on the generalist referring to the specialist.

- The referral is not a surprise. Early in the relationship, when you discover the patient would benefit from specialty care, the patient is informed of the possibility of a referral. When it is time for the referral, there are no surprises.
- You and your team offer strong testimony to the credibility of the specialist. Be specific in your praise, citing the accomplishments and favorable history you've experienced while working with your specialist team member.
- Your team needs to be enthusiastic about the referral.
- Tell your patient what to expect at the first appointment with the specialist. Remove as many unknowns as possible from the referral process.
- Give your patient a sense of your continued involvement in her care even while she's being treated by the specialist. For example, doing postoperative calls following specialty procedures sends a strong message that you're still in touch with her care.
- Your patient knows what to expect in terms of fees and time in treatment with the specialist before she sees the specialist. This requires "behind-the-scenes" work between the general dentist and the team specialist.
- Make the telephone call to the specialist's office while the patient is present. Show the patient that this referral is important to you and that you are willing to handle it personally.
- Whenever possible, have your patient make the referral appointment while still in your office.

- Give your patient maps to the specialist's office and offer brochures on the planned specialty procedures.

In a Nutshell
Chapter Twenty—The Team Approach

- The team approach to dental care is delicate from a relationship point of view. It fails most often because of communication problems during the case acceptance process. The referral process begins with the general dentist going through the examination and post-examination discussion using the Choice and Advocacy Dialogues to discover the readiness and fit issues of the new patient. If the patient is ready and the ballpark fee estimates are within the patient's budget, then diagnostic procedures (models, photographs, facebow, etc.) are completed.

- The diagnostic materials are duplicated (or shared) and sent to the specialist, and together the generalist and specialist treatment plan the patient. This can be done over the telephone or in person. The assumption here is that both practitioners have sufficient clinical experience to look at well-done diagnostics (mounted study models, CT scans, radiographs, etc.) and treatment plan the case.

- The patient returns to the generalist's office for the consultation appointment of the definitive or estimated treatment plan.

- The patient is referred to the specialist for an examination and verification of the treatment plan. The specialist has all the diagnostic materials from the general dentist along with the treatment plan. At this point the patient is already aware of the specialist's fees and financial arrangements from the previous consultation with the general dentist. Once the patient accepts the specialist's recommendations, the specialist completes the technical case presentation and consent procedures. The patient is now ready for right-side dentistry.

Epilogue:
How Would You Practice Dentistry
If You Won the Lottery?

One summer morning Dr. Adam Clarke walked into a Seven-Eleven, bought a gallon of milk and with the change bought a lottery ticket. Later that afternoon while he was watching television at the golf course bar with his cronies, the winning lottery number was announced, and in a heartbeat, Adam Clarke, D.D.S., became a millionaire.

He yanked out his cell phone, called his wife Kristen, told her he had great news and insisted she drop everything and meet him at home.

"We're rich. We're millionaires. I just won $20 million!" Adam sang as he and Kristen danced in their kitchen. *"Let's take a vacation,"* cheered Kristen.

Two months later, Adam and Kristen returned from Tahiti, tanned and mellow.

"So what are you going to do about your practice? We don't need the money," said Kristen. *"I'm not sure,"* Adam responded.

As Adam walked through his quiet office that Sunday afternoon, he realized that he enjoyed dentistry. In fact, he actually missed it. Not all of it, of course. Too much of his practice had become an aggravation. It was the people he missed—Rita, the old-maid schoolteacher, whose face had lit up like a jukebox when she first saw her new smile; Stanley, the lovable barber, who told off-color jokes; his staff, in spite of their "high-maintenance" behavior, had become like a family, a bit dysfunctional but enjoyable nonetheless. Adam decided to stay.

"We're going to do some great dentistry and make this place fun again," said Adam to his staff that Monday morning. *"We're going to make some big changes."* And they did.

****

Twenty years later Adam retired from dentistry. His retirement was honored and celebrated at a black-tie dinner hosted by the community and his fellow professionals. Sitting next to Kristen at the head table, Adam listened to the final accolades of his introduction:

"...and so ladies and gentlemen, our honoree has earned the respect of our profession worldwide. Like an artist with bold and brilliant strokes, he has painted the portrait of his life masterfully and with love, touching and influencing each of us through his leadership, teaching, his numerous books and published articles, and the many innovations he brought to dentistry. A modern day Renaissance man, please help me welcome..."

Adam didn't hear the final words of his introduction as he stood and climbed the stairs to the stage. The standing ovation made him bite back his tears.

Adam began:

"When I became a dentist twenty-five years ago, I had no clue that I'd be up here tonight, enjoying these high honors. In the beginning my interest was on surviving, paying the bills, and maybe, if I was lucky, saving a dollar or two. People called me Dr. Clarke, but I didn't feel like a doctor. Doctors were confident and prosperous, I felt neither.

Then one day I won a twenty million-dollar lottery. I closed the practice for two months, Kristen and I took a wonderful vacation, and when I returned I decided to make my practice a special place—special for my patients and special for those who worked with me.

For twenty years I've heard many times, 'Adam, winning that lottery sure put your practice into orbit!' Let me tell you something, winning the lottery didn't change my practice, it changed me. I let go of my fear, and I realize now that when my fear left, it opened me to relationships. Having a great practice is not about the teeth, it's about the people.

I did some simple things that changed everything in my practice. I spent less time telling people what I thought they needed and more time understanding what they were ready for.

I stopped trying to overcome patients' objections and started looking for ways to help them find a way to fit dentistry into their lives.

I stopped trying to explain every little detail of care and learned to talk to patients in a language they could understand.

I stopped being afraid of talking about money and found ways to discuss fees in a way that made everyone comfortable.

Most importantly, I stopped trying to impress patients with who I am, and started helping them feel better about who they are.

What did it cost me to make these changes? Nothing. These are changes in attitude and perspective. Looking back on it now I realize that you can't buy what it takes to have a great practice.

Let me ask you, how would you practice if you won the lottery? Some of you might say that if you had the money you'd probably do something else. I thought the same thing, but when I started looking at what else I'd do, I remembered how I used to think dentistry was fun. I decided, 'Why not rediscover dentistry, and practice it in a way that's fun and fulfilling? Why not make my work a significant source of my pleasure?'

Some people say that work shouldn't be the center of your life. After all there are more important things like family and community. They say that when you're on your deathbed, you'll never wish you had one more day at the office. I don't know about that–I've had some really great days at the office, and you have too. And I'd wish for my family and community that they'd love their work everyday too.

Being successful and fulfilled in our work shapes how we see and feel about ourselves, and how we see ourselves is the lens through which we see our world.

Our work sounds the beat of the drums of our life. It helps us keep pace with our world. To not love your work is like denying a friendship that urges you to enjoy life's parade.

To work with love is the art of life. Like the painter who uses brushes and colors to reveal the portrait, like the poet who charms his words into rhymes, like the musician who weaves notes into melodies, we too have the portraits, rhymes, and the melodies of our work. And as with the artist, work is our love made visible.

For some, dentistry can be a kind of prison. They see dentistry as a process of solving the same problems year after year. They work hard and seek to ultimately escape from dentistry, hopefully with enough money to do what they really love. The irony is that when you've been in an emotional prison too long, you can forget what it is that you love.

Practicing dentistry is a love-it or leave-it situation. It's too challenging physically and emotionally to be lukewarm about it. If you can't learn to love it, leave it. My choice was to learn to love it. A great day in my life was when I decided I wanted to practice dentistry not because I needed to, but because I wanted to.

Deciding what you want is the only way to live. Deciding brings energy and a focus to each day. Knowing what you want starts the first chapter in the book about the best days of your life. You can't write a book about someone who doesn't know what he wants. So it is with the story of your life; it doesn't get really interesting until you know what you want.

Going after what you want is a kind of gift you give to yourself. And the gift is discovering your unique abilities, creativity, energy, and zest for life. At times you'll find that your gift does not fit in with the traditional thinking of your colleagues. Your gift can be seen as a 'rough edge' that others may say must be smoothed out. Not so. Your gifts—your rough edges—are exactly what will drive the process of loving your life. Make your rough edges your leading edges.

Too many dentists think that dentistry will make them happy. It won't. Dentistry doesn't bring us happiness; we bring happiness to dentistry. It's your passion that's the greatest asset of your practice.

Finally, I'd like to offer you this: having a great practice is about courage to use your gifts. Your life shrinks or expands in proportion to your courage. We cannot grow our practices without first having the courage to grow ourselves.

Thank you all for being here tonight and for loving dentistry."

And the room rose, the applause thundered, and the music began as Adam smiled, walked back to Kristen, took her hand, and danced this very special night away.

****

You're not going to win the lottery, but you can win at dentistry. This book can be the flint to spark the fire in your belly that makes your life as a dentist worth celebrating. The best students of this material tell me that its principles overflow into their lives, affecting their relationships at home and in other areas of their life. When you make it easy for patients to say "Yes," you and your team become better for it.

Our work as dentists is personal; the processes we use are extensions of who we are. Our work and who we are affect each other; change one and it impacts the other. We have no choice in this matter—to have an extraordinary practice you must be an extraordinary person. The best reason for success in dentistry is who we have to become to achieve it.

Dr. Paul Homoly, August 12, 2005

If you'd like to take the next step in experiencing better case acceptance for cosmetic, implant, and restorative dentistry, enroll in my in-office online program *Making It Easy For Patients To Say "Yes"*. This online in-office training program is the most affordable and convenient way to improve your treatment acceptance from modest to complex care patients. You'll learn how to:

- Offer complete care without blowing patients out of the water due to sticker shock;
- Influence patients while never sounding like a salesperson;
- Recommend treatment in half the time with twice the impact;
- Educate patients without losing their interest and;
- Present fees while never feeling uncomfortable

You'll eliminate overwhelming patients and watching them walk out your door never to return from poorly structured and overly complex treatment presentations.

When you complete this program you'll be able to:

- Enjoy loyal and grateful patients;
- Inspire team members;
- Do more of the dentistry you love and;
- Be abundantly rewarded

I also offer live case acceptance workshops. These are two-day hands-on communications coaching experiences where you and your team role play case study simulations of complex care patients. You'll return from this workshop with the confidence and skills to make case acceptance for quadrant to complex care dentistry predictably successful.

To get more information about it visit my web site at www.paulhomoly.com or call us at 800-294-9370.

I hope you enjoyed this book.

About the Author

Hello and thanks for taking a moment to read about my experience and commitment to dentistry's patients, dentists and team members, and profession.

I practiced implant and reconstructive dentistry for 20 years. My clinical career spanned an era of massive transformation in dentistry; implant and cosmetic dentistry, dental advertising, digital scanning and chairside milling, orthodontic aligners, and so much more. What didn't transform was the human nature of patients wanting to be well cared for. I spent the last 10 years in my practice developing a treatment acceptance process that offered patients experiences that signaled they were being well cared for. This work put my practice gross income in the top 1% of general practitioners.

Upon retiring from clinical care due to an eye disability, I put what I know to be true about treatment acceptance into journal articles, seminars, in-office consulting, computer apps, webinars, and have literally been around the world teaching how to make it easy for patients to say "yes" to our treatment recommendations. From meeting thousands of dentists I've learned that many clinically gifted dentists were too often not highly rewarded. My mission for the last 20 years has been to change that.

I've written 3 books on treatment acceptance; *Dentists: An Endangered Species, Isn't It Wonderful When Patients Say "YES"*, and *Making It Easy for Patients to Say "Yes"*. My work spans the entire range of dental practices from mom-and-pop solo general practitioners to all levels of private fee-for-service general and specialty practices. My work with Dental Service Organizations has helped them evolve into world-class dental health care and business entities.

An additional aspect of my career is developing experts into interesting and influential communicators. I authored two books on this topic; *Just Because You're Leading...Doesn't Mean They'll Follow* and *Just Because*

You're an Expert...Doesn't Make You Interesting. I lead speaker development programs for market leading dental companies including Nobel Biocare, Ormco Orthodontics, Pacific Dental Services, Dentsply Sirona, and many others. I hold the highest earned designation in professional speaking from the National Speakers Association – Certified Speaking Professional (CSP). Fewer than 15% of professional speakers hold this designation and I am the first dentist world-wide to earn it.

My newest exciting challenge is to embrace all the opportunities the internet brings to help dentists and teams to do more of the dentistry they love, work with engaged and committed team members, and be abundantly rewarded. Take a look and get involved with my online program *Making It Easy for Patients to Say "YES"* and when you do you'll be partnering with me on my latest journey. Thanks for joining me.

Dr. Paul Homoly, CSP
Buisness address:
1646 West Hwy 160, Suite 8107
Fort Mill, SC 29708

Home office:
26561 W. Vista North Drive
Buckeye, AZ, 85396

paul@paulhomoly.com
www.paulhomoly.com
800-294-9370

Made in United States
North Haven, CT
28 November 2021